Ruth Maleczech at Mabou Mines

Methuen Drama Engage offers original reflections about key practitioners, movements and genres in the fields of modern theatre and performance. Each volume in the series seeks to challenge mainstream critical thought through original and interdisciplinary perspectives on the body of work under examination. By questioning existing critical paradigms, it is hoped that each volume will open up fresh approaches and suggest avenues for further exploration.

Series Editors

Mark Taylor-Batty
Senior Lecturer in Theatre Studies, Workshop Theatre, University of Leeds, UK

Enoch Brater
Kenneth T. Rowe Collegiate Professor of Dramatic Literature & Professor of English and Theater University of Michigan, USA

In the same series

In memory of Daniel C. Gerould, one of my great teachers

Contents

List of Illustrations

Acknowledgments

I first became interested in Ruth Maleczech's work when I was a resident artist at Mabou Mines/Suite. Ruth was my mentor. She had an uncanny ability to look at the work I was making from my point of view. She pushed me—hard—to sharpen my thinking and to take risks. The apparent ease with which she was able to immerse herself in someone else's artistic perspective made me want to know more about her work. As a graduate student I decided I would research it. Not finding much, I went to work. Ruth was extraordinarily generous with her time and energy in granting interviews and consultations, facilitating introductions, and providing access to archival material. I had hoped she would still be alive when the book was published, but I am glad that at least she knew it was coming. I wish to thank her children, Clove and Lute, for their support for the project.

Mabou Mines co-artistic director Sharon Fogarty and former general manager Joe Stackell provided invaluable access to archival material at the Mabou Mines offices. Their continuous encouragement always made me feel that my regular requests for assistance were welcome. I am also thankful to former co-artistic director Julie Archer, who served as a fact-checker in Ruth's absence. This project would not have been possible without the enthusiastic cooperation of so many of Ruth's collaborators who were eager to share their thoughts about her in interviews. Special thanks to JoAnne Akalaitis, Julie Archer, Lee Breuer, Sharon Fogarty, Clove Galilee, Linda Hartinian, Karen Kandel, Paul Kandel, Greg Mehrten, Catherine Sasanov, Joe Stackell, and Doug Stein.

I extend profound gratitude to Iris Smith Fischer, who generously allowed me to consult unpublished interviews she conducted with Ruth. The elegant photography of Julie Archer, Carol Rosegg, James Hamilton, Colm Hogan, Dona McAdams, Jan Meissner, Beatriz Schiller, and Joseph Schuyler is an important illustration of this discussion and I am deeply appreciative to them for permission to include it. Thanks also to Eileen Schuyler for her generous assistance in locating images from *Through the Leaves.*

This study began as a dissertation and benefited tremendously from the insight and encouragement of my graduate mentors. I am profoundly grateful to Marvin Carlson for his incisive advice, steadfast guidance, and unwavering support, as well as for his eminently reasonable perspective. I am indebted to David Savran's shrewd advice and enthusiasm for the project and to James Wilson's perceptive suggestions. The questions these advisors raised during my dissertation defense were important starting places as I began to revise the project. Daniel Gerould's years of kind and wise mentorship prepared me to undertake the challenge of scholarship and his sense of humor and *joie de vivre* taught me to find the fun in it. I am also thankful to Lynette Gibson, who led the way through more pieces of paper and bureaucratic tangles than either one of us probably cares to remember. The City University of New York Graduate Center's Marvin Tackel grant for American Theatre Research provided important financial support for the project.

W.B. Worthen has served as an informal academic advisor, career counselor, and sympathetic ear. I am very thankful for his sound advice, staunch support, and friendship. My colleagues at the University of New Haven have been immensely helpful during the last leg of this journey. I am especially grateful to Erica Haskell and Meg Savilonis for their patience, empathy, and advice.

Presentations at the 2012 American Conference for Irish Studies, the Association of Theatre in Higher Education conferences in 2012, 2013, and 2014 and the 2012 ATHE Women in Theater and Performance focus group pre-conference helped me immensely in developing my thinking about this material. I am grateful to conference organizers as well as to colleagues who contributed important ideas and support. In particular, Jessica Del Vecchio and Catherine Young provided both professional forums and personal space that evolved my feminist perspective.

A version of my discussion on Beckett's *Imagination Dead Imagine* appeared in *Samuel Beckett Today/Aujord'hui* in 2014 and I wish to thank Andrea Moorjani, David Tucker, Mark Nixon, and Dirk Van

Hulle for their excellent editorial suggestions. I am equally grateful to Kathryn Syssoyeva and Scott Proudfit, whose ideas about a related argument I make in a chapter for their forthcoming volume, *Women, Collective Creation, and Devising*, expanded my theoretical framework for this project.

The assistance of staff at the Fales Library Collection at New York University's Bobst Library and the Theatre on Film and Tape Archive at the Lincoln Center Library for the Performing Arts was invaluable.

I am profoundly grateful to series editors Enoch Brater and Mark Taylor-Batty as well as to Mark Dudgeon and Emily Hockley at Methuen Drama for their belief in the project, suggestions that improved the book exponentially, and care and time in shepherding the project to completion. Methuen Drama's external readers contributed constructive ideas that had a substantial impact on the project.

Finally, I am enormously thankful for the emotional and intellectual support of my family and friends, with special gratitude to Liz Brater. I am intensely appreciative of Christopher Silsby's unwavering encouragement and thoughtfulness, technological savvy, editorial suggestions, and very good ideas. Last but not least, thanks to Ezekiel for interruptions that kept everything in perspective.

Introduction

All my work deals with women. It just does.

Ruth Maleczech

When Ruth Maleczech died in 2013, renowned director JoAnne Akalaitis placed a call to make sure the *New York Times* was planning to run an obituary. As a co-artistic director and founder of the company Mabou Mines, Maleczech had been a fixture of American avant-garde theater since 1970. So why was Akalaitis concerned that New York's paper of record in Maleczech's artistic home might not publish an article to mark her passing? Though she was well known as an actor, Maleczech had rarely been credited for her innovative work as an artistic director, producer, and director. As it turned out, the *Times* did run an obituary written by the publication's lead theater critic, Ben Brantley. But Akalaitis's concern was well founded, because the magnitude of Maleczech's contribution to Mabou Mines and to downtown New York theater had never been publicly acknowledged in print, despite the appreciation her work garnered among audiences and artistic peers.

Maleczech was among a group of women who were at the helm of some of the most influential downtown companies during one of the most exciting periods in American theater history. This group includes the Living Theatre's Judith Malina, La MaMa's Ellen Stewart, the Wooster Group's Elizabeth LeCompte, and Maleczech's longtime collaborator and former Mabou Mines colleague, JoAnne Akalaitis. These women, starting with Malina, helped to introduce techniques of early and mid-twentieth century avant-garde theater artists to American audiences. In addition to writers such as Samuel Beckett, Gertrude Stein, and Jean Genet, the Russian director Vsvelod Meyerhold and the Polish director and acting teacher Jerzy Grotowski played a significant part in their emerging work. The director Erwin Piscator and the writer/director Bertolt Brecht, both German, combined trailblazing theatrical strategies with political engagement and also stimulated this new generation of artists in the American avant-garde.

Not only did Maleczech, Malina, and their peers introduce these theatrical strategies to American audiences, but they also adapted them, manipulating them under the influence of the radical counter-cultural politics of the 1960s and, paradoxically, American popular culture itself. Although the work of these women and their male counterparts—Lee Breuer, Richard Foreman, and Robert Wilson, for example—is often described as experimental, its self-conscious roots in the European avant-garde distinguish it from that of the theater artists who emerged in the early part of the twenty-first century. Furthermore, as Maleczech liked to point out, describing theater process and practice as experimental "makes it sound like you don't know what you are doing."

Maleczech thus secures a place in a traditional, male-oriented understanding of the avant-garde—one James Harding suggests has dominated scholarship of the field for the past forty years—but her work is best understood in the context of the new paradigm Harding proposes, which

> positions categories of gender and sexuality not only at the center of stylistic innovation but also at the center of a feminist political aesthetic in which the "critique of the 'dominant male discourse'" and the assertion of a feminist discourse in its stead are recognized not merely as elements of a feminist historiography or of a feminist epistemology but also as crucial components of an American avant-garde aesthetic.[1]

To best elucidate Maleczech's place in the avant-garde, as well as the uniqueness of her contribution, it is useful to view her career both in the context of the work of her peers as well as in this new framework for understanding the multiple dimensions of the movement.

The San Francisco Actor's Workshop and the Living Theatre were two of the first companies in the United States to produce avant-garde plays by writers such as Beckett, Cocteau, and Stein. Maleczech trained at the Actor's Workshop with Herb Blau and later joined an alternative—that is, a consciously noncommercial—theater scene in New York already under the sway of Malina and Julian Beck's pioneering work with the Living Theatre. Maleczech's career parallels Malina's in many ways. The latter founded her company with her spouse in 1947, deploying techniques she inherited from Piscator. Although initially interested in questions of form and style posed by poetic texts as well as political theater, Malina and her collaborators gravitated to collective living and collective creation as well as radical political activism by the mid-1960s, with pieces including *Mysteries and Smaller Pieces* (1964) and *Paradise Now* (1968). Malina was an artistic director, a director, and a performer, as was Maleczech, and both women remained with the companies they founded until their deaths (Malina died two years after Maleczech in 2015).

Ellen Stewart was the first producer to back Mabou Mines's work. She founded La MaMa in 1961, just a few blocks away from PS 122, the converted schoolhouse that was to become Mabou Mines's home on First Avenue and East Ninth Street in the East Village. Stewart was a visionary producer of alternative theater in New York City and beyond, and a prescient founder of off-off Broadway theater. She promoted plays and performances that were unconventional and often controversial, providing space and financial resources to then unknown companies and theater artists, ranging from the Playhouse of the Ridiculous to Sam Shepard to Elizabeth Swados, because she recognized the vitality and dynamism of their work. As with Malina and the Living Theatre, Stewart toured internationally with her New York-based artists and like Maleczech and Malina lived and worked in Europe in the 1960s. As a producer, Stewart also imported cutting edge work by artists such as Tadeusz Kantor and Andrei Serban for the benefit of North American audiences. Initially, Stewart's work at La MaMa was "dedicated to the playwright." Under her leadership, however, the mission expanded to a dedication "to the artist and all aspects of the theatre."[2]

Elizabeth LeCompte, artistic director of the Wooster Group, shares Maleczech's enduring interest in formal innovation and commitment to inventive multimedia performance. The Wooster Group was founded in 1975, though some of its members had already worked together as part of Richard Schechner's Performance Group. From Schechner, LeCompte and her company inherited the Performing Garage, which has been the Wooster Group's permanent home since its inception. As of this writing, LeCompte has directed every production the Wooster Group has produced except for *Early Shaker Spirituals* (2014). Though she has created works based on Stein and Grotowski, she has more frequently been attracted to widely known plays by writers such as Arthur Miller, Eugene O'Neill, and Anton Chekhov than to the less naturalistic material favored by Malina and often by Maleczech. LeCompte is also known for her early collaborations with the autobiographical writer and performer Spalding Gray. As was the Living Theatre's in the 1960s and 1970s, much of the Wooster Group's work in the 1980s was greeted with controversy. While Malina and her collaborators were imprisoned in Brazil for their political agitation and theater for social change in the 1970s, LeCompte and the Wooster Group were at the center of a critical firestorm over their formal and stylistic interest in blackface in pieces including *Route 1 & 9* (1981). They also became a target of legal action by Miller for their unauthorized adaptation of *The Crucible* in what became *L.S.D (... Just the High Points ...)* (1984).

Of these notable women working in American avant-garde theater, it is Akalaitis who worked most closely with Maleczech. When Akalaitis traveled and trained in Europe and cofounded Mabou Mines she was a performer, though she became one of the company's most important directors in its first ten years. Akalaitis was especially lauded for her directing work on Beckett's *Cascando* (1976); *Dressed Like an Egg*, based on the writings of Colette (1977); *Dead End Kids*, a collective creation (1980); and Franz Xavier Kroetz's *Through the Leaves* (1984). Akalaitis gave up performing as she grew more invested in directing, but her early collaborations onstage with Maleczech on Beckett's plays and

Lee Breuer's animations proved formative for the co-artistic directors' concept of the performer's role while shaping the strategies both women employed as directors. When Akalaitis left Mabou Mines in 1990, she served briefly as the Public Theater's first (and, to date, only) female artistic director and subsequently established a distinguished career as an independent director working at institutions including the Guthrie Theater in Minneapolis, New York Theatre Workshop, Lincoln Center, and the Mark Taper Forum. Though Akalaitis's move to the commercial theater world is distinct from that of the other women mentioned here, she has continued to apply the techniques she developed when working primarily downtown. She also established a career as an educator, serving on the Bard College faculty from 1998 to 2012 and as Professor Emerita in her retirement.

Several of Maleczech's aesthetic, political, and organizational preoccupations overlap with Malina's, Stewart's, LeCompte's, and Akalaitis's. Maleczech shared LeCompte's dedication to original uses of multimedia onstage and to formal innovation. Where LeCompte worked with Gray to stage his autobiographical trilogy, Maleczech made use of her own biography in *Hajj*, in which she performed. Grotowski exerted the most apparent influence on Maleczech, Akalaitis, and LeCompte—The Wooster Group's *Poor Theater* (2004) painstakingly investigates some of his techniques in a "series of simulacra" and, as did Malina, Stewart, and Akalaitis, Maleczech lived and created work in Europe, where she trained with Grotowski.[3] The Polish director and acting teacher's influence was widespread among American avant-garde theater makers, including Schechner's Performance Group and Joseph Chaikin's Open Theater, who were inspired by his "poor theater" aesthetic and his rigid training systems for performers.

Maleczech shared Stewart's and Akalaitis's commitment to mentorship and promotion, supporting fellow artists in her community by cofounding ReCherChez and later Mabou Mines/Suite, resident artist programs run by Mabou Mines to provide space, funds, and guidance to new and emerging artists. Maleczech further supported the work of her fellow artists and collaborators as a producer at Mabou

Mines. Although, unlike Stewart, she was not primarily associated with this role, Maleczech was the most sustained producer of Mabou Mines's work. And although not as conspicuous as in Stewart's work, Maleczech shared with her an interest in internationalism and the global reach of theater; this is most evident in her directing of *Sueños* (1989) and *Belén* (1999) but is also apparent in her portrayal of Marie Curie in *Dead End Kids* and Lucia Joyce in *Lucia's Chapters of Coming Forth by Day* (2007).

Malina, Stewart, LeCompte, Akalaitis, and Maleczech can additionally be described in terms of collaborators they share—Greg Mehrten, a former Mabou Mines company member who worked closely with Maleczech and continues to collaborate with Breuer, frequently performing with the Wooster Group as well; Elizabeth Swados, whose work was produced by Stewart, has developed work as part of Mabou Mines/Suite; Anne Bogart (who as artistic director of the SITI Company could easily be included in this group of female leaders of American avant-garde theater) directed Maleczech in Brecht's *In the Jungle of Cities* with Mabou Mines (1991), taught at La MaMa Umbria, and has served on the Wooster Group's emerging artists series selection committee.[4]

Though the members of Mabou Mines did not maintain collective living arrangements for as long as the members of the Living Theatre did, in the early days of the company Maleczech and Akalaitis lived together, along with their spouses. The counter-cultural movement that encouraged collective living also established a creative environment conducive to collective creation. Though Mabou Mines's inaugural production, *The Red Horse Animation* (1970), was written and directed by Breuer, its development was characterized by a nearly collective process in which performers Maleczech, Akalaitis, and David Warrilow exerted control over creative decisions alongside Breuer. This way of working continued to be a hallmark of the company for at least its first decade and was an approach Maleczech employed throughout her career as a performer and a director. As has the Living Theatre, Mabou Mines has also produced collectively created pieces such as *Dead End Kids* and *Belén*.

Among the women in this group, Maleczech's career most closely resembles Malina's. Both trained with central figures in the European avant-garde and were deeply engaged with progressive politics, especially with the ethos of collectivity. Both founded theater companies with a spouse and maintained company leadership for the remainder of their careers. Perhaps most importantly, both women wore the multiple hats of producing, directing, and performing. Maleczech, however, was much more closely associated with her work as a performer.

In fact, one would have to look back at least to the nineteenth century to find well-known figures in theater history to whom Maleczech can trace her provenance. She is perhaps best described as an Actor-Manager whose career finds its closest parallels with David Garrick's and Molière's. As did Maleczech, Garrick and Molière used their virtuosity to confront audiences with surprising subjects and styles. Garrick abolished the popular tradition of seating some of the audience onstage and reintroduced a generation of theater-goers to Shakespeare. Molière, of course, wrote his own material and reinvented Commedia dell'Arte to tackle controversial topics. In the tradition of Commedia dell'Arte, he also created roles within his company for his family members, something that Maleczech did as well. Less widely cited are female predecessors such as Caroline Neuber, instrumental in inventing the German theater; Madame Vestris, credited with introducing the box set in England; and Lillian Mortimer, the American melodramatist. Although these women are less famous than their male counterparts, the position of actor-manager has proven to be an effective vehicle throughout theater history for women seeking independence and self-sufficiency in their careers. This role has nearly disappeared from contemporary theater, however; Maleczech and Kevin Spacey, who ran the Old Vic for eleven years, are notable exceptions.

It is the centrality of Maleczech's identity as a performer that distinguishes her from her peers among the women in the American avant-garde. Though Kate Valk has a similarly visible profile as a performer in the Wooster Group, she is not an artistic director of the company. As such, Maleczech possessed the unusual opportunity to control her own career as a performer, deciding not only which roles she would play but also how she would play them. She used her leadership to create space for other performers to work with similar autonomy at Mabou Mines, stimulating the company to reimagine the performer's role in the theatrical process and challenging performers collaborating with Mabou Mines to restructure the mode, method, and meaning of their work. She also initiated at least ten productions with the company as either performer or director.

Maleczech's performance process is unusual. She was inspired by groundbreaking artists and companies: R.G. Davis and the San Francisco Mime Troupe, Herb Blau and the San Francisco Actor's Workshop, Brecht's Berliner Ensemble, and Grotowski. Maleczech used her training to establish her own distinctive artistic process and set of aesthetic prerogatives, developing an agility of thinking and practice that allowed her to transform the idea of the performer.

This way of working began as often with a concept as it did with a person. Maleczech had a wide appetite for interdisciplinary study as well as experiential learning—in preparation for her role as Winnie in *Happy Days* (1996) she read everything from Stan Gontarski's essay on Beckett's "vaguening" of the text to interviews with the actress Billie Whitelaw. Her research was experiential as well: during the development for *Lucia's Chapters of Coming Forth by Day* (2007), in which she played Lucia Joyce, she visited Nora Joyce's apartment in Galway. Another visit took her to Marie Curie's home in preparation for her role in *Dead End Kids*. Maleczech's interest and investment in research led her to pursue historical and political subjects in her own work; the *Dead End Kids* subtitle is "A story of nuclear power," and at the time of her death she was developing *Imagining the Imaginary Invalid*, a piece that juxtaposes Molière's play with inspiration drawn from the history of medicine.

She was as deeply invested in her collaborators as she was in research and she exhibited an uncanny instinct in selecting them. She was inspired to create *Belén: A Book of Hours* (1999) when she met fellow National Endowment of the Arts (NEA) scholar Catherine Sasanov, a poet, in Mexico City; Maleczech was there to study the work of the

Mexican performer and political activist Jesusa Rodríguez. Julie Archer was a sculptor and babysitter when Maleczech met her. At Maleczech's invitation, Archer became a set designer, then a Mabou Mines co-artistic director, and ultimately one of the most frequent collaborators of Maleczech's career. Maleczech also blurred the boundaries between art and life by co-habiting the roles of mother and collaborator on a number of productions, working with both of her children, Clove Galilee and Lute Ramblin', at Mabou Mines. In the rehearsal room, whether performing or directing, Maleczech extended the same autonomy and independence to her collaborators that she established for herself. She treated elements of language and design as performative, collaborative stimuli in themselves, animating them onstage so that both actors and audience could interact with them. And in performance, Maleczech treated those in the audience as collaborators as well, inviting them to find meaning in her representations by resisting tidy narrative, conventional characters, and obvious symbolism.

This last challenge to the audience was risky, and Maleczech's audacity both onstage and off is what made her work so tantalizing. Her appetite for adventure brought her from the University of California to Los Angeles to San Francisco before finishing college and from San Francisco to a cross-country road trip culminating in a boat ride to Europe. She was bold in choosing her collaborators and brave in staging tricky subjects, complicated language, and complex form. Maleczech was courageous onstage as well—when she couldn't memorize all of the dense text for *Lucia's Chapters*, she utilized an ear bud and performed as someone backstage read the lines to her while she talked. She performed aerially in *Red Beads* (2005), suspended nearly thirty feet above the stage in the cavernous Skirball Center for the Performing Arts at New York University. And as a director, she put the first large-scale hologram onstage in *Imagination Dead Imagine* (1984). As a producer, Maleczech was not adverse to financial risk, either. She worked to put funding together for *Hajj* even as she was rehearsing it and refused to charge admission for *Song for New York* (2007), even though the production was placing Mabou Mines in debt.

But perhaps the most daring and significant aspect of Maleczech's career was her dedication to expanding the possibilities for how women can be represented onstage. Using her position of power as an artistic director as well as the innovative techniques she developed in the context of American avant-garde theater, Maleczech imagined and enacted women who appear as their own fathers; famous fathers who appear as mothers; historical figures we have barely heard of; historical luminaries as individualized and contemporary people; and everyday women as mythical figures. Her roots in the European avant-garde, commitment to exploring progressive social and political ideology onstage, and pioneering approaches to form, narrative, and multimedia design situate her among colleagues in American avant-garde theater, but her singular focus on the representation of women onstage sets her apart from prominent contemporaries such as Malina, LeCompte, and Stewart.

Maleczech's contribution, of course, is inextricably tied to Mabou Mines's, which she cofounded in 1970 with Akalaitis, Breuer, Philip Glass, and Warrilow. The company has, since its founding, been structured as a collective; the founding members were co-artistic directors, an arrangement that remains intact even though the composition of the company has shifted. Its members eschew the notion that the company promotes a single, unified artistic voice. Yet, according to Maleczech, the press has repeatedly attempted to identify the company's "guiding intelligence," usually assigning it to Breuer.[5] Given Maleczech's crucial roles in creating and sustaining Mabou Mines, this persistent myth is troubling.[6] It also excludes the vital contributions of former co-artistic directors such as Warrilow and Fred Neumann, who, as performers, were perhaps less identifiable as guiding forces of the company. That Maleczech, Warrilow, and Neumann have been overlooked reveals a bias in the theater about the relationship between power and certain forms of labor as well as an inability to absorb Mabou Mines's conception of the performer's pivotal and powerful role in the process of organizing, developing, and staging a production.

Akalaitis and Maleczech launched their directing careers for Mabou Mines within its first decade and Akalaitis and Breuer were the company's two major directors during the first twenty years; in this context it is difficult to read attempts to assign central leadership to Breuer as anything other than gender bias. In one of many such instances, a 1975 *New York Times* review of an evening of Beckett shorts refers to the group as "an experimental theater company under the direction of Lee Breuer."[7] Such misattribution has continued to trail the company. Theodore Shank's 2002 updated edition of *Beyond the Boundaries* claims the company was founded "by five artists who worked collaboratively under the artistic direction of Lee Breuer and the musical direction of Philip Glass," subsequently listing Akalaitis, Maleczech, and Warrilow only as performers.[8]

Within the company, however, artistic independence and autonomy extends from creative roles to producing and managerial positions; its members have been encouraged at various times to take on all three. Although those within Mabou Mines (including Breuer) acknowledge Maleczech's central role in arbitrating both artistic and producing choices, the organizational and executive work that consolidated Maleczech's influence within the company has not been critically acknowledged as a meaningful contribution.

Several Mabou Mines collaborators suggest that no one has had more sustained influence on the company than Maleczech. "Ruth is the reason that the company has stayed together," said Sharon Fogarty,

> she thinks of Mabou Mines as this thing outside of her and outside of all of us.... Ruth's opinion is very important to the organization in terms of whether or not we take on something. She's got such a huge heart, but she's tough as nails. She has extremely high standards about work and she's committed to this idea, which the company began with, of making art and not entertainment, not commerce, not conventional theater.[9]

As of this writing, the company exists under the guidance of co-artistic directors Breuer, Sharon Fogarty, Karen Kandel, and Terry O'Reilly; how the company will chart its course in Maleczech's absence remains to be seen.

Maleczech created and maintained an artistic family in Mabou Mines. Using the company's explorations of collective process, its radical reconceptualization of the performer's role, and her own position of power as a founding co-artistic director, Maleczech promoted and pursued risky and revealing artistic choices to reshape and re-imagine the contours of a contemporary theatrical experience. This book identifies key elements of Maleczech's body of work, tracing the outline of her aesthetic imprint through her work with Mabou Mines and pointing to the significance of her contribution to American avant-garde theater.

Background, training, and early influences

Maleczech was born in Cleveland, Ohio, in 1938 to immigrants from Yugoslavia. The family name was Reinprecht, but in 1969 she took "Maleczech" to show solidarity with the Czech reform movement of the late 1960s and to echo her mother's name, Maletiç. "Maleczech" translates loosely to "little Czech." Reinprecht, Maleczech sometimes pointed out wryly, means "probing for cleanliness." Her father was a steelworker and her mother was a homemaker and trained seamstress who made every item of clothing worn by Maleczech and her sister except for underwear, hats, and socks. After Maleczech completed the second grade in 1947, her family moved to Phoenix, Arizona, for her father's health. The story of this cross-country journey would later be dramatized in *Hajj*. In Phoenix, Maleczech appeared onstage for the first time as the witch in *Snow White*. Her mother made her costume and Maleczech, having heard a sound recording, reported that she gave a very effective performance. "I was a great witch," she remembered, "I can tell by the voice. Very high pitched and scary." In high school Maleczech excelled in dance, performed in *Blithe Spirit* and *The Taming of the Shrew*, and was a cheerleader and a drum major. She did well in biology but almost failed math and home economics, the latter of which required that she make a chartreuse-colored dress and subsequently model it in a fashion show. Her seamstress mother told her that it wouldn't be fair for her to help, so Maleczech made and remade the dress three times in order to pass the class. "Oh God! It was murderous," she said, "I remember coming home and cutting it up into a million pieces."

Maleczech studied theater at the University of California, Los Angeles, where she met Breuer, the first and most enduring collaborator of her career, and departed before graduating to join Breuer when he finished his studies. Breuer remembers being struck by Maleczech's intensity and dedication at UCLA. "She had a lot of emotional accessibility and she seemed to have a higher dedication to performing than any of the other students. She was a little more obsessed than the other students," he recalls.[10] In San Francisco, Maleczech was cast as Emily in a production of Thornton Wilder's *Our Town* by a Bay Area theater company, the Interplayers. The main focus of her time in San Francisco, however, was her four years of work with Ronnie Davis and the R.G. Davis Mime Troupe (later the San Francisco Mime Troupe). "It was very thrilling work and I really wanted to do it," she says,

> I wasn't trained enough to actually do it, but Davis was really rigorous, so I learned. He was a marvelous teacher.... We trained for hours and hours every day, and we did standard Commedia dell'Arte, from people like Goldoni. We did a little bit of pantomime, because it was good for physical training, although we didn't ever use pantomime. We used American mime, which is when the body becomes the object, rather than pantomime, which is pretending that you have the object. Instead of everyone pretending that they had a sword, your arm would become the sword. It was based on Chaplin.

This physical training continued to have crucial resonances for Maleczech throughout her career. "Although I've never been a dancer," she says, citing her early work with Davis, "I always take great pleasure in and get great information from movement."[11]

In addition to training with Davis, the students worked with him to put together pieces that they performed in parks or other public spaces. One particularly influential project for Maleczech was *The Black and White Mime Show*, cocreated with his wife at the time, Judy North (then

Davis), a visual artist. "That was the first time that I had the experience of working with a visual artist," recalls Maleczech,

> which I have done ever since. Judy Davis made these shapes and we tried playing with them. Ronnie tried to make a story from them but a narrative didn't work, so he started developing approaches to movement with us that could contain these shapes, or in which the shapes would contain you—you would be inside the shape. It was really eye opening.

Iris Smith Fischer notes that *The Black and White Mime Show* was "the first abstract piece ... in which Maleczech ever performed."[12] The style Maleczech encountered at the Mime Troupe found later resonances in *The Red Horse Animation*; the performers' portrayals of the horse's Heart Line, Outline, and Storyline point to a conceptual approach similar in its emphasis on nonfigurative form over conventional narrative. Where *The Black and White Mime Show* found structure for movement in shapes, in *Red Horse*, Maleczech explained, "David [Warrilow] looked for strong narratives; JoAnne [Akalaitis] looked for strong conceptual ideas. And I looked for strong emotional ideas. And that's how we broke it down."[13]

Another important forerunner of *The Red Horse Animation* and the Mabou Mines productions that followed was the San Francisco Tape Music Center, where Maleczech worked with the composers Pauline Oliveros, Mortin Subotnik, and Ramon Sender, and with the dancer Anna Halprin. "They were looking for actors to be part of their music," Maleczech explains, "maybe to talk while the music was being played or maybe to walk through a series of objects while the music was being played, various things like that. Very discreet, very minimal ... that was another big education for me." Oliveros reappeared in Maleczech's collaborative network when she composed the music for *Mabou Mines's Lear* (1990).

Maleczech's collaborations with multidisciplinary artists in galleries also paved the way for Mabou Mines to present its early work in a variety of nontraditional performance spaces. After *Red Horse* opened at the

Guggenheim Museum in New York with Ellen Stewart as producer, the performance toured to galleries around the country. Maleczech explains that theater producers were unlikely to consider Mabou Mines's early work part of the theatrical genre. Instead, the company was more likely to be programmed by visual and music departments at universities and by independent galleries. Early letters to potential producers around the country reflect the company's struggle to develop a vocabulary with which to describe their performances.

The other crucial component of Maleczech's theater education in San Francisco came from Blau, Jules Irving, and the San Francisco Actor's Workshop, where Maleczech also met Akalaitis, then a graduate student at Stanford. The Actor's Workshop "was the first place where I ever read Genet or Beckett or Ionesco or Dürrenmatt," Maleczech recalled. In order to observe Blau's work on plays that were different in style and structure than anything she had encountered before, Maleczech took on whatever responsibilities were available to her at the Actor's Workshop. This included her job as a dresser on a production of *King Lear* starring Michael O'Sullivan, her first experience with the play that would later figure so prominently in her own career. In 1961, she was also cast in a small role in *Twinking of an Eye* by H.W. Wright and Guy Andros, directed by Alan Schneider, which treated themes of nuclear warfare within the milieu of a domestic comedy. O'Sullivan was also in the cast of this production.

Maleczech says that Blau was interested in "over the top, very explosive" performers, suggesting his affinity for O'Sullivan's work. Of the distinctions she discovered between Davis's approach and Blau's, Maleczech explained:

> Herb did not link acting to psychology, but to what you were using the play to say. And that's very important to me. He was the first person I ever encountered who did that. Ronnie was interested in fulfilling his idea of what the play meant politically, always. Not that Herb wasn't, but Herb also saw the theater as a way of connecting to the audience's intellectual life, or teaching the audience that it could have an intellectual life. Ronnie was very skilled at using theatrical

representations to elucidate his political agenda. Maybe because Herb's agenda was very complicated, it included more than just politics. He had a philosophical agenda. It was very interesting to see a play being used to do something other than what it was written to do.[14]

Maleczech's own point of view about the intellectual relationship between the performance and the audience would later closely resemble the priorities she identifies in Blau's agenda.

During their years in San Francisco, Maleczech also performed in a number of productions directed by Breuer, including Jean Genet's *The Maids* and Federico García Lorca's *The House of Bernarda Alba*, in which she played Martirio. Breuer remembers that in Lorca's play Maleczech performed her first major role under his direction, and, he says, as part of the professional cast "she was very grand, she was brilliant, and everyone noticed." He also recalls that Maleczech played Grusha from *The Caucasian Chalk Circle* for an audition for the Actor's Workshop. "She was a great Grusha," Breuer recalls, "from that point on it was clear that she was ready to do leads."

Maleczech said that she "realized the importance of language" in San Francisco, not only because of her exposure to European avant-garde plays at the Actor's Workshop, but also because of her artistic and political surroundings. "San Francisco was full of poets," she remembered. She recalled seeing Bob Dylan play acoustic guitar in coffee shops as well as performances and readings by Miles Davis, Allen Ginsberg, and Lawrence Ferlinghetti.[15]

Breuer and Maleczech left California for Europe in late 1964 and, after traveling the continent, eventually settled in Paris, where a number of Americans of their generation had established a thriving theater scene. Maleczech earned income by doing voice-over work in English for French films, frequently providing the voice for Catherine Deneuve. Both Smith Fischer and Breuer suggest that this early voice-over work laid important ground for Maleczech's subsequent emphasis on exploring and exploiting her vocal range in performance.[16] "She has a lot of vocal technique and media vocal technique," Breuer said.

When Brecht translator Ralph Manheim learned that they were planning to stage *Mother Courage and Her Children* at the American Theater of Paris, he suggested that Maleczech and Breuer visit East Berlin to observe rehearsals of the Berliner Ensemble. The legendary actress Helene Weigel greeted them when they arrived. "We said, 'we're here,' and she said 'what do you want to know?'" Maleczech remembered,

> and we asked if we could just watch and she said "sure." We watched rehearsals of *Mann ist Mann*, we went to their canteen, we met Ekkehard Schall, who is sort of the doppelganger for Brecht—smoked a cigar and had close-cropped hair, and was married to Brecht's daughter and was a big star in the Berliner Ensemble. We saw the plays that were duplicates of the way Brecht had done them.

Maleczech was deeply impressed by the way Brecht had done these plays, and when they returned to Paris, she and Breuer were inspired to work on their own production of *Mother Courage*.

At the Berliner Ensemble, Maleczech closely observed the precision of the performers' gestures and movements. Actors performed "with great skill," recalled Maleczech, "Exactitude. Timing that was so exact. No wasted gestures. Very economical in terms of the gesture that was used." And the productions were "different than any Brecht that I had seen done or that's been done since," she said,

> they were always revealing of the person. Not even the actor, but the *person* who was on the stage. The opinions, or the feelings or the history of the person playing the part, who the role is then a part of. So it was twice removed from the role. It's very hard to do it. I think Brecht tried often to give them the signals, the signs, the gestures, that would do it for him—say for *him* how Ekkehard Schall should play that moment in *Arturo Ui* or how Helene Weigel should play saying goodbye to Coriolon or how Aufidius and his wife should say goodbye in *Coriolanus*...I think he directed the alienation. I'm not sure that the actors had all that much to do with it.

Maleczech's analysis credits the Berliner Ensemble's acting style entirely to Brecht's direction. The meticulous attention to gesture and the exposure of the actors themselves that Maleczech observed would nonetheless become crucial to her own technique as a performer. She would adapt these strategies to Mabou Mines's collective, pastiched, and research-oriented process.

Mabou Mines's philosophy and methodology were also likely influenced by this visit to the Berliner Ensemble. Maleczech recalls the impact of watching rehearsals in which several assistant directors would call actors to the front of the stage to discuss aspects of the reconstruction of Brecht's staging. These conversations, among several sets of actors and directors, occurred in the open, rather than in the privacy associated with more conventional approaches to the actor-director dynamic. Perhaps more unusual is that several directors were simultaneously exchanging ideas with performers. Mabou Mines's way of working embraces a similar sharing of concepts and techniques from the full range of collaborators.

In 1969, after returning to Paris from East Berlin, Maleczech traveled to the south of France to study with Jerzy Grotowski. After he had narrowed the list to forty or fifty out of the hundred or so applicants for his course, Grotowski asked everyone who was not "good enough to do the work" to step back against the wall to observe. Maleczech did not step back against the wall. The physical work, she says,

> went on for hours and hours and hours. Endless hours. It was really, really tiring. Exhausting. And then around the end of the fourth day we started doing other kinds of things, taking the plastiques and integrating them into some way of talking or some way of waiting or some way of listening. Other things started to be incorporated into what had been purely physical, learned stuff. After the sixth day there were no more gymnastics. It was just performing. And he would give a scene, you had to learn some speech and come out and give it and he would criticize you and he would do things to you to make you do it better—in his terms, better, but you weren't quite sure what his terms were, so it was a very mysterious sort of process to go through. I remember there was a French movie actor there—wonderful

actor—this woman, and she really worked so hard on this thing and Grotowski kept saying, "no, not like that, no, no," and he would tell her some other thing to do, some other way to approach it and she would try again, she would try again, she would try again. And he kept saying to her, "is it that you can't do it, or you won't do it?" And she said, "oh I can't, I can't." He would say "okay," and then he would go again. And this went on until about four o'clock in the morning. There was never any end to these classes until he ended it. And towards the end he said, "is it that you can't do it or that you won't do it?" and she said, "it's that I won't do it." And he said, "leave, and don't ever come back."

Maleczech was willing to do it, and Grotowski told her that the Lady Macbeth "out damned spot" speech she had prepared was "'a proposition.' I thought I'd died and gone to heaven," she says, "that was a huge compliment coming from him. That was major." In response, Maleczech asked if she could study voice work with him. Maleczech says Grotowski, not knowing she was pregnant, "pulled me around the room and punched me in the diaphragm." Grotowski was quite surprised when a visibly pregnant Maleczech arrived in Poland shortly thereafter to see his work in production. Maleczech and Akalaitis went on to teach what they had learned from Grotowski to Breuer and Warrilow, and Maleczech continued to teach these techniques and to use them in her own work with Mabou Mines.

Samuel Beckett's work played a fundamental role in shaping the approaches of the founding co-artistic directors equal to their experiences with Blau, Grotowski, and the Berliner Ensemble. Maleczech and Breuer were fortunate to have their first taste of Beckett at the San Francisco Actor's Workshop, the first theater in the United States to produce his plays. In her chapter on the company's history with Beckett, Ruby Cohn notes that the San Francisco Mime Troupe (then the R.G. Davis Mime Troupe) also worked with Beckett's texts during the time that Maleczech and Breuer were in San Francisco. Describing the various European theatrical influences on the members of Mabou Mines, Cohn suggests that they evolved an approach to acting that Breuer called Mr. [sic] Outside (Brecht) combined with Mr. Inside (Grotowski). Less schematically than this contrast would suggest a Beckett play became the linchpin of their exercises—*Play*, the very play that occasioned Beckett's own step into a new dramatic phase.

As Cohn describes, before the famous collaboration between the playwright and Warrilow, the actor worked with Maleczech, Akalaitis, Breuer, and Glass on the production of *Play* in Paris. Work on *Play* began as an experiment in acting, one that, according to Cohn, would help them to "work their way through and beyond realism." [17] Although Cohn credits Breuer with this initiative, it was Maleczech and Akalaitis who taught what they had learned from Grotowski to Breuer and Warrilow, suggesting that the search for a nonrealistic approach was a group endeavor, and one in which each individual collaborator was already engaged. In Maleczech's case, the journey had begun when she sought out artists such as Davis and Oliveros in San Francisco in the 1950s.

Play evolved into a production in which the performers adorned their faces with pancake batter and oatmeal, which Cohn reports, "flaked off in the rapidity of their delivery."[18] Mabou Mines's *Play* premiered in Paris at the American Cultural Center in 1967, before there was a Mabou Mines, and was performed again in New York City under the imprimatur of the newly minted company. The New York production ran in tandem with *Come and Go*, which premiered under the Brooklyn Bridge in 1971 featuring Maleczech, Akalaitis, and Ellen McElduff under Breuer's direction. Along with Warrilow's performance of *The Lost Ones* (1974), these productions later formed a program entitled "Mabou Mines Performs Samuel Beckett" at Theater for the New City, which at that time occupied space at the Jane West Hotel, an SRO (Single Room Occupancy) on Jane Street. This evening of Beckett is what first drew Joseph Papp to see Mabou Mines, leading him to offer the company a residency at the New York Public Theater. Maleczech recalls that "he came and he said afterwards, 'why don't you come over to my place.' And that was the first inkling that maybe we could do this kind of work in a theater."[19]

Though she derived inspiration for her work from each of the men she referred to as her "three great teachers," the most important lesson was one Maleczech learned from Grotowski. He suggested Maleczech use his principles and techniques as well as those from the Berliner Ensemble; from Blau; from her first great acting teacher, R. G. Davis; and from the group's experiments with Beckett to establish her own aesthetic approach. Grotowski "said that he didn't think that people should take his aesthetic, that the ideas behind it were for everyone to use but that it shouldn't come out looking like him," and, says Maleczech, "I took that very much to heart."

A brief history of Mabou Mines

Upon leaving Paris, the Mabou Mines founding co-artistic directors scattered to several cities, where they planned to explore the feasibility of starting a company. Akalaitis and Glass were in New York and, finding fertile artistic ground, Akalaitis encouraged Maleczech, Breuer, and Warrilow to join them there.

The company's name comes from a town in Nova Scotia near a house of Glass's, where they rehearsed *Red Horse*. Maleczech said that the cofounders liked "Mabou Mines" because they thought it could just have easily been the name of a rock band or the title of a record album. Mabou Mines made its company debut at New York City's Guggenheim Museum with *The Red Horse Animation*. Maleczech played the horse's Heart Line. Though it was written and directed by Lee Breuer, *Red Horse* was created collectively with Maleczech and collaborators Akalaitis, Glass, and Warrilow. The show set the stage for the intensively collaborative development process that is a hallmark of the company. The making and presenting of *Red Horse* also established a context for the work Maleczech would generate for the rest of her life. At the February 2014 memorial service for Maleczech organized by her family and held at La MaMa in New York's East Village, Breuer described her unique ability to find a structure for feelings onstage. He was speaking of her performances, but Maleczech's imaginative work as a director and dedicated role as a company producer were also characterized by her capacity to transform rich emotion into theatrical experience. When Mabou Mines performed *Red Horse* in art galleries around the United States, it helped to establish a place for American performance in nontraditional theater spaces. *Red Horse* was also a foray into the technically ambitious staging that the company is known for; in this early production, Glass amplified the specially designed flooring so the movements of the performers could be aurally (as well as visually) perceived by the audience.

The company is celebrated for its ambitious adaptations of prose to the stage as well as its reinventions of classic plays from a traditional repertory. In addition to *Dressed Like an Egg* (1977), directed by Akalaitis and based on the writings of Colette, and *Wrong Guys* (1981), directed by Maleczech and based on a Jim Strah novel, prose adaptations include Patricia Spears Jones's reinvention of Gorky's novel *Mother*, directed by John McGrath and featuring Maleczech (1994), who also commissioned Jones, in the lead role. Breuer directed Mabou Mines's adaptations of *King Lear* and Henrik Ibsen's *A Doll's House* (*DollHouse*, 2003). Adaptation took another form when Fogarty staged *FINN*, based on the Celtic legend of Finn McCool, in 2010.

As already mentioned, Mabou Mines is recognized for its extensive work with plays and texts by Beckett in the 1970s and early 1980s, including their productions of *Play, Come and Go, The Lost Ones* (1975), and *Mercier and Camier* (1979). Warrilow and co-artistic director Fred Neumann are best known for their interpretations of Beckett's plays and texts, though, in addition to Breuer, Akalaitis and Maleczech also directed works by Beckett for the company; in 1984, Maleczech staged Beckett's short story *Imagination Dead Imagine*. Mabou Mines's work with Beckett's texts displays the company's commitment to language, an interest that has endured throughout the company's history in work with a variety of writers, including Breuer himself.

In addition to Mabou Mines's early residencies at La MaMa and the Public Theater, in the 1970s the company enjoyed the support of the organization Arts Services, which helped Mabou Mines and other artists to manage funds and secure touring engagements that would pay their bills. Mabou Mines benefited early on from substantial support from the NEA and other government agencies, but the company has seen those funds dwindle in recent years and their development and production budgets have suffered as a consequence. The company was also successful at securing private funding from corporations including AT&T and Sony, especially in the late 1980s and 1990s. Mabou Mines in turn has given back through its ongoing residency program, Mabou Mines/Suite, which provides mentorship, funding, and space to emerging artists.

Mabou Mines has called the converted East Village schoolhouse PS 122 home since 1980. Originally they used the school's cafeteria on the main floor, moving later to the second story, where their offices and the small ToRoNaDa studio space were located. The ToRoNaDa provided the company with a rehearsal and an occasional performance space. As of this writing, PS 122 is undergoing renovations by the City of New York and Mabou Mines occupies temporary offices near Union Square. Improved office space and a new performance venue are slated to open in 2016, but in the context of decreased funding the displacement from a regular rehearsal space has created challenges for productions in development. The company has a repertoire of touring works, however, including *Lucia's Chapters* and *DollHouse*, and they have continued to stage productions regularly in New York and around the world during their absence from PS 122.

The fluid constellation of artistic directors has also affected the company's work, both practically and artistically. Starting in the mid-1980s, Maleczech began to take on an increasing number of featured roles in projects such as *Hajj* and *Lear*. Although Mabou Mines has continued to emphasize the importance of creating an ensemble of performers, this work of Maleczech's marks the emergence of a pattern of productions highlighting particular performers, begun in the 1970s with Neumann in *B. Beaver* (1974) and Warrilow in *The Lost Ones*. This continues in recent work such as *Peter and Wendy* (1996), which features Mabou Mines co-artistic director Karen Kandel, and *Lucia's Chapters*, which featured Maleczech.

Although Mabou Mines is organized as a collective, not every artistic director participates in each production; performances have resulted from collaborations of almost every imaginable combination of artistic directors and associates. There are, nonetheless, a shared set of concerns among the co-artistic directors, such as a highly collaborative development process that sometimes borders on the collective; an integration of design elements with performance; an effort to encourage the autonomy of performers; a dedication to language and research; an interest in a multimedia approach to storytelling (though not necessarily conventional narrative); and a blending of comedy and sentimentality. These characteristics, however, have tended to influence the approach to creating work rather than resulting in a "house style;" for example, though Breuer and Maleczech are both founding artistic directors, it is hard to imagine two productions more dissimilar in mood, style, and scope than her *Belén* and his *DollHouse*, despite the fact that both stage fundamental questions about representations of gender. Breuer, who does not believe that the company has a house style, suggests that if there is a common stylistic thread among productions, it may come from the sheer number of them that Julie Archer designed during her tenure starting in the mid-1970s and ending in 2013. "I honestly don't think there is a discernible Mabou Mines style that spreads to a number of different people," Breuer says, "just like there is no Wooster Group style—it's just Liz [LeCompte]." Mabou Mines is distinct from the Wooster Group, of course, because of its structure of shared artistic directorship, but Breuer points to the distinct nature of the aesthetic of Mabou Mines's co-artistic directors.

As Maleczech noted, the company is collective but not necessarily democratic. This extends to the way in which it approaches aesthetic as well as producing concerns. "Ruth has the power of being the elder statesman," Breuer said before her death, "If you have to come down to it, it's Ruth's company. It's not my company. And that's unquestionable. I think if anything came up that Ruth said no to it wouldn't happen. And most things that she says yes to will happen." Co-artistic directors have the power to turn down a collaboration on a production that does not interest them and performers have a great deal of leeway in choosing which avenues to explore during development, but since the late 1970s the director has usually had the final say on artistic decisions. Because not every co-artistic director has worked on every production, because the composition of co-artistic directors is not the same today as it was at the time of the company's founding, and because collaborators are given permission to develop production work with a great degree of autonomy, each co-artistic director has developed an independent body of work. It is thus possible, even important, to isolate the aesthetic concerns of artistic directors (which frequently overlap) in order to treat individuals in the collective with the complexity that each artist's work deserves.

Maleczech participated continuously in the company's daily operations and its fundraising, even though co-artistic director Sharon Fogarty has been the company's central producer since 1999.[20] Former General Manager Joe Stackell supported the producing and managerial work of the company until his retirement in 2015.

In addition to her managerial role, Maleczech directed regularly for the company. Her first directorial venture was *Vanishing Pictures* (1980). *Vanishing Pictures* was quickly followed up by her multimedia adaptation of Strah's *Wrong Guys*, premiering at the Public Theater. Her staging of *Imagination Dead Imagine*, which featured the first large-scale hologram onstage, showcases Mabou Mines's characteristically inventive use of technology. *Song for New York: What Women Do While Men Sit Knitting*, was staged on a barge off of the Long Island City pier in Queens and was the first Mabou Mines production since *Come and Go* to be staged site specifically.

Maleczech also used her position as co-artistic director to initiate projects as a performer, as she did with the company's production of Mabou Mines *Lear* and as she did just before her death with *Imagining the Imaginary Invalid*. That she was able to do so is evidence of Mabou Mines's success in promoting the independence of performers.

Although not all of the artistic directors agree on the success of wearing multiple hats, it may be that Maleczech's extensive experience as a producer and director helped to instill the confidence and competence that allowed her to create the kind of self-driven performance she was known for. Of Maleczech's ability to craft her own performances, Breuer, her collaborator from 1957 until her death, said, "I think Ruth is best in the stuff that she practically does herself, and that goes for me and for other directors. I think what I can offer Ruth are good ideas, and sometimes other good directors can too, but probably not as good as the ideas she can come up with herself."

Though Maleczech's commitment to Mabou Mines meant that she took on outside projects on a highly selective basis, she and other co-artistic directors have sometimes produced notable work with other collaborators. Her 1996 production of *Happy Days* with director Robert Woodruff was first produced by the La Jolla Playhouse. Maleczech was the winner of five OBIE awards, a USA Gracie Fellowship, the Otto René Castillo Award for Political Theatre, TCG's Zeisler Award for contributions to American not-for-profit theater, and other prestigious citations and awards from organizations including the NEA, the Fox Foundation, and the Foundation for Contemporary Arts. She was posthumously granted an Off-Broadway Hall of Fame award. Brief biographies of other prominent past and present co-artistic directors are available in the appendix.

Methodology, scope, and structure

By considering Maleczech's production and performance choices thematically, and by juxtaposing previously unpublished interviews with reviews in print, production archives, and critical analysis, this book points to patterns in Maleczech's body of work that highlight the interrelationship between process and product. Case studies illustrate Maleczech's social, political, and emotional aesthetic for the contemporary theater. The theoretical framework engages with gender studies scholarship and takes into consideration new strategies for developing a critical methodology to approach theatrical landscapes that are by their very nature ephemeral and fleeting. I have engaged with both journalistic and academic writing about Maleczech's work whenever it is relevant, though the paucity of attention that focuses on her contributions in particular is what makes this effort to point to the significance of her work so crucial.

The work I examine in depth was created between 1980 and her death. This may be because Maleczech emerged in the 1980s as an artist independent of the collective of performers she worked with at Mabou Mines in the 1970s. She began directing in the 1980s, and she also began to take on featured roles in Mabou Mines productions with increased frequency during this same period.

This project builds on the pioneering work of Iris Smith Fischer, whose 2010 book, *Mabou Mines: Making Avant-Garde Theater in the 1970s*, is the first and only full-length study of the company. Smith Fischer covers the company's founding and gives comprehensive accounts and insightful analyses of processes and productions in the 1970s, engaging with the work of each of the founding artistic directors and a number of early artistic associates. My work is indebted to Smith Fischer's research and ideas.

Bonnie Marranca is one of the first scholars to have considered Mabou Mines in depth, and her introduction to Breuer's *Animations: A Trilogy for Mabou Mines* (1979), which Marranca coedited with Gautam Dasgupta, as well as their treatment of *Red Horse* in *The Theatre of Images* (2005), are foundational to my work on Maleczech.

Alisa Solomon, who served as dramaturg on *Lear*, also provides a particularly useful approach in terms of methodology and theoretical framework in *Re-dressing the Canon* (1997). I draw on Solomon's suggestion that Mabou Mines asks audiences to make contact with their performances in new, different, and challenging ways as well as her emphasis on close readings of productions.

A number of scholars who have written on Mabou Mines (Solomon included) position their analyses of the company's work within a feminist theoretical framework. This study of Maleczech's work does the same. This is no accident; the political and social leanings of the company members make for leftist aesthetics, and Maleczech, among others, acknowledged that the work of the company is intentionally socially engaged, though she noted that only certain pieces are intended to be overtly political.

Feminist theater critics such as Elin Diamond, Lynda Hart, and Sue-Ellen Case were among the first to use analyses of the live body onstage to focus on questions of gender and sexuality, as Jill Dolan notes in her introduction to *A Sourcebook of Feminist Theatre and Performance* (1996). This book draws upon these interpretive strategies as well as on Dolan's idea of the feminist spectator. Hart's anthologies *Making a Spectacle* (1989) and *Acting Out* (1993, coedited with Peggy Phelan) challenge readers, artists, and audiences to expand possibilities for who is seen, how s/he is seen, and who sees him/her. The art and artists theorized in these anthologies confront and defy traditional representations of gender, identity, and truth, paving the way for my close reading of Maleczech's work. Judith Butler's significant contributions on the performativity of gender (most notably in *Gender Trouble*, 1990) also play a crucial role in my analytical framework, as does the rigorous deconstruction of gender and sexual identity pioneered by queer theorists including Eve Kosofsky Sedgwick, Adrienne Rich, and Diana Fuss. There is a striking correspondence between the queer and feminist theory of that period and Maleczech's preoccupations in the productions I examine. Indeed, the earliest productions treated here are contemporaneous with the emergence of these theories. Maleczech's career was dedicated to staging some of the very conflicts articulated in such landmark works.

Because Maleczech's crucial and distinctive contribution to downtown New York theater—the site of many of the United States's most innovative performances from the 1960s to the present—and to Mabou Mines in particular has not been given the critical credit it deserves, this book functions in part as a recuperative history. It is my premise that the full significance of Maleczech's work has been ignored in part because she was a woman and in part because she was best known as a performer. Until her death, she and Breuer were the only founding artistic directors who remained with the company, and yet Breuer is credited with contributing substantially to the company even as the importance of Maleczech's contributions has been largely overlooked. This project thus responds to Harding's challenge that scholars of the avant-garde consider "whose history one ultimately produces or reproduces ... whose work scholars ultimately discuss, to what end, and in whose interest?"[21]

Stephen Bottoms's 2004 rewriting of the founding of the off-off Broadway movement, *Playing Underground*, provides a valuable example of recuperative theatrical history. The central figure to whom Bottoms brings overdue credit is Joe Cino, and this belated examination of Cino's contribution provides inspiration for what I hope to accomplish with this project, though Maleczech begins as a more widely known figure than did Cino. The recuperative projects that Anne Fliostos and Wendy Vierow undertake in *American Women Stage Directors of the Twentieth Century* (2008) and *International Women Stage Directors* (2013) also establish significant precedents for my focus on Maleczech as a director.

Finally, David Savran's 1988 book on the Wooster Group, *Breaking the Rules*, provides a model for interspersing critical analysis with interviews with the artists themselves. I was fortunate to be in regular communication with Maleczech in the years between 2006 and her death and have used her as a resource while at the same time forming my own critical judgments of her work. Savran's and Solomon's thematic organization also suggest a useful alternative to chronological organization.

The Mabou Mines archives are housed at the Fales Collection at NYU's Bobst Library and I have relied heavily on these materials. More recent material has not yet been given to or catalogued at Fales and has been made available to me at the Mabou Mines offices. A small number of video recordings related to my research are also available at the New York Library for the Performing Arts's Theater on Film and Tape collection. The most central archival materials are video recordings of performances, but I have also relied on production photographs, company-generated publicity material and grant applications, programs, letters, and reviews. Interviews I conducted with Maleczech and many of her collaborators as well as some live performances are equally vital to this discussion.

The first chapter traces connections between Maleczech's approach to acting and her performances in Samuel Beckett's *Happy Days* and Franz Kroetz's *Through the Leaves*. These productions reveal her interest in making ordinary women important onstage. Here, Maleczech's ordinary women achieve the status of Everywomen in spite of, or perhaps because of, the theatrical particularity with which she invests them. I also chart connections between Maleczech's background and training and her performance choices in these productions.

The next chapter centers on Maleczech's predilection for resurrecting extraordinary women from history and finding their resonances in a contemporary theatrical context. This chapter treats the productions *Dead End Kids, Lucia's Chapters of Coming Forth by Day,* and *Belén: A Book of Hours* as history plays establishing an interrogative relationship with the past, exploring the ways in which Maleczech uses theater as a historiographic device to reconsider representations of women from the past.

The third chapter puts two productions about fathers, *Hajj* and Mabou Mines's *Lear*, in conversation with one other, demonstrating an interest on Maleczech's part in destabilizing traditional notions of the father figure and, by extension, all family roles and relationships. These works further reveal Maleczech's investment in redrawing the boundaries of what women are allowed to say, onstage and off.

The final chapter investigates *Shaggy Dog, Red Beads,* and *Summa Dramatica*, works by fellow founding co-artistic director Lee Breuer, as well as Beckett's *Imagination Dead Imagine*, all productions on which Maleczech collaborated with her daughter, Clove Galilee. By looking at the ways in which Maleczech positions Mabou Mines with regard to family relationships, this discussion considers how collaboration with her own daughter challenges theoretical notions of both familial and artistic hierarchy. Constructed and represented in such a way, the physical and emotional intimacy of these family ties advances the development of the productions and deepens the emotional investment for both artists and audiences.

The conclusion examines eulogies of Maleczech and includes some of the views of her long-term collaborators as they ponder the significance of her work. A brief exploration of her final work in progress, *Imagining the Imaginary Invalid*, suggests ways in which the project draws together a range of Maleczech's enduring theatrical commitments. These reflections draw together the patterns identified in the earlier chapters and paint a convincing portrait of Maleczech's social, political, and emotional aesthetic for the theater.

Maleczech invented Mabou Mines with her cofounders, and it, in turn, gave her the license and flexibility to repeatedly reinvent her own role as a theater artist. Mabou Mines's marriage of process and product meant that the women Maleczech put onstage retained a similar elasticity, stretching and reforming the relationship between how we might expect to see them and how they actually appear to us.

1

Ordinary Women

Oh, this woman's life, it's like mine.

Ruth Maleczech quoting an audience member

Maleczech's ability to transform ordinary women into important ones onstage is among her most spectacular feats of her enterprising theatricality. Her performances in Samuel Beckett's *Happy Days* (1996) and Franz Kroetz's *Through the Leaves* (1984) demonstrate her investment in this project. In these performances, Maleczech's ordinary women become Everywomen because she endows them with particularity; she invites the audience to recognize the individuality with which each character approaches both the quotidian and the unusual aspects of her situation. Douglas Stein, the set designer for both productions, says that what struck him most about Maleczech's performances in these plays was "the extraordinary detail of her work."[1] Well positioned to bring the particularities of ordinary concerns to the stage, she grew up in a working-class family in the Mid- and Southwest, earning international distinction as a result of hard work, dedication, and determination. This chapter traces the influence of Maleczech's personal history and professional training on her political and social commitment to acknowledge the significance of commonplace women onstage.

Through the Leaves is a collaboration with director JoAnne Akalaitis and performer Fred Neumann, both co-artistic directors of Mabou Mines at the time of the 1984 production, which premiered at the Women's Interart Theatre and transferred to the Shiva Theater at the New York Public Theater. Akalaitis, Neumann, and Maleczech received

OBIE Awards for their work, and the production garnered the award for Best Production at the Festival of the Americas in Montreal the following year, where Maleczech also picked up the award for best performer. The production traveled to the Israel Festival in 1986 before returning to the Public Theater in 1990, shortly before Akalaitis resigned from Mabou Mines and began her brief tenure as Artistic Director of the Public. *Happy Days*, directed by Robert Woodruff, was first commissioned by and produced at the La Jolla Playhouse in 1996. Despite its origins in California, this was by no means a conventional regional theater production, which may account for Maleczech's involvement. The show was produced in New York at Mabou Mines's ToRoNaDa studio in 1999. In her portrayals of Annette and Winnie, Maleczech's rich and detailed depictions make the women she represents more important onstage than they would be in daily life. Maleczech, taking her cue from the writers whose voices she interprets, brings our attention to bear on the everyday struggles of these ordinary women.

It should come as no surprise that Maleczech gravitated toward Winnie; by the time of the La Jolla production she had established an impressive history of performing Beckett with Mabou Mines. Winnie is a significant milestone in building Maleczech's reputation for putting noteworthy roles for women on the stage. *Happy Days* marks Beckett's first foray into a highly detailed and expansive female role for the theater.[2] It also requires the demanding vocal acrobatics that Maleczech's training prepared her for and that Mabou Mines has continued to pursue; Akalaitis describes this as an interest in "different ways of speaking."[3] As Enoch Brater notes,

> Although *Happy Days* is a two-character play, the work is, in effect, Beckett's first female solo … Beckett once said that he selected a woman for this role because the contents of a handbag would provide an immobile character with more "business" to do onstage. And yet this statement belies his growing fascination with the vocal range of a female player, the quality of sound he was able to get from an earthy Maddy Rooney, an ethereal Miss Fitt, or a sentimentally "canned" but philosophically correct Nell

... *Happy Days* exploits the higher timbre of Krapp's female counterpart, a vocalizer whose rising action climaxes in a song of songs, the waltz duet from *The Merry Widow*.[4]

It is no coincidence that Maleczech, who had honed her instruments on *Play* and *Come and Go* (both 1971), wished to tackle the multidimensionality of this middle-aged Beckett woman as a more mature performer.

Furthermore, Winnie's middle-aged, middle-class—in short, ordinary— concerns likely appealed to Maleczech's interest in treating everyday women with extraordinary dignity onstage. Linda Ben Zvi writes:

> Winnie could well be described as a caricature of the middle-aged woman from Borough Green, but Beckett prevents this interpretation by allowing her an awareness of her own predicament and her own limited means to ward off the despair she experiences ... Beckett's Winnie is thus not only a woman; she is the physical embodiment of the condition of being a woman in her society. Not a stereotype, she is the result of stereotypic views of women. Beckett suggests what culture offers as ballast for a woman like Winnie. Not much.[5]

Though Winnie cannot rely on her cultural context to extract her from her circumstances, a sophisticated performer such as Maleczech can bring her predicament to bear on our cultural consciousness, reminding us how little has changed for Winnie and women like her in the three decades that transpired between Beckett's writing and the La Jolla production.

Kroetz, too, provides a meaty role for a mature female performer. Both Annette and Victor are working-class characters with lower to middle-class concerns. Annette's tastes are the more elevated of the two: she serves caviar at dinner and likes to go to the movies, while Victor prefers drinking beer and flipping through girlie magazines. And instead of taking the vacation Annette dreams of, the pair plant themselves under sun lamps on the floor in the back room of her shop. Roger Downey argues that Kroetz's concerns with the stark realities of everyday life made him attractive to the postwar German world in which he emerged by eschewing classical texts in favor of realistic, contemporary concerns.[6]

Akalaitis was also drawn to *Through the Leaves* because of her admiration for Kroetz's dramatization of blue-collar daily life. "I was very struck by his tremendous empathy for the working class," she says, "there's almost no playwriting about that that's not folkloric, that's real. And his writing is very real." She knew immediately that she wanted Maleczech and Neumann to play the roles: "They are both working-class people. They both have that great roughness that comes with the working class and I thought they could handle the material to do it."

Maleczech's representations of Annette and Winnie are symptomatic of her commitment to engaging with ordinary women on the stage. Iris Smith Fischer links Winnie to yet another of Maleczech's representations of a not so stereotypical everyday woman, Mother in Patricia Spears Jones's play of that title, produced in 1994:

> Like the character Maleczech played in Patricia Spears Jones's play *Mother*, inspired by Gorky's novel, Winnie is difficult. She is full of prosaic grousing, as was the Mother when she packed up her I-love-New York shopping bag and left her old life behind. Winnie has fewer options than the Mother; yet she too occupies a new world. In a sense Winnie's situation mirrors that of Mabou Mines—a company that speaks in the multiple voices of the postmodern while remaining defiantly modernist, i.e. avant garde.[7]

The material Maleczech chooses and the technique, texture, and tonality of her performances elevate these women from commonplace to archetypal. Along with Rose in *The Shaggy Dog Animation* (1978), and, but for their historical significance, the women of *Belén* (1999), representations discussed in subsequent chapters, her roles in *Through the Leaves* and *Happy Days* establish a pattern in which she dedicates her energies as a theater artist to making visible onstage the concerns of women whose ordinariness makes them nearly invisible in daily life. Maleczech marshalls her background, her training, and her determination to put herself in a prominent position from which to do so; she used her power onstage to advocate for the significance of working- and middle-class women.

A process of her own

Though their approaches diverged in many ways, Maleczech was deeply impressed by the rigor with which each of her "three great teachers," Davis, Blau, and Grotowski, approached his work. Future generations of students, she suggested, might find a similarly strict system of training in, for example, classical acting. "Sometimes when things are very prescribed, defined, outlined, and narrow you can bang against them," she says:

> It's the resonance of doing something that is other than the thing itself. Lots of rules, lots of strictures, lots of insistence on form and content are all good things because you will formulate your own aesthetic response. First you'll have to experience it, then you'll respond to it, and then it will be part of your skill set. It can be very valuable to study things that are antithetical to what work you might end up making.

The rigid training Maleczech advocates aims at establishing a set of technical tools that will allow artists to develop a creative vocabulary and articulate an individual artistic point of view; this is precisely what Grotowski suggested Maleczech and others who followed his training should do. Maleczech promoted classical training (or other similarly strict approaches) as a strategy for the kind of dialectical theater Breuer and Maleczech generated themselves:

> Classical work also teaches you counterpoint and opposition, which I consider to be very important in creating any kind of work. I hate one-to-one correspondences. I really don't like that. I think that the audience isn't well served by that kind of work because they don't really have work that *they* do. It's more or less the sense that "we did this for you and now we put it in your lap for you to enjoy."

While Judith Malina developed her training in Epic Theater techniques with Piscator in a rather different direction, Maleczech's view is influenced by the trip she took with Breuer to observe the work of the Berliner Ensemble in the mid-1960s. It was soon after this that they began to make new work under the auspices of Mabou Mines in 1970.[8]

Maleczech emphasizes a new disciplined, dialectical approach to performance in order to facilitate and foster communication with the audience. As part of the Mabou Mines tradition, she considers spectators a crucial element of the performance, even during the development process. "Mabou Mines has always had the idea that the way an audience looks at a piece is as important as the piece itself," Maleczech has said.[9] Contrary to what she and Mabou Mines advocate, she complains that

> almost all contemporary theater is done to please the audience. Not only Broadway. And of course the artists assume in the making of this work that they know what the audience would like to eat for dinner that night.

Influenced by Brecht and Blau, Maleczech advocates for a theater that challenges the audience to engage intellectually and politically with what they see onstage. Maleczech "leaves it in the audience's hands to make their own judgment," Breuer says. "It does make the audience work."

Such dialectical strategy is quite different from the interactive tactics Malina and the Living Theatre used to elicit politicized responses from the audience in the moment during performances such as *Paradise Now* (1968). Mabou Mines, and Maleczech in particular, aims to reach the audience on a more profound visceral level. Maleczech brings to her performances "one hundred percent honesty, real emotional honesty," said Breuer. The juxtaposition of intellectual rigor and emotional vulnerability is one of the distinctive aspects of her aesthetic, one she brings to bear in both her physical and vocal approaches to the text. Her exploration of this technique is the key that allows her to create, as Breuer has said, a structure for feelings. It can be traced to her first role at Mabou Mines: the Heart Line in *Red Horse*.

Mabou Mines's famous inaugural production, although written and directed by Breuer, was an ensemble piece influenced by contributions from the acting company throughout the development process. The company's early forays into Beckett's precise texts in *Play* (1971) and *Come and Go* (1979) encouraged Maleczech to develop a technique for approaching the language of a writer who was not in the room while she was working; one that combined her training with Davis and Grotowski and her keen observations at the San Francisco Actors' Workshop and the Berliner Ensemble. The result was precisely what Grotowski advocated, something that was distinctly Maleczech's.

Maleczech described her tactics for tackling language and narrative in nonnaturalistic, nonlinear plays as a three-tiered process meant to address "levels of language which are not natural to us." Her first point of entry is with the writer. Maleczech tries "to hear the voice of the writer—not what the writer puts on the page, not the character—the voice of the writer. I don't play roles," she says. "I don't even know what that is. I try to imitate the voice of the writer with my voice and physically. That's what I do." Her method for identifying this voice emphasizes research; she relies on other texts by the writers whose works she performs as well as critical examinations and historical/biographical context. In fact, Maleczech describes production research as her favorite aspect of the development process, citing as examples visits to see the Joyce apartment in Paris and Nora Joyce's "awful apartment in Galway" in preparation for the 2003 premiere of *Cara Lucia*. "You can get a lot of things by osmosis that way," she explains. In addition to helping Maleczech locate the writer's voice, research guides her in making determinations about the "music and pitch" of the language.

Maleczech's second point of entry into the text is "what the collective artists make." Because Mabou Mines typically introduces design elements into the rehearsal room early on, she responded to "how all the other people, the objects, the light, and the clothing impinges on me." The company's history of initiating probing and sometimes heated conversations about artistic decisions among the entire company—performers, designers, directors, designers, and technicians—was also crucial to Maleczech's interpretation. In addition to the tangible contributions she mentioned, Maleczech relied on her collaborators to generate "ideas about what the writing could mean. This is rarely questioned in the normal theater," Maleczech argued, adding that, in the case of what she describes as avant-garde plays, "they are *your* conclusions about the language." This is especially fruitful in the context of Mabou Mines's development process. Maleczech suggested that "most of the work of this company is about ideas" and those "ideas can be turned into theatrical moments." She likened Mabou Mines's theatricalization of ideas to American football:

> you throw the ball and you know somebody's going to catch it because they're in the right part of the field. So you throw the idea out and somebody catches it and runs with it all the way to the end zone and makes a big touchdown. A touchdown being an idea from a previous scene or an idea you know well but might have seen done in a different way before. That kind of process is very unwieldy, very ungovernable, and difficult for the director too, because there are so many strains going all at once and so many electric spin offs from one person's idea or another. [10]

Finally, Maleczech suggests, the meaning of language can only be determined in performance when an audience is present:

> The third thing has to do with the audience. This is more difficult because the audience is changeable, fickle. If you care about them, and I do, you have to be on your toes.

For Maleczech, spectators are crucial in the equation to decipher meaning. The interpretation of a given production, she says, is "in a very brief, very ephemeral moment what it *does* mean on a given night, to a given audience." Borrowing Grotowski's terminology, Maleczech says the relationship between audience and performance "is the proposition—our work has to meet their work."

In performance, Maleczech says, the three levels she describes are "bouncing around. It's very athletic. And that's why so many avant-garde artists gravitate to movement. Meyerhold and American Naturalism are after the same thing: the elimination through performance of this text." According to Maleczech, it is the means to this end that differ. In a naturalistic play, she contends, one might see an actor who plays a British character sipping a cup of tea in a manner that is particularized by the context and history of the play. In biomechanics, by contrast, the audience may derive meaning from a performer standing on her head. Elizabeth LeCompte and the Wooster Group engage in similarly corporeal tactics to invigorate naturalistic text in their adaptations of Eugene O'Neill's *The Emperor Jones* (1993) and *The Hairy Ape* (1996).

If the Mabou Mines process is football to Maleczech, avant-garde performance, she says, is closer to basketball. "It happens really fast. You're running the whole time, and you get really tired." Performance is "a 360 degree experience," requiring that the player have a sensory understanding of what is happening everywhere on the court at all times, without necessarily being able to see it all.

Although, for Maleczech, the process for deciphering meaning requires an audience, she insists that she does not make adjustments to her performance based on audience response. "No," she says, "that would be a deep, dark, black hole in the universe that you never get out of. I wouldn't even know how to do that." She does, however, describe an interaction with the audience that positions them as key players in performance. In order to attract their interest and attention, Maleczech explains, "you startle them or you push what you are doing so far that you get them to laugh, or you do the opposite of what you're doing, and you have them for a second, and then you lose them again." Paul Kandel, who performed with Maleczech in *Lucia's Chapters of Coming Forth By Day* (2007), suggested that Maleczech possessed a quality of liveness onstage. "If you care about what you do," he said,

> you have to come to the theater each evening a blank slate … you have to find a way to come to this material that you already know fresh, as if you don't know it. That's hard to do. Ruth is very good at it…. She's incredibly flexible. She is not a creature of habit. I don't think we've ever done *Lucia's Chapters* the same way twice, nor would it be in her to do that.[11]

Maleczech's facility to remain in the present moment allows her to take the kind of risks in performance that will jolt the audience into paying attention. The distinction between making adjustments based on audience response and engaging their concentration may appear slight. The contrast for Maleczech, however, was in the difference between playing *to* the audience and playing *with* them. She passed the ball to the audience as well as to fellow performers, casting the audience as players in the game of performance.

As Maleczech suggested, one of the best techniques for startling an audience is to make them laugh. Comedy is central to the work Mabou Mines makes, especially when Maleczech is involved. "Most of what we do is comic," Maleczech explained, and "I'm not so sure there's much difference between comedy and drama. I think it must be the distance to which you take it—how far you're willing to go."[12] Maleczech liked to take risks onstage; the notion that comedy necessitates extremity illuminates her affinity for this form. Breuer agrees with Maleczech's assessment that Mabou Mines has a sustained interest in comedy— "dark comedy," he notes. "She's a great comedian," Breuer said, "I actually think that's her forte. She's aggressive, and most great comedians are aggressive." Maleczech's forceful exploitation of comedy is another part of her inheritance from Beckett and Brecht; Maleczech and Breuer in particular use it as counterpoint to the emotional honesty in their work. "Mabou Mines uses comedy to cut through sentimentality," says Mabou Mines artistic associate Clove Galilee, Maleczech's daughter with Breuer.[13] Used in such a way, comedy becomes integral to the dialectical strategy that Maleczech promoted, and Breuer continues to exploit.

Maleczech's deployment of humor finds roots in her investigation of strict and rigorous forms that provide structure for the performer; her facility with comedy lies in her attention to detail and strong emphasis on mechanics. "Ruth knows funny," said Mabou Mines co-artistic director Karen Kandel, "She knows how to be funny. She says, 'well, you know it won't work if I say it only two times. I have to say it three times.' It's amazing." It was Maleczech's seemingly paradoxical pairing of a carefully calculated approach with the risk of coming fresh to each performance that elicited the audience's surprise. This works particularly well with comedy, which will not work if the audience anticipates the joke.

Maleczech's emphasis on process is endemic to avant-garde productions such as those by the Wooster Group, which categorically invite artists to collaborate in bringing meaning to text in production. More rare, however, is, as Maleczech suggests, the egalitarian nature of that collaboration at Mabou Mines; each artist is expected to contribute original ideas to the production. Although in most cases (evident in the company's more recent history) the director is the final arbiter of such input, each artist has, during the development process, left an indelible mark on the work. While this links Mabou Mines to the Living Theatre to a certain extent, Mabou Mines's primary emphasis on promoting the independence of performers is unique. "In the case of this company," Maleczech explained, the actor "is central."

Furthermore, although here Maleczech outlines her technique in relation to what she describes as "avant-garde" text, a similar approach is evident with scripts of a more naturalistic style, such as Kroetz's *Through the Leaves*. "This company is very involved in language," she said, and the performer is at the crux of this relationship. "The idea is, how does the performer meet the language," Maleczech said of Mabou Mines's performances. "It's like the language just sits out there and until you can sort of put your hands on it and eat it, you can't perform it. The language is the mysterious part."[14] Maleczech established a rehearsal process that allowed her to invest language with specific ideas and at the same time avoid transparency; Douglas Stein, who designed the sets for both *Through the Leaves* and *Happy Days*, describes Maleczech as "precise with words." In performance, Maleczech balances concepts that have been carefully considered and debated during the development process with inscrutable gestures, expressions, and intonations that preserve the enigmatic qualities of poetic language. The strategy aims to tantalize the audience to draw their own conclusions about what they see and hear.

Stein's suggestion that Maleczech is precise with words applies both to her performance and to her way of working. Maleczech has said of Mabou Mines: "We don't really do plays here, we make work," highlighting a shared, collective approach to material regardless of stylistic concerns. In this way Mabou Mines has developed an aesthetic that blends abstract ideas with traces of the discussions that have given the production meaning for the artists whose work we now see onstage. At the same time Mabou Mines estranges language we may take for granted by coupling it in production with remnants of the development process. Similar techniques have been employed by American avant-garde companies and artists such as the Wooster Group and Richard Foreman, who regularly fold elements of the artistic process into staged narrative. "The process itself is very complex," Maleczech has said,

> and usually it is the process that ends up being the piece. In fact, that's what you see when you go to the theater. You see the distillation of the process. That's why it's very often nonlinear. The narrative is often very deep in the piece so it doesn't surface so readily as it does in other people's work.[15]

Here Maleczech alludes to texts that have originated with the company, work like *Hajj* and *Red Horse*, both written by Breuer, yet the same applies to the company's work with nonoriginal scripts as well, in productions such as the adaptations of *King Lear* (1990) and *A Doll's House* (2003) in which new contexts and surprising metaphors explode the audience's preconceptions about such well-known plays. This approach makes artists adept at interpreting plays with abstract and nonlinear text in production, as the company has done repeatedly with Beckett's texts ever since its founding.

Despite Maleczech's willingness to explain her rehearsal and performance techniques, some aspects of her method remain mysterious. Galilee, Maleczech's collaborator on *Imagining the Imaginary Invalid*, the project she was developing at the time of her death, recalls finding her mother sitting up in the middle of the night, thinking, with the washcloth she used as a prop for Argan on her head. In *Happy Days* and *Through the Leaves*, Maleczech synthesizes material aspects of her technique—developed through her training and her work with Mabou Mines—with her ability to hover in the elusive space and time of liveness to turn ordinary women into extraordinary individuals onstage.

Happy Days: Maleczech's Winnie

Beckett's influence on Mabou Mines extends well beyond the founding artistic directors' experiments with his texts in the late 1960s and early 1970s. Although the company's work with Beckett's drama and Warrilow and Neumann's stage presentations of Beckett's prose are better known, Maleczech sought and received rare permission from Beckett in the early 1980s to stage his short story *Imagination Dead Imagine*. Her 1984 production premiered at the Performing Garage (discussed in depth in Chapter 4). *Happy Days*, however, is unique among Mabou Mines's Beckett productions because it was first commissioned and produced by La Jolla Playhouse during Michael Greif's tenure as Artistic Director; Maleczech worked with Robert Woodruff rather than with a Mabou Mines company member.[16]

Maleczech says that the Mabou Mines co-artistic directors struggled early on over the question of whether or not to take on outside work, ultimately deciding that they would do so only in cases where they could bring something back to the company. In some instances, outside work has meant that Mabou Mines could reconnect with former company members, as Maleczech did in Minneapolis when she performed at the Guthrie Theater in Akalaitis's 1989 production of Jean Genet's *The Screens*. Stackell, Mabou Mines's former General Manager, recalls that this production was a genuine point of pride for Maleczech because of the play's notoriously and intentionally difficult staging. Maleczech was attracted to outside projects because of the artists involved; among other productions, in 1987 she codirected *Fire Works*, featuring traditional Chinese music, with Valeria Vasilevski, one of Maleczech's major collaborators on *Imagining the Imaginary Invalid*. Also in 1987 she performed in Peter Sellars's production of *Zangezi*, which also featured her longtime colleague Warrilow, at Museum of Contemporary Art (MoCA) in Los Angeles. In the case of *Happy Days*, Maleczech had an opportunity both to work with a new colleague, Woodruff, whose work she admired, and to bring a production back to the company; the show was produced at the ToRoNaDa studio in 1998, two years after its La Jolla premiere.

Maleczech had wanted to play Winnie for some time; she recalled discussing the possibility of doing *Happy Days* with Akalaitis while they were working on *Prisoner of Love* at New York Theatre Workshop in 1995, but that production never materialized. Maleczech remembered that Akalaitis wasn't so keen on the idea. As for collaborating with Woodruff, Maleczech said she "didn't know him at all." "I'd only seen one thing that he had ever done—an adaptation of Dostoevsky's *The Devils* at New York University; five hours long, divine. I mean really, really good. People were just complaining—you had to sit on these little plastic chairs at Tisch on Second Avenue. And I thought, 'he can really work it.'"

It might seem an unusual choice for a regional theater to cast a major downtown New York theater player rather than an actress with more commercial appeal, but it seems that Greif was looking for ways to stretch traditional regional theater boundaries. Michael Feingold has suggested that casting Malina in commercial film and television roles may have held a similar kind of appeal for producers.[17] In August 1996, Greif told the *Los Angeles Times*'s Jan Breslauer that Maleczech's "acting 'is extreme in many ways.'" He continues, in what appears to be an effort to contextualize his comments for his regional theater audience, "She has great technical precision and makes really bold choices, but it's always informed by a detailed and deep emotional life."[18]

Pairing Woodruff with La Jolla also proved to be atypical of the regional theater milieu, especially in terms of the development process. Maleczech remembered that Woodruff negotiated for a rehearsal period that extended far beyond the usual six weeks allotted by regional theaters. "He's a wonderful director, but I thought, 'what are we going to do in a room alone together for all that time?'" As it happened, the time was spent on something close to Maleczech's heart: research. The production team included several dramaturgs who supplied Maleczech with what now amounts to an overstuffed binder of material that includes excerpts from Linda Ben Zvi's *Women in Beckett*; Stanley E. Gontarski's chapter on Beckett's "vaguening" of *Happy Days*, interviews with the renowned interpreter of Beckett, Billie Whitelaw; Beckett's essay on Proust; and even a short essay by Maleczech's mentor, Herbert Blau.[19]

Maleczech's exposure to Beckett's several drafts of the play (through Gontarski's chapter and other research material) influenced Maleczech's project by allowing her to find the voice of the writer in preparation for her performance. Research provided an understanding of Beckett's "vaguened" final draft. "He cut part of the sentences out," Maleczech says, "he took out the connective tissue so you don't know how to get from one to the next. Winnie has all these weird jumps."[20] References to previous versions of the text would be useful for the purposes of filling the syntactical gaps to which Maleczech refers because, as Gontarski puts it, "the earlier version ... is in places more concrete and reveals more clearly the sort of images with which Beckett began, then grew away from ... toward an abstract clarity, an image free of cluttering detail."[21] Beckett's decision to move from the "concrete" to the "abstract" provides a crucial clue to the performer seeking to understand the playwright's intentions.

Maleczech relied upon documentation of Beckett's interest in musicality and pacing in shaping her performance. "It's important to know that he cared about the music, only the music. The sense will make itself clear," she said. These comments echo Billie Whitelaw, whose interview with Ben Zvi on the subject is included in Maleczech's production notebook. Whitelaw explained that "it is so important to get the music right in Beckett, and I do think of the parts in terms of music. Beckett sometimes conducts me, something like a metronome."[22] Maleczech noted that the pacing in *Happy Days* is "clearly set out. Pause means one thing, period means another, and dot-dot-dot means another. The precision is part of the challenge, actually."[23] The physical approach to Winnie is demanding as well. "It's a very tricky play because you're trapped. You can't move at all by the end—no shoulder movement. You have your face, your voice, your being." The precision required of the

Beckett performer—both vocal and physical—clearly appealed to her interest in rigorous systems of training and preparation.

An examination of the performance notes from Woodruff that survive in Maleczech's production notebook give us a valuable glimpse into the performer's and director's shared priorities in their representation of Winnie. These notes reveal that the director was equally as concerned with precision in performance; a substantial number address the concern for detail that Beckett is careful to outline in his stage directions. In her record of Woodruff's notes from the third preview at La Jolla on August 8, 1996, Maleczech wrote, among other notes, "small gesture to collar bone for 'strange feeling' touching" and "further extension of arms, deeper for 'perhaps the moon.'" For the third performance on August 14, Maleczech recorded, "'What claws!' smaller reading, look up length of arm to nails." Woodruff's involvement in Malaczech's physical script reflects his underscoring and interpretation of Beckett's intricate stage directions. Other notes from Woodruff underline his attention to building an overall arc in performance. In a direction that accommodates itself to one of Winnie's repeated physical tropes, Maleczech noted on August 9 "smiles—only wisps throughout."

Woodruff emphasized vocal precision as well as physical rigor. On August 13, Maleczech wrote "sounds—don't use upper register—keep it low and fierce" an overarching vocal direction from Woodruff. Specific vocal instructions from Woodruff for particular lines such as "brighter," "flatter," "whispered," "more separated," and "up to down" run throughout Maleczech's notes. Woodruff's effort to highlight the rigor and music of the text indicates that he and Maleczech were well matched in this pursuit.

Maleczech's reliance on rhythm and research and her insistence that she doesn't "play characters" is also a good match for a writer who manipulates pacing and punctuation for drama and dynamism. "Winnie could be anyone," Maleczech told Breslauer,

> but she can't be anyone, because she speaks in this very broken kind of a way. So if you just speak that way, you learn more things about her

than by trying to investigate her psychology. It's surprising what you find out about her just by saying it the way Beckett set it out. Sometimes deep things are revealed just because of the way it's punctuated.

Maleczech's comments suggest one of the reasons why her American colleagues seeking nonpsychological approaches to performance have been attracted to avant-garde plays in the first place—Judith Malina and Elizabeth LeCompte, for example, to Gertrude Stein.

The focus on rhythm and pacing that Maleczech described was evident in performance as well; in his review for *Daily Variety*, Julio Martinez notes a "music-like pacing to Maleczech's dialogue."[24] Laurie Winer's review for the *Los Angeles Times* extols Maleczech's "extraordinary rhythms," making a case for her success as a comedienne, a comment that links Maleczech's performance to Mabou Mines's investment in the comic. Citing Maleczech's take on Winnie's *lazzo* with the toothpaste, Winer writes

> in Maleczech's hands, Winnie's inability to read those next words is a delicious little vaudeville; they seems to contain the meaning of life, these words on her toothbrush. As frustrated as she is, she performs a delicate, resigned "ah, well" shrug each time she fails. [25]

Here, as Winer describes, Maleczech takes her cue from Beckett, using rhythm in service of comedy that lends poignancy to Winnie's unenviable situation. As Nell says in *Endgame*, "nothing is funnier than unhappiness."

Maleczech's supremacy of rhythm over traditional character development was not, however, universally applauded. Writing for the *New York Times* on the ToRoNaDa production, Wilborn Hampton complains that Maleczech "occasionally appears uncertain of her character."[26] In retrospect, Maleczech, too, wondered about some of her choices. "The problem with that play is, who is she talking to? Because she talks continually and there's nobody out there. I just talked. I didn't have a goal. That might not have been right. Maybe we should do that play again." Beckett's text indicates that Winnie is talking to Willie, at least for part of the time, even if he is only "on the semi-alert."

Maleczech's question suggests a choice on the part of the performer, whether or not her own choice in this case left her entirely satisfied.

Maleczech and Woodruff made several adjustments between La Jolla and New York that Maleczech did find satisfying, however. At La Jolla, Stein's set was a thirty-foot-high mound of sand (despite Beckett's specification that the mound is made of earth). Maleczech recalled having to walk up stairs to get inside it: "It was really tall and I was really tiny at the top of it. The audience was very far away. There was no question of being in touch with them." This is likely to have complicated Maleczech's "proposition" for the audience. At the Mabou Mines studio, Stein reconceptualized the mound into one made of glass, significant for Maleczech because sand itself is finely ground glass. Constructed of old car windows and built over steel, the hill was reduced to accommodate the scale of performance space at the ToRoNaDa. In photographs it contrasts sharply with the stark La Jolla setting—an enormous mound of scorched sand. No recording of this version survives, though Iris Smith Fischer describes the ToRoNaDa scene:

> Douglas Stein's set for *Happy Days* ... filled one corner of this space. A scalloped, sand-colored curtain rose to reveal, as though in her boudoir, Winnie slumped over her mound. Yet this hillock, in which Winnie was embedded to the waist, was itself spiked down with a pile of cracked and broken windshields that seemed the deadly detritus of a wrecked civilization. Like Winnie, these vehicles are mobile no more.[27]

Although Stein notes that his decision to alter the set was dictated by the more limited financial resources available for the Mabou Mines production, Maleczech said she preferred it artistically; although neither design provides the grass that Beckett describes in the text, Stein notes that the glass of the windshields in the ToRoNaDa set was green. Maleczech preferred the more intimate setting in New York to her separation from the audience in California. "The lights were so hot they burned me," Maleczech recalled of her proximity to the ceiling at the ToRoNaDa. Mabou Mines co-artistic director Sharon Fogarty remembers that the alarm was so loud that it caused Maleczech ear

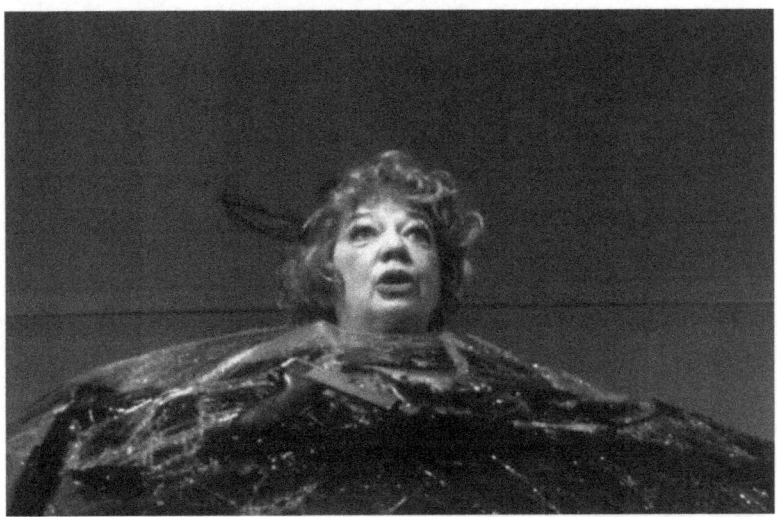

Photo 1.1 Ruth Maleczech as Winnie in the Mabou Mines production of Beckett's *Happy Days* at the ToRoNaDa studio in New York, 1999. Photo: Dona Ann McAdams.

problems. "Everything is set up to be exaggerated," Maleczech explained. Perhaps this sense of hyperbolic expression is easier to communicate in the small space of the ToRoNaDa. Maleczech's desire for intimacy with the audience marks a crucial distinction between her work in the regional theater and her priorities for Mabou Mines's productions and audiences, one that resonates across the small spaces of downtown New York, such as La MaMa's Ellen Stewart Theatre.

Aside from the possible attraction of bringing a production back to Mabou Mines and her interest in revising a production (which she and Mabou Mines have done regularly), *Happy Days* appealed to Maleczech on a thematic as well as linguistic level. Maleczech's comment that "Winnie could be anyone" but for her syntax is revealing; the condition that finds her up to her waist in a mound of earth rising at an alarming rate establishes Winnie as an ordinary woman in an extraordinary stage situation. The objects she handles—a handbag, a toothbrush, an umbrella—are familiar ones. Indeed, Beckett warned one director "not to make Winnie too capable a woman." She is "a mess," according to the playwright, who was careful to specify that the mess should nevertheless be "organized."[28] Winnie must be commonplace to the point of mundane. But Beckett's meticulous language and Maleczech's musically precise delivery elevate Winnie from ordinary to astonishing.

Although Beckett describes Winnie as being in her fifties—middle-aged—he doesn't specify Winnie's social class, and actors and directors have approached this in a variety of ways. Maleczech treats Winnie as a woman with bourgeois aspirations, if not bona fide credentials. In her review of the New York production, Smith Fischer writes that Maleczech's Winnie "is matter-of-fact but never simple in her brutal doting over Willie. It seems almost a portrait of a working-class woman who aspired to a middle-class respectability that she never quite achieved."[29] As with *Through the Leaves*, in which she plays the working-class, middle-aged Annette (who might also be characterized by her "brutal doting" over her paramour, Victor), here Maleczech transforms someone who might not be terribly interesting or important in real life into a fascinating, large-scale portrait.

Maleczech is by no means the first performer to find Winnie's behavior in the face of her predicament heroic; Whitelaw has said that

> Winnie is terribly brave, terribly courageous. She is marvelous; she hangs on and hopes things will be better.... Who's to say that just sitting and opening your bag and taking out your lipstick and this and that isn't courageous—perhaps the most courageous thing one can do.[30]

There is a certain bravery required of the performer playing Winnie, at least as far as Maleczech is concerned. Of tackling nonnaturalistic text she says, "You just literally jump. You don't think about where you'll land, and then you're in some other structure." Woodruff gave Maleczech a note along much the same line, urging her to have "no fear about going to another place" during the La Jolla previews.[31] Although they are talking about structure rather than subject here—Maleczech's comments are about playing language while Woodruff's come in the context of staying ahead of the audience in performance—these impulses also apply to the idea of what it means to represent Winnie, as articulated by Whitelaw. Although Maleczech notes her physical difference from Whitelaw—the latter is "delicate" and, despite the touch of cockney in her voice, "has a cultured way of speaking"—they are kindred spirits in their respect for Winnie.

Maleczech rarely felt completely satisfied with past productions, which likely influences the regularity with which Mabou Mines has revisited them. Of Winnie, she said, in addition to her desire to reexamine her strategy of speaking without a goal, "I think it would be interesting to see somebody younger stuck in the hole. She's about fifty-five, but you can be twenty years old and have a very long past." Even after two productions of *Happy Days*, Maleczech continued to ponder interpretive possibilities, influenced, no doubt, by Mabou Mines's emphasis on ongoing process. One aspect of Maleczech's Winnie would certainly have remained consistent: the performer noted that Winnie "never stops talking, and that's important in itself." In *Through the Leaves*, she takes on another loquacious lady.

Through the Leaves: Maleczech's Annette

Through the Leaves began as a coproduction between Mabou Mines and Women's Interart Theatre, founded in 1970, the same year that Mabou Mines came into existence. The relationship soured, however, when, according to a letter from Akalaitis to Women's Interart, the latter withdrew funds from a joint production account, causing a check to Kroetz to bounce and damaging Mabou Mines's relationship with him.[32] The partnership between Mabou Mines and Women's Interart further deteriorated when Margot Lewitin, the Interart Theatre artistic director, began to negotiate directly with Kroetz, circumventing both producer Spence Halperin and Mabou Mines. This prompted Halperin to ask Lewitin to cease further negotiations with the playwright if he and a representative of Mabou Mines were not both present.[33] Despite these difficulties, Women's Interart Theatre is credited as a coproducer and the production premiered at Interart Theatre on March 13, 1984. The recording that exists of the production is from the 1990 iteration at the Public. Logistical troubles continued to crop up in the revived version; in a letter dated September 19, 1990, written during the show's previews, Kroetz expresses his displeasure at not having received a signed contract from Mabou Mines.

The trail of reviews suggests that there were subtle but significant changes to the performances in the years between the Mabou Mines premiere and the revival. If there is any refrain among the reviews, however, it is one of inconsistency—some find praiseworthy what others criticize. Kroetz himself appears to have been unhappy with the 1990 production. In the same letter in which he requests a signed contract, the playwright complains of uproarious and inappropriate laughter in response to comic moments onstage during previews.[34] Comedy seems not to be what Kroetz had in mind. But for at least one critic, this was one of Akalaitis's most striking interventions: "What is good about this evening's theatre is its brevity and its strangely memorable quality. What is surprising is its humor. We laugh at the predicament that these middle-aged, overweight lovers are in," wrote Robert McNamara for the *Washington Review*.[35] The wildly contrasting opinions of critics, audiences, and the playwright are typical of the stir Akalaitis's work has by now developed a history of inciting. Significantly, Akalaitis's approach is linked to Mabou Mines's inclination toward comedy. Once again, the company relies on humor to expose the profound desolation of Annette and Victor's circumstances.

In another of Mabou Mines's interpolations, this production transports Kroetz's German context to Queens, New York, changing Maleczech's character's name from Martha to Annette and Neumann's from Otto to Victor.[36] "We make American work," explained Maleczech, noting that from her point of view, the transposition fit "like a glove." There is a stylistic suitability for Kroetz's terse language in the Queens accents employed by Maleczech and Neumann and a gritty realism enhanced by a New York audience's familiarity with the context. The choice to use accents is characteristic of Maleczech's vocal approach and what Akalaitis describes as Mabou Mines's interest in "different ways of speaking." Maleczech also employed accents in productions including *Dead End Kids* (1980), *Summa Dramatica* (2009), and *Lucia's Chapters of Coming Forth by Day* (2013).

Through the Leaves had its English-language premiere at the Empty Space Theater in Seattle in March 1982. The play, translated by Downey, follows the emotional life of a female butcher, who struggles to reconcile her role as an independent businesswoman with her desire to maintain a relationship with her macho and less professionally successful boyfriend, Victor. Annette runs her own butcher shop, although Victor disparages it because the cuts she sells are used for pet food. She is described in the stage directions as "between 30 and 40 years old, dark-haired, moderately ugly; usually wears a butcher's smock."[37]

There is no mention in the stage directions of Victor's physical appearance. His profession also remains unspecified, although Downey notes, "he appears to work indoors on some kind of packing line. Construction worker would seem to fit better with his casual working habits."[38] Maleczech recalled that she thought of Victor as an out-of-work truck driver. He hates Annette's dog and disappears for weeks at a time. Despite Victor's erratic behavior, Annette is determined to coax him into staying by her side. As Feingold puts it in his review of the 1984 production, although Annette is "terrifically clearheaded as a businesswoman, she is an unawakened romantic of the most old-fashioned kind in her private life."[39] At the end of *Through the Leaves*, Victor has neglected to make contact with Annette for more than two months.[40]

Most of what we learn about Annette's inner life comes from her diary. The audience is privy to these entries, which she reads aloud, sometimes sharing them with Victor, and sometimes in voice-over. Feingold suggests that Kroetz's inclusion of the diary entries in *Through the Leaves* "makes the play more distinctly" Annette's,

> as well as dramatizing the disparity that is the source of their conflict: the man would never commit the unmanly act of sharing

his inner feelings with anyone else.... We get to gauge her honesty from the way her monologues reaffirm her behavior in the scenes. She becomes familiar and dear to us; he, in effect by his own choice, remains aloof.

Annette's diary entries allow her to create a more intimate relationship with the audience than Victor has. As with Winnie, we come to know Annette largely because of what she tells us about herself. Victor remains a mystery, both to the audience and to Annette. Even Victor's description in the stage directions is less colorful than Annette's—he is "a worker, about 40 years old, average"—and though Maleczech is careful to note that Annette and Victor are "awful to each other," it is difficult not to feel more empathy for Maleczech's Annette as the action unfolds onstage.

There are correspondences between the way in which Maleczech explains her approach to text and the way she described her performance in *Through the Leaves* to Alisa Solomon in 1984:

> "The only way to perform Annette," she explains, "is to find a parallel between what I think the fantasy of the playwright was when he wrote the character, and my response. So there's his Annette and there's my Ruth, and when you put them together, they make my Annette—it's a combination of him and me. But not in the sense of trying to get inside of his character because I don't think that's what actors in the theatre should be doing."[41]

Although explained in different terms here, the performer's description of seeking the writer's voice as an entry point echoes her 1984 description of discovering the fantasy of the playwright. Maleczech maintained a consistent point of view about character. The 1984 position that Solomon records regarding the actor's relationship to character is nearly identical to her later contention that she does not play roles.

Maleczech's performance as Annette is a major source of the conflicting opinions that surfaced among critics, particularly in the 1984 production. A recurring concern in these critiques involves her vocal approach. In his otherwise positive review, Feingold expresses concern over one element of the company's interpretation:

> My one minor reservation about it, ironically, concerns what is actually its strongest and most gratifying element, Ruth Maleczech's performance. For certain key moments, Maleczech uses a gratingly shrill voice (homage to Helen Hanft) and a stereotype dumb-broad laugh to underscore the woman's fallible side. My complaint is that these are used inorganically, as mere alienating devices, not integrated with the rest of her portrayal; they obtrude a sense of directorial effect which slightly mars what is otherwise a full and enrapturing performance.[42]

Feingold's reservation regarding Maleczech's voice is echoed by Frank Rich, who writes that "Miss Maleczech affects a mannered, distracting laugh that recalls Thelma Ritter's."[43]

The critical response to Maleczech's voice raises a central point concerning her application of process in performance. Maleczech's vocal approach results from the research she uses to identify and imitate what she perceives to be the voice of the writer, establishing the music and pitch of the language she uses in performance. Downey's translation of the play begins with Annette "giggling," a direction that was significant to Maleczech and Akalaitis. That reviewers of the 1984 production make note of this aspect of Maleczech's approach suggests that it was both noteworthy and intentional, whether or not it was appreciated by reviewers.

The critics' view of Maleczech's vocal delivery, considered in the context of her stated intention of locating the writer's voice, evokes the notion of theater as ventriloquism. What Maleczech describes in her own process positions her as a vessel through which the writer's voice is channeled to the audience, much as the dummy functions as a mouthpiece for the ventriloquist. Perhaps what Feingold and Rich identify in Maleczech's shrill voice and mannered delivery points to a false note in Maleczech's positioning as medium for the writer's point of view, or an unsettled relationship between Kroetz's Annette and Maleczech's presence. Maleczech's 1984 OBIE for her performance demonstrates that the complaints of these critics were not by any means universal. Neither were they fatal—Feingold has been a fixture on the award committee, including for the 1984 season.

However, the 1990 production may have given Maleczech the opportunity to make adjustments to the correlation between the character of Kroetz's fantasy and her own appearance onstage. Indeed, the recording of that version bears little trace of a shrill voice or grating laugh, and a *New York Times* review of this version describes Maleczech as "less brassy, but tougher."[44] In answer to the script's call for Annette to laugh repeatedly, here Maleczech's voice is full-bodied and throaty, dissimilar to the one Feingold describes. Once again Maleczech used the opportunity of remounting a production to reevaluate her approach, tinkering with her vocal relationship to the writer's point of view.

Maleczech's carefully calculated point of view about her technical strategy expands beyond a straightforward evaluation of the effectiveness of her technique into an ideology about the political efficacy of the performer's training and methodology. This philosophy goes to the heart of Maleczech's investment in Mabou Mines. As a co-artistic director, she said,

> You get to call some of the shots without people questioning your authority to do so, which is important to me because I don't think I would function very well in the world at large—the theater world at large, where you try to get a job and somebody says no a million times.... I don't like the idea of working for somebody else. I've never liked it.

Maleczech shares this sensibility with Annette, who prides herself on her ability to sustain self-employment. Annette has a dream of a shared life with Victor (one that echoes the overlap of life and work at Mabou Mines, especially in the company's early days) and suggests more than once that he come and work at her shop. In the first such exchange, Victor insists that he earns more than she would be able to pay him. Annette proceeds to one-up Victor, telling him that she can "do better" than the $1,400 he receives from his employer after taxes, which may be a savvy negotiation tactic in the world of business, but makes her, as Victor will repeatedly tell her, sorely lacking as a female specimen. But it isn't just the money to Annette:

Martha [Annette]	On top of that, I'm my own boss, and you're not.
Otto [Victor]	Who needs independence, it don't buy you a beer.
Martha [Annette]	You never been your own boss, if you were you'd talk different.

Victor accuses Annette of counting her pennies, which she readily admits to: "Sure," she tells him, "because every penny's mine!"[45] Not only does this philosophy echo Maleczech's own in establishing a framework for making independent career choices, it resonates with her guiding role in a financially strained, nonprofit theater company. In other words, Maleczech, too, is an experienced penny-pincher; her concerns about finances and her head for figures spill over into the themes of *Hajj* (1983) and Mabou Mines's *Lear* (1990), discussed in detail in a subsequent chapter.

For Annette and Maleczech, work is a family business. Breuer is the father of Maleczech's two children, and both Clove Galilee and Lute Ramblin' have collaborated with her at Mabou Mines, while Annette inherited her shop from her parents. When Victor derides her for selling pet food rather than "steak," Annette explains that her father was also in the "utility" meat business, relying on the precise terminology of a specialist. As Stein describes, Maleczech too chose her words carefully to describe both her own work and Mabou Mines's, hence her insistence on referring to herself as a "performer" rather than as an "actor" and to the company's work as "avant-garde" rather than "experimental." Language mattered to Maleczech, both onstage and off.

Maleczech treats Annette's profession with the same importance with which she regarded her own; both Akalaitis and former Mabou Mines member Greg Mehrten remember that Maleczech wanted actually to acquire the skill set Annette would need for her work. "She went to a butcher and learned how to chop the meat there," Akalaitis recalls. Mehrten elaborates:

> She had this real butcher teach her how to sharpen knives (and then she had to do it for me once because I didn't really know how to do it). And she learned exactly how, she was so conscientious about not faking it, doing it the real way, which wasn't easy. That's what I remember about her most—going for it, not taking the shortcuts. She's going, "oh, well, I'm playing the butcher. I guess I have to learn how to be a butcher."[46]

Photo 1.2 Ruth Maleczech chopping meat as the butcher Annette, while Fred Neumman embraces her as her deadbeat boyfriend Victor, in Franz Xavier Kroetz's *Through the Leaves*, 1984. Photo: Joseph Schuyler.

Maleczech, finding her cue in the text, takes Annette as seriously as a butcher as Annette takes herself. This approach paid off with critics as well; among production elements that Feingold finds "unbetterable" is "the professional way Maleczech deals with activities like dicing a beef heart."[47] Maleczech honors Annette's career choice and professionalism by recognizing its complexity and imbuing it—and by extension, Annette—with significance onstage by means of her detailed and knowledgeable portrayal.

After Annette successfully parries Victor's jab to undermine Annette's credentials as a "real" butcher, he tries another tactic:

| Otto [Victor] | But a woman butcher, that's not normal, say what you like. |
| Martha [Annette] | There's nothing not normal about it, it's just damn hard for a woman, that's all, but I did it! |

The two can agree on one thing: it is easier to be a man. But Annette, seeking to establish mutual understanding, wants Victor to comprehend and appreciate the context for her dedication to her profession. Victor, interpreting Annette's efforts to communicate as braggadocio, interrupts Annette:

Otto [Victor]	Listen to her talk, nothing feminine about her!
Martha [Annette]	I say what I think, that's all.
Otto [Victor]	But a woman's got to be female. Sometimes you got to look to be sure.

When Victor becomes overwhelmed by Annette's business acumen, he attempts to humiliate her sexually by calling both her gender identity and biological sex into question. "I read it on the sports page," he tells her, "where they got these Russians who dress themselves up like women so they can win gold medals. Lift up the old apron there and let's have a sex check."[48] Victor's comments make it clear that his discomfort with nontraditional gender roles extends beyond his dislike of Annette's role as a businesswoman.

Despite Victor's protestations, we know that Annette is a woman because Maleczech strips down to the buff onstage. There are several sex scenes in Akalaitis's staging of *Through the Leaves*, all of which are consensual, but few (if any) of these encounters seem to be pleasurable for Annette. This is because Victor uses sex and desire to humiliate Annette and to put himself, for once, in a position of power. McNamara describes these copulation scenes: "at times, as they furiously cavort making love, they resemble beached whales or merely the brute animal force that is trapped in all humans."[49] In the recording of the 1990 production, it appears that the "brute animal force" is all Victor's. Although Maleczech plays Annette as an eager and willing participant, sometimes even an instigator, she lapses into passivity even before the act commences. Early on, Annette complains that Victor is hurting her. Next he threatens that she "won't get any loving" from him if she refuses to get rid of her dog. The game of chicken escalates until, refusing Annette's repeated pleas to come home with her and spend the night (the two pass their time in the back room of Annette's shop—the stage-left half of Stein's bifurcated set), Victor gives her an ultimatum. "Here or nowhere," he tells her, "You never know, it might be a long time until the next one." She consents. The humiliation escalates: "Just get rid of the underpants, that's good enough," Victor advises. Maleczech starts to take down her underpants. She freezes for just a moment, and we see that something just barely perceptible has shifted. "I don't want to do it after all, I thought it over," she says. Victor wants to be sure she has considered the consequences. She tells him she has. After he exits, Maleczech's Annette tells herself, "You were right."[50]

This moment of resistance is not an isolated incident. Although Annette repeatedly tries to placate Victor, she never completely sets aside her own agenda. Having no one else from whom she can expect support or constructive criticism, she uses her diaries as an outlet for expression and reassurance. Maleczech's Winnie, continuously talking to herself, functions similarly. Through sheer force of will, both women are able to keep themselves going. Maleczech herself never looked for the affirmation of the audition system for casting that so many other actors seek. Instead, she started her own company and selected her own roles, approaching them with aspects of the technique she developed with her collaborators but never according to the whims of what Akalaitis describes disparagingly as the all-powerful director.[51]

Maleczech's point of view about what she was doing on a technical level reflects and supports her assertion that Mabou Mines is interested in the theatricalization of ideas. Alisa Solomon ties Maleczech's technical approach to the ideas the performer has about the meaning of the play and the performance, noting that Maleczech's

> distanced stance allows for a heightening of the feminist aspect of the play. "I think of the performance as feminist," she says, "but I'm not sure if the play is. I try to let the audience know that Annette, or my Annette anyway, is not to be taken for granted. By texturing moments, and actions, and physical business, and spatial relationship to Fred [Neumann], and tone of voice, and quality of accent, and the way that I stand or sit or move, I let them know some things that Annette doesn't know. But not so much that they wouldn't be able to believe [Kroetz's] Annette."[52]

Her assertion here suggests that her performance is political, right down to its technical details. Rather than reinvent Kroetz's naturalistic world, as LeCompte did in her deconstructions of O'Neill, Akalaitis relies on Maleczech's process to invest Annette with a particularity that endows her with power onstage that she would never have in daily life. Solomon lauds Maleczech for what is, in her terms, a feminist performance technique. And despite Maleczech's doubts about Kroetz's intentions, the production itself, with her performance and Akalaitis's direction, comes across as profoundly feminist as well.

Putting up with the rustling

The politics of Maleczech's approach and aesthetic are inextricably tied to her founding role at Mabou Mines. As a co-artistic director, Maleczech wielded a rare degree of control over her own career as an actor. Along with Akalaitis and other founding members of the company, she developed a philosophy about the role of the performer that defies the audition and casting system at work in most professional theater. Accordingly, Maleczech sought projects outside of the company only when they appealed to some aspect of her aesthetic. She was less active than Malina in pursuing commercial work as a means of supporting her art.[53] Maleczech's determination to carve out a position of theatrical power for herself reflects her insistence that it is necessary to speak up onstage for all the Winnies and Annettes around the world.

In her book on Akalaitis, Deborah Saivetz reports that the director credits Mabou Mines with establishing an "empowerment of actors." Saivetz describes Akalaitis and Maleczech's position on the performer this way:

> Mabou Mines's perception of the actor as an autonomous, intelligent being able to function creatively both onstage and off contributes to what Akalaitis describes as the "strong sense of performance" that permeates the company's work. It is not surprising that the members of Mabou Mines more often refer to themselves as "performers" than as "actors," particularly when speaking about their work within the company. Asked whether she thought there was a difference between performer and actor, Maleczech replied that she thought most people who call themselves actors tend to think of themselves as interpreters. In her view, performance is a kind of active, public mediation in which the performer moves out of self into the performance of self. "Every once in a while," says Maleczech, "it does happen that you are only performing the performance. That's the ideal."[54]

Though Maleczech did not seek approval from casting directors at auditions, Mabou Mines is deeply invested in the audience's perception of its work. "We want them to like it, to love it," she said. But Maleczech wants the audience to love on its own terms, to do the work it requires to establish a relationship with the performance—that is the proposition she offers us. As for her mixed reception from critics, Maleczech once mentioned that she used to keep a post office box where she would mail her reviews, unread. Kroetz's play opens with an epigraph of a Bavarian proverb: "If you go walking through the leaves, you'll have to put up with the rustling."

Maleczech hopes it is the audience that will hear the "rustling" of the ordinary women she portrays. And in her performances of Winnie and Annette, the sound of rustling reverberates. She recalls an encounter with an audience member after a performance of the 1984 production of *Through the Leaves* at Interart:

> There were no dressing rooms, so I was in the bathroom trying to wash the meat off my hands and the makeup off my face. There was a woman in the bathroom in a beautifully tailored suit, beautiful hair— glamorous in a New York way—she looked fabulous, the way a New York woman can look really fabulous. And she was crying. And I said "are you ok?" And she said "oh, this woman's life, it's like mine." And I thought, "with that suit, that hair?" And she said, "it doesn't look like my life, but it *is* like my life." Then she patted her face, and she left.[55]

Extraordinary Women

Rats will nest in the archives:
Our history nibbled into beds

Belén: A Book of Hours

Maleczech's commitment to making ordinary women important onstage complements her reexamination of historical female figures in a contemporary context. The work of several of her co-artistic directors displays the same concern for developing contemporary characters based on figures from the past and using historical events to present new stories for the stage. The result is a number of unconventional history plays in the company's repertoire: *Dead End Kids* (1980), *Belén: A Book of Hours* (1999), and *Lucia's Chapters of Coming Forth by Day* (2007). These productions highlight Maleczech's and Mabou Mines's interest in adaptations of history by troubling the relationship between women and conventional narratives about the past. This chapter explores Maleczech's role in reimagining for the stage women and events from the past in the context of each production's distinctive theatrical historiography.

In *Dead End Kids*, *Belén*, and *Lucia's Chapters*, Maleczech and her collaborators change identifiable source material in order to challenge accepted notions of history, confronting audiences with a new way of thinking about people and events of the past. *Dead End Kids*, with its intricately embroidered patchwork of adapted research material and imagined scenarios, relies on historical pastiche. Meanwhile, *Belén*'s imagistic fictionalized scenarios are better described as political iconography. *Lucia's Chapters* is shaped by the singular vision of an invented version of a lone figure from the past; the resulting world is a wistful autobiographical dreamscape.

These three productions are history plays that establish an interrogative relationship with the past. The nature of this relationship is different in each case; each theatrical world establishes a distinct methodology particular to the way it positions itself in relation to the past it investigates. These productions, nonetheless, have several characteristics in common. They are never realistic attempts at historical reconstruction. Nor do they pretend to be objective. They are, as Peter Weiss describes his documentary drama, frankly "partisan."[1]

In *Past Performance: American Theatre and the Historical Imagination*, Roger Bechtel writes that his aim is to

> investigate and understand what I perceive to be new and complex theatrical strategies for representing—or perhaps a better word might be *engaging*—history. History, in the plays and productions I examine, is not understood as a mere reference to the historical record; rather, these productions marshal historical reference to interrogate history—the idea of history, its uses and abuses, as Nietzsche would have, rather than its facts alone—and our relation to it.[2]

This is a useful framework for examining *Dead End Kids, Belén*, and *Lucia's Chapters* within the milieu of historical drama. The productions involve an energetic and muscular approach to wrestling with their respective histories, inserting themselves assertively into the record of the past and insisting that we do not take the idea of history or the figures and stories it has documented for granted.

Dead End Kids, Belén, and *Lucia's Chapters* use poetic language and imagery, manipulate our perception of space and time, and invoke the art of good, old-fashioned entertainment to stage histories that have been previously overlooked, ignored, or willfully repressed. The subtitle of *Dead End Kids* is "A History of Nuclear Power," signaling that Mabou Mines selects certain thematic historical episodes and weaves them together with imaginary ones in order to shed light on the rise of nuclear power in a politically engaged way. Neither *Belén* nor

Lucia's Chapters confront such contentious issues. Yet the productions are no less committed to righting historical wrongs. They, too, expose unexamined points of view about the past.

Such performances ask audiences to integrate new perspectives into their understanding of historical figures and events. "I like work that requires of the audience that they do something other than witness," said Maleczech,

> Grotowski's thing was witness, and I think that's very important, but it's not enough. It would be good if the audience actually had work that they needed to do in order to take that piece of work that they're watching into themselves and think about it and talk about it and go home and bat it around a little bit.

Dead End Kids, Lucia's Chapters, and *Belén* establish a historical discourse with the audience about the subjects they stage. Indeed, they elevate the importance of the histories they engage by retracing the motions of representation night after night, designed for different spectators. As Freddie Rokem writes of the repeated appearance of the ghost in *Hamlet* in *Performing History: Theatrical Representations of the Past in Contemporary Theatre,*

> What can be seen in *Hamlet* is how a burden (some kind of unfinished business from the past) becomes transformed into an actor's being and doing "this *thing*" on the stage, appearing again in tonight's performance, continuously performing a return of the repressed on the theatrical stage. History can only be perceived as such when it becomes recapitulated, when we create some form of discourse, like the theatre, on the basis of which an organized repetition of the past is constructed, situating the chaotic torrents of the past within an aesthetic frame.[3]

In the same way, the characters and stories in these productions haunt the stage in order to remind us of those who have been ignored (such as the women of *Belén*), those who have been misunderstood (such as Lucia Joyce), and those, like Marie Curie, whose discoveries unwittingly led to tragedy.

Dead End Kids, one of the most famous productions in the company's history, was conceived and directed by JoAnne Akalaitis and produced during Mabou Mines's extended residency at the Public Theater. The production premiered in November 1980 and was adapted into a film in 1984. The company of actors, which included Maleczech, researched, wrote, and helped to develop scenes and text. Maleczech played Marie Curie, one of the few well-known female figures in the history of science. Akalaitis saw this role as central to the relationship between patriarchal and nuclear power.

In *Belén: A Book of Hours*, Maleczech explored gender, power, and history again, this time as a director. The production premiered in March 1999 in Mexico City as part of XV Festival del Centro Storico at El Claustro de Sor Juana in Mexico City, using poems by the American writer Catherine Sasanov and performances by Mexican artists and political activists Liliana Felipe and Jesusa Rodríguez.[4] *Belén* was performed internationally, opening in the United States at Mabou Mines's ToRoNaDa studio in April 1999. It subsequently toured to Chicago, San Francisco, the University of California at Northridge, and back to Mexico City, this time to Rodríguez and Felipe's Teatro de La Capilla.

In contrast to Marie Curie, the women in *Belén* have been lost to history. The research, development, and production of this piece functioned as an excavation of sorts, unearthing fragments of personal histories and daily living and then inventing characters and stories that tell us who these women were and how they spent their days. The Catholic Church built Belén in 1683 as a refuge for prostitutes and pregnant, indigent women. It gradually underwent changes that made life for the women there increasingly restrictive. The *Belén* production program notes that, "once a woman entered, she could never leave." Belén was converted into a prison in 1860 by the Mexican government and became so notorious as a site of torture that it was torn down in 1935. The production was not Maleczech's first foray into staging the history of women in Mexico—in 1989 she adapted and directed writings by Sor Juana Inès de la Cruz for *Sueños*, but this lacked the sophistication and complexity of her later work in *Belén*.

As she did in *Dead End Kids*, Maleczech played a notable woman from history in *Lucia's Chapters*, portraying James Joyce's troubled daughter. The production, directed by Sharon Fogarty, opened as *Cara Lucia* in 2003 at New York's HERE Arts Center; the adapted version, *Lucia's Chapters*, was shown in 2007. This version subsequently toured the United States and traveled to Ireland's Kilkenny Arts Festival, appearing again in 2011 as part of the First Irish Festival at New York's Performance Space 122 (PS 122). Two years later it toured to the National Theater of Norway.

Lucia Joyce, a known figure, is an underestimated one. She was raised across more than three countries including Italy, France, and Ireland and some suspected that she was the true inheritor of her father's genius. She began to exhibit eccentric behavior in her teens. At the urging of her brother Giorgio, she was committed after an outburst in which she threw a chair at her mother. Except for the few years shuttling among family, friends, and various hospitals in France and Switzerland, she spent the rest of her life in mental institutions. She died in 1982 at the age of seventy-five. As with Belén's women, there is limited documentation about Lucia Joyce's life; much of it was destroyed in an attempt to protect her father's image. Some evidence about her feelings, interests, and health does survive, however.

Because James Joyce's writing is in many ways related to the life of his daughter (scholars suggest that the writer took the portmanteau language of *Finnegans Wake* directly from his conversations with her), Lucia Joyce's story is interwoven with her father's. Thus, the discussion that follows would fit nearly as well in the context of *Hajj* and *Lear*, Maleczech's dramas about parents and children. What separates them, however, is the significance of James and Lucia Joyce as historical figures and this production's emphasis on revisiting and revising the records of the past.

Maleczech's dedication to putting historical women onstage in these productions was inspired in each case by female collaborators: Akalaitis in *Dead End Kids*, Sasanov in *Belén*, and Fogarty in *Lucia's Chapters*. Maleczech's investment in the passions of her creative partners demonstrates her openness to new ideas and an ability to recognize the potential for theatricality in historical research material.

Maleczech's interest in alternative history is characteristic of her work. "I think a woman's perspective of history is something that is important to Ruth," says Fogarty:

> She's looking at our world and saying, where's the woman's voice in this point of view? What can women add, especially women who have been repressed or kicked aside or left out of the conversation, as in *Belén*.... And I suppose Lucia Joyce is one of those. Marie Curie was a very brave female scientist, but her exploration also brought her in contact with things that ultimately killed her. So, it's the bravery of being an individual, whether you're male or female. And especially for those who've been sidelined or oppressed or warehoused ... these are hot buttons for her, I think.[5]

The processes for developing stories of these "warehoused" women, in addition to the stories themselves, are all characteristic of Maleczech's intuitive connection with her creative partners. They also invoke Mabou Mines's signature brand of collaborative development. Maleczech's dedication to staging these histories and the unique approach she and her collaborators established for each production reveal priorities in the method and meaning of her innovative work.

Dead End Kids

Just as, fifteen years earlier, Malina and the Living Theatre had been inspired to present *Paradise Now* in response to increasing public dismay about the Vietnam War, Akalaitis created *Dead End Kids* as a "response to the tremendous political movement in the country" surrounding the use of nuclear power.[6] "It seemed kind of natural to me that Ruth would play Marie Curie," she says, describing the similarity in looks between the women and Maleczech's facility with foreign accents. Akalaitis recalls that Maleczech's vocal approach to Marie Curie "was a kind of comedic Polish accent. It was very, very funny and I have no idea how she did it, but she did it. I think it is because Mabou Mines is very interested in accents and different ways of speaking." Maleczech remembered the role fondly. "I loved doing that part," she says, echoing Akalaitis's emphasis on the vocal approach to Curie,

> because she had a Polish-French accent, and of course I'd never heard Polish, so I would make it up! And then in the *Faust* section, which was done in German, I was the translator—Marie Curie was the translator—and so I had to translate Goethe's *Faust*.... But it had to be funny, so at first it was improvised and eventually it was scripted because I said the same thing over and over.[7]

Akalaitis and Maleczech's use of comedy reflects the deployment in *Dead End Kids* of a strategy that Mabou Mines has regularly pursued in order to establish both distance and contrast. *Dead End Kids* avoids the polemical by incorporating satire and parody as well as visual

Photo 2.1 Ruth Maleczech as Marie Curie in *Dead End Kids* at the Public Theater in New York City, 1980. Photo: Carol Rosegg.

gags: in one scene, Marie Curie appears with a black poodle (on a walk through Central Park in the film version), framed by scenes of Faust and Mephistopheles (the latter in human form). Akalaitis even parodies comedy itself by incorporating a decidedly unfunny stand-up comedian, played by David Brisbin. By contrast, Maleczech's performance *is* funny; her ability to control the comedy invests her Curie with power that moves beyond the stage.

Although Maleczech suggested that Ellen McElduff played the more crucial role in *Dead End Kids*, Akalaitis insists that "Ruth was at the center of the piece." Curie provided the fulcrum for Akalaitis; when the director adapted the work for film in 1984, she seized the opportunity to expand and enrich Maleczech's role. Curie was, Akalaitis says, "a woman who was a preeminent scientist and basically killed herself doing her work, who was incredibly important in a world where women are not important." Greg Mehrten, a former company member who also performed in *Dead End Kids*, remembers that Maleczech was intent on learning the specialized activities she portrayed onstage as the Nobel Prize-winning scientist. "She had this scene where she was taking the radioactive elements and she really learned how to do that," Mehrten says. Such attention to detail is characteristic of Maleczech's method for creating authentic portraits of women for the stage. She pursued a similar strategy when she portrayed a female butcher in *Through the Leaves* (1984), also directed by Akalaitis (see Chapter 1). Curie was important in her own contemporary context in a way that Lucia Joyce and the Belén women were not; the science that secured Curie's place in the historical record was the key to Maleczech's performance.

In reviews of the production, Akalaitis is sometimes credited with writing as well as directing *Dead End Kids*, just as she is in the film version. The Mabou Mines website, however, attributes the text to Akalaitis "with the company," with excerpts from documents by a lengthy list of figures from Paracelsus to General L.R. Groves.[8] Akalaitis has herself stated that the script was indeed written "with the company." Performers involved in the production recall that they engaged in the research process with her. The subject was "too vast for one person to do all the research," Maleczech says, "it needed all the people in the piece to do it." Mehrten recalls a process of interdisciplinary collaboration:

> Originally it started out as a workshop where a lot of people who weren't in Mabou Mines were invited to think in collaborative ways— musicians and filmmakers, all kinds of people—because it wasn't meant to be like a normal play. It had all these vignettes from different periods in history all around the subject of nuclear power.[9]

The collective creation Mabou Mines employed in *Dead End Kids* can also be seen in a number of the Living Theatre's political performances, including *Paradise Now* and the 1970s cycle, *The Legacy of Cain*.

Maleczech readily responded to the development process, with its heavy emphasis on research. She said she developed a performance that eventually became scripted, though Akalaitis remembers each performance as "always slightly improvised." Curie's representation, central to the director's interpretation of the piece, was "all Ruth," Akalaitis says, crediting the creation and representation of the role entirely to Maleczech. Engagement with the research that facilitated her creation of Curie is an early example of her investment in this phase of the process, which she describes as her favorite part of development. Her costume for Curie, Maleczech recalled, was copied from a dress she and Akalaitis saw slung over the back of a chair when they visited the scientist's home, now a museum in Paris.

Akalaitis, Maleczech remembers, selected material to include in the piece based on research conducted by the company, refashioning and structuring it to develop the script. "JoAnne is a structuralist," Maleczech says in describing Akalaitis's directorial approach,

> she structures everything. She doesn't ever want anything on the stage that isn't a structure. It can be an emotional structure, it can be a physical structure, it can be a movement structure, it can be a language structure, but it's got to be structured. That's where her heart goes. When we made *The Red Horse Animation* we each had a part of the red horse. David Warrilow's part was the Storyline. My part was the Heartline, and JoAnne's part was the Outline. And it's very appropriate that that was her part.

The process Akalaitis employed for *Dead End Kids* is also characteristic of Maleczech's as a director. Both focus on bringing together artists from multidisciplinary backgrounds. But where Akalaitis intervenes to give shape to contributions of company members, Maleczech works with what they offer in an unmediated state. "Julie Archer could have made any set for *Belén*," Maleczech says, "it's up to her what she makes. I'll work with it, she makes it."

A staged history of nuclear power

Much of the critical attention surrounding *Dead End Kids* centers on the notorious scene in which Brisbin's sleazy male stand-up comedian taunts a naïve female audience member, played by Ellen McElduff, with a series of sexually exploitative manipulations of a raw roasting chicken during his act in a nightclub; as he does so, he suggestively reads excerpts of a document regarding the consequences for livestock in the event of a nuclear war. In "Staging the Obscene Body," Elinor Fuchs describes her own discomfort as an audience member during this sequence and notes the widespread disdain with which critics greeted the scene. In the end, however, Fuchs writes, "most critics, sympathetic with the director's political intentions, finally 'allowed' it on political grounds." Fuchs also documents an audience walkout during a presentation of the same scene:

> In an interesting sequel, the nightclub scene was presented as a single excerpt at a joint anniversary celebration of the War Resisters' League (WRL) and Performing Artists for Nuclear Disarmament in May 1983.... Women in the hall began to shout to the female character, "Don't do it honey, don't let him do it to you!" Within moments, accompanied by mounting booing and hissing, there occurred a full-scale feminist walkout from the hall.... The performance was broken off and an angry confrontation with the director followed.[10]

The melee Fuchs describes followed a presentation of one scene of the play, not a presentation of *Dead End Kids* in its entirety. Nonetheless,

Akalaitis subsequently developed a reputation for courting controversy—she is the well-known veteran of a showdown with the Beckett Estate over her production of *Endgame* (1984), followed by a dismissal by the Board of the Public Theater that ended her brief and tumultuous tenure as the organization's only female artistic director. It should come as no surprise, then, that her earlier provocation was so wildly controversial.

The confrontational nature of this scene makes it an excellent microcosm for examining the larger patterns at work in this piece. As it plays itself out, the scene reveals the intentions of Akalaitis and the company had in mind. *Dead End Kids* situates familiar figures, images, and historical events onstage in a provocative and deeply subversive way. What results disrupts what the audience knows about the threat of nuclear power on the political landscape. In doing so, it forces the audience into what Maleczech designs as a transactional relationship with the performance.[11]

There is no video of the stage production, but the film adaptation is available for streaming through a number of library systems. Though the Wooster Group has regularly adapted its productions to film, Mabou Mines has done so only rarely—*Dead and Kids* and the 2003 film of *DollHouse* are notable exceptions. The *Dead End Kids* film opens with a scientist drawing on a chalkboard, delivering an enthusiastic explanation of the atom. Less than five minutes later, the actor Fred Neumann's cigarette-smoking armchair intellectual sets the stage for a reconstruction of medieval-looking attempts at its alchemical transformation. An evening talk show is dedicated to pseudo-scientific inquiry ("Welcome to the incredible, unbelievable world of alchemy," one co-host beams), in which a magician makes a handkerchief into a dove and enacts other improbable feats as the co-hosts discuss the history of alchemy. Then, of course, there is the stand-up comedian. These narrative threads establish unexpected juxtapositions between familiar situations and figures, pairing birthday party magicians with ancient alchemical theory.

Such contrasting scenes highlight another unlikely and in this case ultimately lethal pairing: the American government's machismo and jingoism, and its easy access to science with the capacity to create an atomic bomb. As Fuchs notes (despite her discomfort with the nightclub scene), she "recognized ... the most unsettling version of the connection Akalaitis had been making all along between the war state and the sexist state, male nuclear fantasies and the exploitation of women...."[12] Where the Living Theatre used political pieces such as *The Legacy of Cain* to highlight what were, in its view, universal issues, *Dead End Kids* emphasizes the dangers of male patriarchal power at the expense of women's equality. Mabou Mines's piece thus develops two trains of thought. One has to do with the abuse of nuclear power, both in the real world and in male fantasies. The other has to do with the science that gave us the capacity to make a nuclear bomb in the first place.

This question, how we ended up with the capacity to make a nuclear bomb, brings us back to Aristotle and subsequent proponents of alchemy. The first third of *Dead End Kids* functions as a sort of history of alchemy, or, at the very least, a history of the gestational period of science. As the drama unfolds, alchemy and modern science collide at the moment when Marie Curie is introduced to stage. Once she appears on the scene, she haunts the production: lurking in the corners, she demonstrates the centrality of this character to Akalaitis's overall conception of the project.

As we first glimpse Maleczech's Curie, strolling through Central Park with her poodle, the scientist recounts the story of Faust in a voice-over. Later Curie relates her own biography, which interconnects personal and professional triumphs. She describes meeting her husband, Pierre Curie, not in the language of romance, but in terms of their shared commitment to science. "A conversation about science began between us," says Maleczech's Curie, "soon he caught the habit of speaking to me about his dream of a life consecrated entirely to scientific research and he asked me to share that life." Among the *Dead End Kids* characters, Curie is unique in demonstrating this sense of an integrated professional and personal life; Maleczech and Akalaitis are careful to embed this correspondence throughout Curie's story.

Curie and her husband Pierre worked in a shed that served as their laboratory, just outside the home they shared with their daughter. In the film's continued voice-over Maleczech explains, "it was in this abandoned shed that the best and happiest years of our life were spent entirely consecrated to work.... This period was for my husband and myself the heroic period of our common existence." It is in this shed that Curie decided to "devote" herself to the purification of radium. "In 1902 I possessed one decigram of radium. It had taken me four years to produce it."

> The baby had been put to bed and cried again. I stayed with her until she fell asleep; then I went down and tried to sew, but I was too restless. I suggested to Pierre that we go to the laboratory. We opened the door in the dark. I begged Pierre not to light the light. The reality was more entrancing than we had wished. It was spontaneously luminous.[13]

Here, Curie's husband, child, and scientific innovation are linked together in the pride she feels for her accomplishments. Maleczech's voice is warm, and we have the sense of Curie as a particularized individual because of the slightly untraceable yet charming accent Maleczech uses. She describes the qualities of radioactivity, its ability to make images on photographic plates through black paper and to disintegrate the paper in which it is wrapped in the tones of a proud parent talking about a precocious child. "What could it not do?" she asks.[14]

Marie Curie is the only character in *Dead End Kids* whose view of science and domesticity are so securely interwoven. This makes her the ideal figure to haunt the later, post-Hiroshima and post-Nagasaki scenes. As a mother, she is a poignant presence in the doorway of the auditorium, where she watches the schoolteacher (played by McElduff) read eyewitness accounts of the horrors of Nagasaki to children in a sing-song voice. The schoolteacher holds a large picture book in her hands and pauses occasionally to make sure the children understand the more difficult words. "Those people who managed to get out by some miracle," she intones in a sweet, soothing voice, "found themselves surrounded by a ring of fire and the few who did make their way to safety died twenty to thirty days later from the delayed effects of the deadly gamma rays."[15] Marie Curie looks on with a mixture of regret and wonder.

The sinister intermingling of nuclear activity and innocent daily life also inserts itself into a scene in which high school girls, played by Maleczech and Akalaitis's daughters, Clove Galilee and Juliet Glass, demonstrate the wonders of nuclear power in their science-fair exhibit. They admiringly describe a nuclear-powered coffee pot, plutonium-heated long johns, and a nuclear-powered pacemaker. "Radiation is the most recent step in man's ancient quest to preserve food," they rave, eating irradiated hamburgers.[16]

Marie Curie stares out the window at a nuclear power plant as she travels past in a train and later sits in an armchair watching a television program in which McElduff plays a crazed mother helping her son assemble a hydrogen bomb as a scout project. Curie silently observes the consequences of her scientific contribution; her appearances are infused with regret. Curie haunts her own legacy, unable to detach herself from her beloved radium, while at the same time witnessing unforeseen consequences that have spiraled out of control.

Marie Curie may be at the center of the drama for Akalaitis and the audience, but *Dead End Kids* is ultimately an ensemble piece. It builds its dynamism by making use of the pastiche that results from a process of collective creation, presenting its story of nuclear power as a collage of fact, fiction, science, and stage magic. Blending selected history with imaginative invention, *Dead End Kids* suggests that we can alter the course of the future. The juxtaposition between Curie's maternal presence and the "manifestations of the sexist state" that Fuchs identifies is a unifying motif functioning to humanize a major political problem, aiming to provoke the audience to take action. The coupling of the real and the fictional in its use of scientists and their stories underscores *Dead End Kids* as a partisan "story of nuclear power" and emphasizes the subjective nature of historical narrative.

In search of lost time: *Belén's* Book of Hours

Dead End Kids marshals history to suggest changes for the future; *Belén* asks the audience to alter the way we think about the past. One of the projections that appears in blackout during the performance reads: "History is an archive of deeds undertaken by men, and all that remains outside history is forced to the realm of conjecture, fable, legend, or lie."[17] In *Dead End Kids*, scientific deeds undertaken by a female scientist become deadly in the hands of a male-dominated, militarized power structure. *Belén's* vision of the past reminds us that women are often limited to quotidian deeds and seeks their more prominent role in the historical record. Maleczech's directing work pairs her investment in ordinary women with her dedication to a vigorous reexamination of history.

Contrasting her own directorial approach to Akalaitis's and Breuer's, Maleczech said that, "neither one of them gives their collaborators the leeway I do, but it's not leeway really—that's not the right word because it sounds like permission. No, neither one of them involves their collaborators at the level that I do. The collaborators have completely free reign." Maleczech was drawn to colleagues with backgrounds in independently created forms of art, such as sculpture and poetry. This explains why Sasanov, a poet, and Archer, who began as a sculptor, responded so enthusiastically to her inclinations. Maleczech embraced artists capable of bringing a strong point of view to the project at hand. "I like it when it's feisty," she said,

> and I like it when things are messy for a long time. I trust that a lot. I'm not much one for "let's get this all organized and put together and let's get it up there." ... I'm not very satisfied by the results when I've had to do that. I'm a real appreciator of people rooting around and coming up with whatever comes to mind and then trying to figure out why exactly that came to mind and how that crosses with somebody else's mind and feeds into somebody else's passion.

Maleczech's directing style is eclectic. Relying heavily on intuition, she invites creative partners into the process. Nowhere is this more apparent than in Maleczech's collaboration with Julie Archer.

The story of *Belén* begins long before the piece itself began to take shape. It starts, in fact, when Archer first met Maleczech in the 1970s. Archer moved into an apartment on Avenue A in New York's East Village below the one inhabited by the Maleczech/Breuer family. She had already worked for a year as the babysitter for Maleczech's children. Archer relates that Maleczech "would come down after the kids were in bed and we would smoke cigarettes and talk."[18] During one of those conversations, "I said that I think of myself as a sculptor." Several months later, Mabou Mines ran into trouble during rehearsals for *Dressed Like an Egg* (1977; Maleczech was performing under Akalaitis's direction). The sculpture of a dog they commissioned began to crumble and "this eleventh hour panic about this thing set in, and out of that statement to Ruth that I think of myself as a sculptor, Ruth went to JoAnne and said, 'Let's let Julie do it' and JoAnne said 'What!' You know, 'Why would we do that?'" But Maleczech insisted, and Archer had her first job with Mabou Mines. "That's how Ruth rolls," said Archer, "she's really not afraid of putting 100 percent in somebody with very little evidence—obvious evidence anyway—that they're up to the task." Archer was not the first visual artist to work with Maleczech; her collaborations with multidisciplinary artists can be observed as far back as her early work in San Francisco at the Tape Music Center and on *The Black and White Mime Show*.[19]

Maleczech drafted Archer to design the set for her directing debut, *Vanishing Pictures*, in 1980.[20] By that time Archer had moved to Los Angeles; Maleczech and Breuer were visiting when Maleczech approached Archer to propose that she design the project. First Maleczech asked if she would design the lights for *Wrong Guys* (1980), another project she was developing for Mabou Mines:

> I didn't know a thing about lighting and I couldn't fathom why she would want me to do it. She said, "Because I want the lighting to be 'sculptural.'" Oh, and by the way, will you design the set for this other ReCherChez project I'm directing, *Vanishing Pictures*.

This was not unusual, according to Archer: "It wasn't an isolated way of working.... She believes in casting that line out and then sort of seeing if it will play out to her satisfaction." In Archer's case it did. Maleczech and Archer won an OBIE Award for the design of *Vanishing Pictures*; they sustained their collaboration over the next thirty-two years, working together on Mabou Mines's projects that included *Wrong Guys* (1981) and *Belén* (both directed by Maleczech) and *Lucia's Chapters* and *Hajj* (1983), in which Maleczech performed. Archer was co-artistic director of the company from 2005 to 2013. "Julie and Ruth have a bigger shorthand than anybody else," said Fogarty.

Maleczech gathered the rest of her collaborators on *Belén* in the same intuitive manner. In 1995, Maleczech was in Mexico City on a NEA fellowship to observe the work of performer and political activist Jesusa Rodríguez. At El Habito, the political cabaret that Rodríguez ran with Liliana Felipe, Maleczech first saw Felipe perform songs she had composed herself. Maleczech knew immediately that she wanted to work with Felipe, though on what she was not yet sure. Coincidentally, Maleczech was staying in the same hotel as the American poet Catherine Sasanov, who was also in Mexico City on an NEA fellowship. As Sasanov recalls,

> I wanted to stay downtown, in the area of the Zocalo, and not in the suburbs of Coyoacan where everyone else pretty much went. It was where I wanted to do my work, and it was wonderful, but rather lonely, too, at times. Then, one evening I came back and found a note under my door from another NEA recipient who was also in the hotel; in fact, she had been in the hotel almost a week before she was told there was another kindred soul in the hotel as well. She gave me her room number and asked if I'd like to have dinner. And so, Ruth and I met.[21]

Over lunches and dinners during the following weeks, they talked about Mexico City. "One night," Sasanov remembers:

> I told Ruth about something from Mexico City's history that interested me greatly, and that I was sleuthing around, trying to find out more about, el Recogimiento de Belén (the sanctuary of Bethlehem), a Catholic-run sanctuary for women without means of support, run like a prison, and eventually, turned into a secular prison.

As in her casual conversations with Archer, Maleczech listened closely. What began as a personal connection with an artist working in a different medium soon blossomed, with Maleczech's urging, into a theatrical collaboration.

When the poet left Mexico City on December 13, 1995, Maleczech saw her off. Sasanov gave her a copy of the galleys for *Traditions of Bread and Violence*, her first book of poems. Maleczech "liked Catherine's writing a lot," Fogarty recalls. Six months after parting ways in Mexico City, as Sasanov recalls, Maleczech contacted her to say that she was interested in Belén. She asked her if she would like to write a libretto for a new theater piece about it. Maleczech's recollection varied slightly; in her version of events, it was Sasanov who suggested Belen as a topic. But both women remember that from the beginning the idea was for Felipe to set the poems to music, and that she would sing the poems live as Rodríguez performed. Because Felipe didn't speak English, Sasanov worked with a translator so that she could set the Spanish translation of the poems to music.

Maleczech remembered that Sasanov sent her a number of poems, almost all of which she promptly returned because she thought the poet could do better. Sasanov recalls an interactive fluidity in the early days of the process:

> I would write a poem, then pass it by Ruth for her blessing. We might talk about a type of poem she would like to see in the piece (or a tone, a viewpoint), and I would go back with that and see what I could do (this became more common as the piece began to take form; at the beginning, I was free to see what I came up with). If she liked the poem, it then went to the translator.

Maleczech worked in a similar manner with the five writers she engaged to create the poems for *Song for New York* (2007).[22] *Belén* was developed in a series of intense three- and four-week sessions, and via mail. The artistic team exchanged ideas this way until they were granted residencies in 1998 at the Sundance Theatre Laboratory in Utah and the Rockefeller Foundation Bellagio Center on Lake Como in Italy.

There they were able to work directly with Archer, the designer, who had previously done her own visual research for the project in Mexico. Sasanov and Maleczech had difficulties with the translator, Alberto Blanco; they eventually returned to Bellagio with a new translator, Luz Aurora Pimentel. According to Maleczech, during the residencies, Sasanov and Pimentel worked in the mornings, handing translations to Felipe in the afternoon. Maleczech and Rodríguez worked throughout the day, developing a scripted series of gestures and movements depicting household chores. These would unfold in a nonverbal parallel track as Felipe performed the songs. Sasanov, who is nearly fluent in Spanish, recalls working closely with the translators "to make sure each translation was as close as possible to the original." When they were satisfied with the translation,

> it was passed to Liliana to set to music. Amazingly, it was rare that Lili needed to make much of any change in wording for the music to fit. Once she had a song ready, we gathered around her and listened (or, if we were all scattered long distance, we listened via cassette tape). At this point, Jesusa and Julie Archer came in, thinking about movement and visuals. I was exceedingly lucky to be present at all the rehearsals as *Belén* was created. I loved how the work came together, all very organic. I didn't just write a finished piece and pass it on to Ruth. Each of us had our part with each individual song/poem that I created. At times, I might make suggestions of images I had seen that my collaborators might be interested in working with or incorporating into the visuals or as part of the movement of the piece. Or I might bring up one of my obscure details that we'd consider working into the piece.

This overlapping interchange—cultural, linguistic, and multimedia in nature—was crucial to *Belén*'s development. It also proved to be characteristic of the final product. A program note describes the process:

> A challenge in developing a theatre piece with artists that speak different languages is to work in a way that the collaborators are not struggling with language as they create. Catherine Sasanov wrote the

twelve poems in English. Ruth Maleczech suggested they be translated into Spanish so that Liliana Felipe could freely set them to music. Julie Archer then worked to integrate the English of the poems into the visual life of the work. Ruth Maleczech wrote a silent scenario for Jesusa Rodríguez to be understood by all. By this process *Las Horas de Belén—A Book of Hours* became a truly bi-lingual, bi-national, bi-cultural collaboration."[23]

This international and intercultural exchange situates *Belén* within an American avant-garde tradition championed early on by Ellen Stewart at LaMaMa. It proved to be successful for critics and creators alike; Felipe and Rodríguez were given OBIE Special Citations for their performances, the first Mexicans to receive the award. Sasanov says that "working on *Belén* was one of the great events of my life" (though Mabou Mines producers recall some difficult negotiations with Rodríguez and Felipe when the production went on tour).

The subtitle of the play, "A Book of Hours," refers to Christian devotional books, drawing attention to the religious origins of the institution in which the women in this story find themselves. It also underscores the hours that made up the days and years spent at Belén in captivity. In performance, indignities perpetrated against Rodríguez's characters are rendered in the guise of normality, unfolding as part of the rhythm of daily life. The sense of the quotidian surrounding episodes of oppression and abuse underscores the production's message that subjugation is, in fact, part of everyday life for many women.

Sound, light, projection, and performance are calculated to evoke this reference, and this is clearly accomplished even in a recorded version of the performance at the ToRoNaDa. Before the lights come up onstage, a projection appears on the wall: "like certain refined forms of torture, household chores must be repeated as soon as they are done."[24] The words disappear abruptly, accompanied by a jarring aural effect that seems a cross between thunder and the door to a prison cell clanging shut. According to Archer, the mysterious sound "is an audio composition by Miles Green that consisted—in part—

of the sound of old-time photographic flash powder and exploding/ falling glass, slowed and run backward." This aural trope will recur throughout the performance. As the play begins, four distinct tracks emerge. Felipe, at a piano, sings Sasanov's poems in Spanish while English translations are projected on the wall. At the same time, Rodríguez enacts a variety of household tasks—the ones we were warned about in the opening projection. Sometimes she is the woman in the poems and sometimes she is another woman entirely, engaged in routine work that complements the lines of the poem. All of this is punctuated by outbursts in English delivered by a woman (played by Monica Dionne), our contemporary, who looks back on the history of Belén. The fourth track is provided by Archer's design. Images collected by Archer of saints and photographs of women line the walls. Projected outlines of plants and flowers, giant in scale, infiltrate the stage with a mysterious menace.

In her review of *Belén* for the *Village Voice*, Alisa Solomon notes that "sound, text, and movement follow separate trajectories that sometimes intersect, sometimes run parallel, and sometimes, by contradicting each other, collide." The clash and confluence of these events," Solomon argues, result in

> a complete, disquieting universe. More associative than narrative, the performance never actually tells the history of Belén. Rather, it summons Belén's ghosts—and their cousins from all the places women have been tormented—for a ghoulish yet gorgeous encounter.[25]

Space is crucial to the encounter Solomon describes; although Rodríguez and Felipe are near to each other, it is clear that they inhabit discrete playing areas. The outbursts come from a site lofted above, away from Rodríguez and Felipe, while the projections appear on every available surface, including Rodríguez's body.

Roslyn Costantino's 2001 article in *Theatre Journal* mines the production's visual imagery for its subversive retelling of the history of racism that played an insidious role in the oppression of women in Mexico. In one arresting scene, Rodríguez sets out flour and whisks eggs. We expect her to make bread. Instead, she undresses, smears herself with egg, and covers herself in flour, whiting up before our eyes. "Without speaking a word during the play," writes Solomon,

> Rodríguez enacts women's timeless chores—ironing, sewing, cooking—in exacting ways, sometimes transforming these labors into stark images of women's subjugation. Her movement, neither realistic nor romantic, jerks and sputters ever so slightly, as if to emphasize the archetypal nature of this endless drudgery. Maleczech likens it to Meyerhold's biomechanics; Rodríguez says she found inspiration in watching stop-action films of growing plants.[26]

Rodríguez's distancing mode of performance juxtaposes Felipe's impassioned singing as well as the tortured outbursts. Maleczech's use of binary tension, the alienating style of Rodríguez's performance, and epic storytelling techniques force the audience to confront a brutal history of women without sentimentality.

Maleczech and Rodríguez rely on comedy to create a sense of alienation, rejecting any temptation to romanticize or victimize the women Rodríguez represents. The actor's physical interaction with objects onstage contains an element of the macabre, and her use of comedy occasionally establishes an unnerving sense of confrontation with the audience.

Motherhood plays as poignant a role in *Belén* as it does in *Dead End Kids*. In one memorable sequence, we see Rodríguez bundle a watermelon as if it were an infant and try to climb the walls of the theater, as if to escape. The episode is prefaced by this projection:

> If a mother was arrested, no one was left to take care of her children. But if she brought them to prison, she lost them to the worst examples of criminals, or the frequent epidemics of typhus. Nothing made her wilder to escape than the suffering of her child.[27]

Later Rodríguez slices open the watermelon and sews it back together. As with many of the unfolding images, the significance of this action, perhaps elusive, nevertheless communicates a feeling of violence, loss, and inadequacy.

Both *Dead End Kids* and *Belén* use everyday life as a backdrop for horrors that Maleczech and company insist the audience acknowledge. In *Dead End Kids*, manifestations of daily life appear as distinct episodes, such as the high school science fair. Other scenes, for example the one in which a nine-headed Mephistopheles appears to Faust, are infused with magical feeling. In *Belén*, moreover, there is no escape from the ordinary turned ominous: everyday elements become surreal as Rodríguez and Maleczech manipulate familiar objects. A trench coat on a hanger begins as a sewing project and becomes a dance partner, and then a rapist. Costantino reports that the collaborators were moved by the news of "unsolved rapes and murders of hundreds of young women working in the *maquila* factories in United States-Mexico border towns. Official indifference to this violence echoed the stories" that they discovered about Belén's women.[28] In this case, elements of everyday life morph into monstrosities.

As if nightmarish versions of recognizable objects were not enough, additional interventions further unsettle the audience. Flashes of light, the clanging sound that repeatedly signals the end of an episode, and the outbursts from the chained contemporary woman above our heads foster the experience of disjunction. Rodríguez's stop-motion movement style further disrupts the audience's comfortable position. For the American audience, singing in Spanish and outbursts and projected words, both in English, become part of the interruptive strategy. Although projections of the poems allow non-Spanish speakers to understand the words, the simultaneous use of two languages helps to establish a more complex process of reception. It is these interruptive techniques that unravel narrative threads and unsettle our sense of time.

Maleczech's unmooring of linear time offers the audience the opportunity to experience what it might be like to be in prison. Routine days, with little to distinguish one from the next, deprived Belén's women of any sense of progression—a problem that Fogarty's invocation of Lucia Joyce's "chapters" suggests she encountered as well. Maleczech's strategy of interruption is also a practical method of undermining conventional narrative structure, one advocated by feminist critics as a tactic for fostering nonpatriarchal representation onstage.

The resurrection and reclamation of Lucia Joyce

In *Lucia's Chapters of Coming Forth by Day*, Maleczech undertakes another project designed to theatricalize historiographic complexities. The project was initiated by Sharon Fogarty, Mabou Mines's newly appointed co-artistic director, and was first produced as *Cara Lucia* in 2003. Fogarty, who had seen *Dead End Kids*, began working with the company in the mid-1980s in the touring version of *Cold Harbor* (she shared a dressing room with Maleczech).[29] She also worked on Mabou Mines's *Lear* (1990), first as understudy for Gloucester and Albany as the company developed the project and later in various minor roles when the production opened in New York: "I held down Gloucester when she was getting her eyes gouged out." She also brought the dogs who played Lear's entourage to the theater and helped Maleczech with her wig. "She trusted me," Fogarty remembers. Her appearance on the scene coincided with what she recalls as "a bad time in the company." Akalaitis had just left Mabou Mines, and Mehrten, McElduff, and Bill Raymond departed after the production of *Lear*. Nevertheless, Fogarty liked working with Mabou Mines anyway; in 1994, after receiving a master's degree in Ireland, she returned to New York to discover that the company was looking for someone to work in the office. Fogarty applied for the job. She interviewed with Maleczech and board member Esther Fortunoff. Maleczech, Fogarty remembers, was confident that Fogarty possessed the requisite business skills for the position, despite her own uncertainty.

Fogarty took the job as company manager. "I arrived the first day," she says,

> and I'm the only one there. There had been nobody in the office for eight months. There was mail, boxes and boxes of mail that nobody had opened. And there was some bad stuff in the mail, tax letters and things that needed attention and nobody had been dealing with it. It was in terrible shape. I spent the day opening mail and trying to get the desk in order and trying to figure it out.

Fogarty hired someone for a development position and soon "things started happening." She pursued her organizational work at Mabou

Mines while working as a director for the Irish-American theater company Daedulus. The office work was "not fun," but she began to realize that she liked being part of an organization. "I liked having a home," Fogarty says, "and it came to me that what I wanted was to be an artistic director."

She became one at Daedulus, but the situation was far from ideal. Fogarty found that she was not given credit for the substantial contributions she made and that the executive director consistently "undercut" her at meetings. Fogarty began to suspect sexism. "I have an Irish temper," she says ruefully, and the situation was "getting a little contentious." As Fogarty began to consider leaving Daedulus, the Mabou Mines's co-artistic directors began to consider the future of the company. It was "Ruth mostly," said Fogarty, "she's the one who thinks about the personality and cohesion of the organization. She's gifted at that." As Maleczech, Breuer, Fred Neumann, and Terry O'Reilly began "fishing around to cast somebody" as co-artistic director, they considered the idea of offering the position to Fogarty. "It all came about in casual conversation over a long period of time," Fogarty says,

> and finally they were ready to bring it up in discussion within the board, so they brought me into Lee's tiny office. I remember sitting in there and Lee said, 'so we've been talking about inviting you to be an artistic director and we all know about the organization and how we run and how it works and doesn't work' and all that. But Ruth says, 'what kind of work do you want to make?' And it sounded like such a loaded question. I felt like I was in front of the firing squad or something.

With the Irish playwright Elizabeth Whyte, Fogarty had researched the life of Lucia Joyce. She was deeply impressed by what she learned. She knew that the material had enormous potential, but she was not certain she wanted to continue her collaboration with Whyte. "In the Irish theater world," says Fogarty, "it's pretty much realism or even magical realism, but it's pretty stuck in straight drama. And I felt there was more to explore."

When Maleczech asked Fogarty what kind of work she wanted to make, Fogarty mentioned her research. The company's history of staging Samuel Beckett made the co-artistic directors receptive to a project involving James Joyce's daughter, given the close personal relationship between the two master writers. "They all got very excited." As for the developmental process she envisioned, "I had seen Mabou Mines in action," Fogarty explains,

> with *Lear* and with *Epidog* and a few other things, but it didn't seem like anybody was the author per se. I mean, Lee was the author of *An Epidog*, but it certainly felt like other people had some authorship and certainly with *Lear*, everybody in the room was rewriting this thing. So, I didn't feel too worried about the writer part.

Fogarty embarked on an extensive phase of research. "And then I had all this material," she says, "and here's the composition part and I don't know what the hell to do. I was trying to channel JoAnne Akalaitis." Eventually Fogarty discovered that, despite working with performers of such high caliber, "we weren't going to sit around the table and hash it out together, although we had come up with some decisions together. Really it was my job to go off and figure it out." Fogarty went to Ireland to work with dramaturg Jocelyn Clark and returned with one script and three Lucias: a young dancing Lucia, an old incarcerated Lucia, and the Anna Livia Plurabelle from *Finnegans Wake*.

Fogarty suggests that Lucia Joyce became important to Maleczech as the performer came to believe, through the research process, that Lucia Joyce had been shut away "because she was too much trouble." Once Fogarty discovered her project would be a Mabou Mines production, she knew immediately that she wanted Maleczech to play a version of Lucia. Maleczech "could take Lucia's extremities and make them reachable or accessible to the audience," said Fogarty,

> and she's a great comedian and I found this woman to be really funny, whether she was really crazy or she wasn't. She's crazy like a fox. There's someone in there laughing at everybody in a way, even though she's suffering. I thought Ruth could get the darkness, the anger, and

frustration, she could embody that and help us to connect with Lucia, to Lucia's anger.

By investing their Lucia with humor, Fogarty and Maleczech emphasize her strength, playing against any preconceptions that this figure was frail and hysterical.

As with *Dead End Kids*, accents figured largely into the vocal approach to *Cara Lucia* and *Lucia's Chapters*. The pronunciation that Maleczech and Fogarty developed for Maleczech's portrayal enhances Lucia's humor and works to establish a detailed portrait of her in the context of the staged world of the play rather than as a generalized figure from history. "We spent a long time trying to figure out if she had an accent," says Fogarty of Maleczech's Lucia. If she did, Fogarty, Maleczech, and their collaborators decided, it certainly would not be an American one. Lucia Joyce's parents were both Irish, of course, but Fogarty suggests that the woman herself might have had more of a "polyglot" accent:

> her dad probably spoke a more proper, almost English Irish. And she lived in England for twenty-five years. She might have had a slight French accent, but that didn't seem right. We ended up going with a British accent, a very light old lady British accent.

Maleczech played an important part in these discussions. Fogarty also consulted her as she considered adapting *Cara Lucia* into what became *Lucia's Chapters*. They decided to revise the production to focus on a single Lucia. Fogarty did away with the roles that had been performed by Rosemary Fine and Maleczech's daughter, Clove Galilee, and added James Joyce, played by Paul Kandel.

Despite the addition of the Joyce character, *Lucia's Chapters* became almost entirely a solo piece for Maleczech, who spends most of the performance seated on a chair that occasionally propels her around the stage. "I really do most of the work in the performance," she says,

> Paul doesn't come in—except as a shadow, an important shadow but a shadow—until later in the piece when he speaks. But for a long time it's just me. And there's not a lot of blocking. I mean, the chair flies and rocks, but there's not a lot of blocking to divert the audience.

Maleczech continued to hear the voices of Fine and Galilee as she read the lines now assigned to her; she decided, rather than memorize the new material, that she would prefer to have the lines fed to her through an electronic earpiece as she performed. Maleczech had done this once before, when Mehrten read Rose's lines to her in *The Shaggy Dog Animation* (1978). Mehrten recalls that Maleczech had a complicated sequence in which

> she was manipulating the puppet and she was talking in this puppet voice, and she was doing all these things, and she just couldn't remember the lines.... I was doing live sound effects on the side ... and we came up with the idea that she would have a little earphone and I had a little mic and then a wire connected to her, and I would feed her the lines in this one scene that was so complicated.

Maleczech enjoyed what the dual tracks of the voice in her ear and her own live action did for her performance. It allowed her to let go of her memory of Fine and Galilee's performance of the same text. It also introduced an element of surprise, leaving Maleczech at times unsure of what text was coming next (though Fogarty notes that, in her view, Maleczech was very familiar with the script). Maleczech placed value on arriving at unexpected discoveries in performance, as a number of her colleagues suggest. "I never felt that if I had an instinct I wanted to follow that Ruth wouldn't come for the trip," Kandel said of performing with Maleczech in *Lucia's Chapters*, "and same way the other way around. If Ruth needed to make a right, I would go. And that's why we have such a good time onstage, because each night is unexpected."[30] In *Lucia's Chapters*, though, Maleczech spends most of her time onstage alone. Thus, her use of the ear bud fulfilled one of the functions that a partner such as Kandel might in other scenes—taking Maleczech by surprise.

While Lucia's mother is absent in *Lucia's Chapters of Coming Forth By Day*, her father looms large. Because *Lucia's Chapters* is concerned with reexamining a historical record that positions the daughter only in relation to her father, Fogarty's and Maleczech's production provides

Photo 2.2 Paul Kandel in silhouette as James Joyce and Ruth Maleczech as Lucia Joyce in *Lucia's Chapters of Coming Forth by Day* at the Kilkenny Arts Festival, 2009. Photo: Colm Hogan.

her with her own point of view, albeit an imagined one. The real Lucia Joyce had a point of view too—as a young woman, she painted her face black, refused to wear undergarments, and spent six days on a friend's couch in a near-catatonic state after quarrelling with her parents (they had invited ex-boyfriend Samuel Beckett to her father's fiftieth birthday party, even though he spurned her romantic advances). It was such behavior that troubled the Joyce family.[31] Carol Loeb Shloss suggests that the young woman may have been a moody young artist, highly anxious and probably depressed, though she was by no means the full-fledged mentally deranged menace her brother Giorgio feared she was. Shloss cites, among other evidence, largely unheeded advice from a number of Lucia Joyce's doctors.[32]

Her book, *Lucia Joyce: To Dance in the Wake* (2005), heavily influenced Fogarty as she researched and developed *Lucia's Chapters*. The production does not, however, proclaim Lucia Joyce as a wrongfully incarcerated victim (neither does the book). Rather, *Lucia's Chapters* paints a complex portrait of a person physically shut away against her will. All the while she has a vivid imagination and a rich store of memories that allow her to travel exhaustively in her mind. This sets the character of Lucia apart from the women Rodríguez portrays in *Belén*. Lucia's unfettered imagination and extensive creative resources have been nurtured by her unorthodox upbringing. Perhaps neglectful, her parents nonetheless provided her with a privileged access to art, literature, languages, and travel. This is the sophisticated and promising young dancer Shloss describes.

Most of Lucia Joyce's life was spent in confinement. In contrast to the frenzy of physical activity of Rodríguez's imprisoned woman in *Belén*, in *Lucia's Chapters* it is the protagonist's frenzied mind that roams in response to her captivity. The historical Lucia Joyce and the women of *Belén* are linked by the stigma of being social outcasts, badly behaved, and therefore undesirable women who must be shut away. The women are also connected because their confinement is associated with sexual deviance. This is a more straightforward situation in the case of Belén's women: prostitutes or unwed mothers. Discomfort with Lucia Joyce's sexuality played a more ambiguous but no less insidious role in her incarceration. She had an open attitude toward sex and was known to have lovers. For a brief time she and her parents even feared her mental illness might be the result of syphilis contracted through her promiscuity (this proved not to be the case). There are also the allusions to incest in Joyce's novels, more than likely based on the unnatural desire Lucia Joyce supposedly harbored for her brother. In *Lucia's Chapters*, however, the remnants of a lively and accomplished young woman are refracted through the memories of an older woman who has been robbed of the possibility of fulfillment and maturity. Her incarceration has denied her any measure of professional, creative, or emotional development.

In the first version of this production, *Cara Lucia*, Lucia in her three manifestations effectively severs the tie with her father. One of the Lucias who appears is the Anna Livia Plurabelle of *Finnegans Wake*; the novelist's absence and Lucia's presence onstage make the words of that text hers rather than his. *Cara Lucia* takes words that James Joyce may have taken from his daughter and gives them back to her.

Lucia's Chapters, on the other hand, condenses the three Lucias into one figure played by Maleczech. What is a more integrated character offers the audience a more harrowing experience. Because James Joyce is physically present in this version, the fragments of text from *Finnegan's Wake* (spoken mostly by James but also occasionally by Lucia) assume a joint ownership. The notion of shared possession of text is heightened by our impression that the author, who first appears in shadow through a scrim, is merely a figment of his daughter's memory and imagination.

Mindful of the legal entanglements the Wooster Group encountered in 1984 when it used Arthur Miller's *The Crucible* in an unauthorized way in their production of *L.S.D. (... Just the High Points ...)* and aware of the Joyce Estate's strict policies, Fogarty was careful to adhere to fair use laws in drawing upon the novelist's text for her play. Though Fogarty initially made the decision to refrain from using Joyce's text out of necessity, the result, which centers the script more directly on Lucia Joyce's own words, allows Fogarty and Maleczech to present a figure guided largely by what she said about herself rather than by what others said about her. *Lucia's Chapters* provides its female figure with retrospective power, dramatizing her own point of view and casting aside the negative opinions she was subjected to during her lifetime. In doing so the production challenges the historiography that consigned her to a madhouse. The three personas in *Cara Lucia* become a single character in *Lucia's Chapters*, creating a more nuanced and complex character for Maleczech to play. "While the other two were interesting pieces of the Lucia puzzle," Fogarty says of the young Lucia and Anna Livia Plurabelle,

> Ruth's character was the one that I understood the best, because the young Lucia was really taken from reports. People would quote her in various reports about what she did and said. Whereas the basis for all of the language for the older Lucia was directly from her writing, from her letters, her memoirs, kind of a biography.

This single and solitary Lucia is more powerful in her ability to draw upon her memory and her own creativity. She is also lonelier: the only other character she can summon is her dead father. Maleczech and Fogarty locate a deep bond between father and daughter. This is supported by their research; we know that James Joyce was deeply conflicted about his daughter's confinement and was the only person to visit her regularly. But instead of overshadowing his daughter in this relationship, James appears only in relation to Lucia rather than the other way around. Less than a minute into the play, Lucia tells us, "My name is Lucia Joyce. My father is James Joyce, the famous Irish writer. I am seventy-five years old, I like to smoke, and it costs a lot."[33] She introduces her father to us on *her* stage and mentions two other facts about herself that she wants us to know. She begins to read aloud to us from her own book, not from one of his. And she calls this book her "chapters of coming forth by day." The title suggests her namesake, an emergence from darkness into light, from obscurity to prominence.

Despite the bond *Lucia's Chapters* establishes between father and daughter, the figure Lucia conjures for us here is distant and a little frightening. "I really felt like Joyce was there, however the hell I tried to keep him out," Fogarty explains. "He was this big shadow that hovered near her to the end of her life. So I decided to make him a shadow and then bring him out at the end to help her cross the River Styx, or whatever you want to call it." Joyce first appears to us as a sharply delineated shadow on the scrim, appearing in full form only toward the end of the play; we are unsure what to make of him when he eventually appears before us in full form on the stage. Eventually we discover James is there to usher his daughter into the hereafter, as his narrator has done with Nuvoletta in *Finnegan's Wake*.

Lucia's Chapters sharpens what Fogarty describes as "the afterlife metaphor" she hoped to communicate in *Cara Lucia*. Inspired by Lucia Joyce's habit of prefacing communications with the phrase "bad news," Fogarty begins the piece with an expository line used by the historical figure herself. "Bad news. I'm dead," are the first frank—and funny— words Maleczech's speaks.[34] Perhaps, then, the time Lucia spends onstage before us amounts to a semblance of purgatory. If it is, it is hard to distinguish it from the days at Saint Andrew's Hospital, where she lived between 1951 and her death in 1982. This is precisely the point. *Lucia's Chapters* gives us a heightened sense of a purgatorial existence. "She's looking back," says Fogarty, and

> fearfully looking forward, and the thing that helps her transition is this language that her father wrote for her. She's at the end of *Finnegan's Wake*. I believe he wrote it for her because it's all about, "I go back to you my cold father, my cold, mad father." So that to me is where they sort of come together. He truly understood her and she was somewhat free in his thoughts.

In Fogarty's afterlife metaphor, James appears to release Lucia from her confinement in an institutionalized purgatory.

Yet the impression that Kandel's Joyce is a menacing figure remains with us. In addition to appearing as the father she loved, he also haunts Lucia's stage as the embodiment of regret: she has been robbed of her chance to fulfill her artistic potential. Lucia Joyce was forced to give up her career as a dancer because her parents believed this was the source of the stress that caused her severe anxiety. Historiography has recorded James Joyce's literary achievements as his alone, setting aside the inspiration he derived from his daughter. Maleczech and Fogarty convey the profound sense of frustration, even fury, that a talented Lucia Joyce must have felt at the circumstances that conspired to ruin her life. At the same time they paint a compelling portrait of her potential. When one yearns to be a creative modern dancer, it is probably of very little comfort to be relegated to the role of muse.

Virtuoso performance

Dead End Kids deploys the ensemble to reenvision the past and present of nuclear power; *Belén* and *Lucia's Chapters* rely on virtuoso performances to magnify the lives of women who have been historiographically minimized. Maleczech portrays a Lucia Joyce of mythic proportions; this eccentric figure is the motor for the entire play. We see her story unfold from what Fogarty and Maleczech imagine as her own point of view, amplified by symbols of the afterlife and invested with dreamlike qualities. In *Belén*, larger than life stage presences intersect as they occasionally cross paths but each remains distinct under Maleczech's careful direction: a striking performance by Jesusa Rodríguez, a forceful and exuberant cabaret style music composed and played by Liliana Felipe, and Archer's prominent and arresting projections that appear and disappear as if they have a performative life of their own. Sasanov's poems animate the stage, sung by Felipe, projected on the wall, and enacted wordlessly by Rodríguez. Maleczech and company make the history and lives of their subjects in *Belén* and *Lucia's Chapters* as large in performance as they have been small in recorded history.

Maleczech's direction in *Belén* creates a space between Rodríguez and her performance and between the performers and each other, thereby expanding the scale of presentation. The distance between performers is emphasized by Felipe's singing and Rodríguez's near silence, Rodríguez's apparent detachment from Felipe's presence for much of the performance, and Maleczech's placement of Dionne in an entirely separate area above and away from Rodríguez and Felipe, where she conveys the "outbursts." The projections give an impression of giant, two-dimensional puppets and appear to be driven by an unseen force, creating a mood of hyperreality in which images and emotions are invested acuteness and intensity.

The actors' and musician's performance styles establish distance between the performer and the audience. Rodríguez, Maleczech noted, is a seasoned cabaret performer and as such her natural instincts were for broad, bold, and fluid physicality. Maleczech worked with Rodríguez to circumvent her conventional physical routine, breaking down her movement into a precise unfolding of small gestures that add up to a much larger picture. This is typical of Maleczech's interest in restructuring routine physical and vocal patterns, paving the way for unanticipated discoveries. What results here has a jarring effect on the viewer: a physical landscape that seems to unfold in time lapse. Felipe's singing and piano playing are ferocious and forceful, so much so that they prevent the audience from relapsing into the easy comfort a performance by such an accomplished musician can induce. Felipe's passion and volume in the small space of the ToRoNaDa juxtapose Rodríguez's finely tuned alternation between stillness and hyperactivity. The gallows humor she and Maleczech incorporate into her scenarios keep the audience engaged but at the same time at bay, providing them with a space to process on an intellectual level what they are experiencing on a visceral plane.

Fogarty realized that Maleczech's performance in *Cara Lucia* needed to be featured more prominently, leading to her decision to collapse the three roles into one in *Lucia's Chapters*. Paul Kandel remembers lobbying Fogarty for a revised production that would do just that. "I made a big push with Sharon that *Lucia* should be done in New York, that Ruth should be seen in New York in a solo piece." He initially suggested remounting the production as a fundraiser for Mabou Mines. "It would be a special event that would be centered on Ruth," Kandel said.

> I wanted it to be about Ruth and this stunning performance she was doing.... I wanted people in New York in the theater community to see her at the center of a piece, which she has done already, but this would be a triumphant return.... She's an extraordinary artist and creative performer and deserves that kind of attention, I think.

Mabou Mines has a history of mounting productions featuring individual performers, including Maleczech herself. As far back as the 1970s the company produced Breuer's *B. Beaver Animation* (1974), featuring Fred Neumann's performance, as well as David Warrilow's solo presentation based on Beckett's *The Lost Ones* (1974). And although the role of Rose was divided among company members in *Shaggy Dog Animation*, Galilee points out that Maleczech's Rose was really the center of the piece. As the composition of the company changed over the years, with the departure of regularly featured performers such as Warrilow, McElduff, and Mehrten, Maleczech assumed an increasing number of featured roles (they have also occasionally gone to other performers, including Karen Kandel—then an artistic associate—in the 1996 *Peter and Wendy*). Fogarty's decision to expand Maleczech's role in *Lucia's Chapters* is part of a Mabou Mines tradition, one tied to Maleczech's central position in the artistic life of the company.

Lucia's Chapters is part of a dynamic American avant-garde tradition that uses theatrical imagination to reinvigorate ideas about a figure from the past. Robert Wilson and Philip Glass did so in *Einstein on the Beach* (1976), as did the Wooster Group in *Poor Theater*, based on the work of Jerzy Grotowski and William Forsythe (2004). But while these productions speculate on the accomplishments of widely celebrated figures, Fogarty and Maleczech make use of a politicized theatricality to reassess and reevaluate Lucia Joyce's place in history. What is at stake is nothing less than recuperation.

Maleczech's performance in *Lucia's Chapters* relies on a set of performance strategies that make Lucia Joyce a star in her own right. Balancing the three Lucias from *Cara Lucia* who inspired the single figure in *Lucia's Chapters* requires a juggling act on Maleczech's part. It also allows her to blur the lines between one persona and another. Fogarty describes Maleczech as a distinctively intuitive performer; indeed, Maleczech has always been adept at conveying delicate internal shifts to an audience. Her performance in *Lucia's Chapters* offers us a constant push-and-pull that lures us at the same time that it keeps us at a calculated distance. Maleczech establishes such distance with strategic shifts of internal focus. The tension the audience senses is rooted in the nonlinear text, in Lucia's portmanteau language, and in Maleczech's muscle memory of performance history; this is a departure from the largely externalized shifts in focus that moved from one performer to another in *Cara Lucia*.

Maleczech's sensitive and understated alternations between personas insist that almost as soon as we are captivated by one Lucia, we are redirected to another. The rerouting of our attention means that even though Lucia is not able to disappear from us physically (or from the caretakers presumably lurking somewhere on the periphery), she is able to keep some part of herself private. This gives Lucia Joyce power; she has access to information that only she can choose to share or keep to herself.

Maleczech's choice of accent fosters both intrigue and alienation in her performance. Although, as Fogarty describes, she and Maleczech finally settled on a gentle, "old lady" British accent, there is a trace of something more hovering beneath the surface: it might be the "polyglot" accent they considered that combines various traces of Lucia Joyce's multinational upbringing. As with Maleczech's accent for Marie Curie, this one combines familiar with invented qualities. The result, in both cases, brings sophistication and complexity to the women she portrays. Both accents attract the attention by combining familiar sounds with ones that are mysterious, even strange. We hear Maleczech's accent for Lucia almost continuously throughout the hour-long performance; for most of the time, she is the only person talking. Maleczech's unique pronunciation enables her to assert her presence in performances just as Rodríguez's nearly unbroken silence in *Belén* highlights hers.

Archer's projections advance the feeling of estrangement that Maleczech's Lucia establishes. Taking its cue from the play's title, Archer's visual track is influenced by Egyptian symbols of the next world, inspired in turn by James Joyce's incorporation of the Book of the Dead in *Finnegans Wake*. The projections contribute to the unreal, often nightmarish quality of the world we see before us, providing an appropriate context for a mythical Lucia. Another scenic element that creates this mood is the set design by Jim Clayburgh, a fantasy world that includes a flying chair. In *Cara Lucia*, Maleczech's seated position found a counterpoint in Galilee's fevered dancing as she struggled against a tether that bound her to the floor. Although the lone Lucia dances a bit in *Lucia's Chapters*, it is clear that the aged woman we see before us has lost the physical agility and elegance of her younger self. Maleczech's restricted choreography also draws our attention to the physical condition of the performer herself, someone who is no longer capable of executing the sort of intricate dances for which the young Lucia Joyce was favorably reviewed. When Maleczech's Lucia orbits her place onstage in her chair, however, she is airy, whimsical, and surprising. Lucia's flying, dancing chair is a graceful and masterful expansion of her physical presence in this space. We are never sure whether she controls the chair or the chair is controlling her, but either way, she seems to enjoy the ride. Lucia's duet with the chair parallels her mental

Photo 2.3 Jesusa Rodríguez in *Belén: A Book of Hours* during its run at the ToRoNaDa studio in New York, 1999. Photo: Julie Archer.

and emotional travels, which wander far and wide and sometimes catch her unawares. It also joins her physically to her environment, as do the images projected directly onto Rodríguez's body in *Belén*.

In *Belén*, however, the images projected onto Rodríguez's body are part of a pattern of tactics underscoring her corporeal presence. Costantino makes the case that Rodríguez's figure embodies the struggle of Mexican feminist activists:

> For the last 30 years in Mexico, where the female body has served as the stage upon which national identity has been constructed, feminist scholars, writers, and artists have devoted much energy to the task of locating the persistence of women's intervention into spaces to which they supposedly were denied access as well as to representing women's resistance to systems designed to control every aspect of their life.[35]

Costantino points to the importance of the images Archer selected in Mexican history, noting that they are drawn from popular religious paintings, codex drawings of an Aztec market from the sixteenth century, and the eighteenth-century *castas* paintings and photographs that recorded the process of "miscegenation" among Indians, Spanish, and African peoples. Two things are happening. First, Rodríguez's body becomes subject to Mexican history; Archer's images and Sasanov's projected words flicker over and around it. At the same, this dualism slyly inserts her live body into conversation with the disturbing records of the past. The episode in which Rodríguez whites up with flour and the one in which she dances in her underwear with a knife, holding its glinting form against her skin, are also associated with this trope, as is her nudity in such close proximity to the audience. Such images serve to spotlight Rodríguez's body, emphasizing its hypersensitivity to outside stimuli and establishing a dichotomy between these forces and her powerful, performative physicality. Rodríguez's live presence does not, alas, have the retrospective power to free the women of *Belén*, who remain trapped as eternal prisoners. "The hand that stretches out to strangle operates in full daylight and has many names," a projection reminds us: "Oppression, Poverty, Injustice, Dependence."[36]

Both *Belén* and *Lucia's Chapters* make us conscious of the relationship between physical scale and social significance. In one of Sasanov's poems, a young girl makes herself smaller by speaking of herself in diminutives. In *Lucia's Chapters*, Lucia advocates for her own full-fledged personhood by insisting, "I'm a grown woman and I don't need looking after!" By putting these women and the history surrounding them in letters and images writ large onstage, Maleczech and her artistic partners insist upon their value for both past and present. These productions bear ghostly imprint of the women who suffered and died unacknowledged and misunderstood, the very opposite of the women artists who were free to make these pieces.

The close of the first poem in *Belén*, "A Memory of Things to Come," reads

> From Belén, I can see
> how they'll lock prisoners away
> in the arms of a star
> Rats will nest in the archives:
> Our history nibbled into beds.[37]

Here Sasanov speaks simultaneously of a desire for acknowledgment of lost histories and the improbability of recovering records that would make such recognition possible. In *Belén*, *Dead End Kids*, and *Lucia's Chapters*, Maleczech and her team sift through scraps of the past and piece them together to revisit forgotten episodes, reconstructing them from a point of view that has been relegated to the off-site storage of history. What these artists lack in historical documentation, they make up for with political conviction and theatrical imagination.

Although each production proposes a distinct model for theatricalized historiography, all require that the audience, in Maleczech's words, "do something other than witness" what is unfolding before them onstage. Each production asks its audience to formulate its own "idea of history." This is no less than what the highly collaborative development process for each production demanded of its co-creators. The eclectic backgrounds of those involved make them particularly suited to such a task, providing each production with a variety of approaches with which to interrogate research and respond theatrically. Maleczech's openness to the ideas of her collaborators makes her distinctly suited to capitalize on the expansive possibilities these artists present. It is no coincidence, then, that these productions are characterized by Maleczech's instinctive ability to recognize theatrical potential in colleagues from varied disciplines, the trust she places in them as fully invested creative partners, and her dedication to resurrecting the outcasts of history. Maleczech insists upon a place for these figures and stories in the collective historical record by assuring their place on the stage night after night in performance.

While Maleczech's project is in part a recuperative effort to revitalize forgotten and misunderstood figures, her engagement with the famous scientist Marie Curie demonstrates that her initiative is an even more expansive one. What distinguishes Maleczech's staging of history from that of her fellow artists is the degree to which her interpretations are shaped by the contributions of her team. The resulting representations encompass a range of points of view about Maleczech's subjects, underscoring the suggestion that our understanding of history must acknowledge the multiple perspectives of its players and storytellers. Rather than present her audiences with neatly bundled packages, she hands them a puzzle to take home, inviting them to construct yet another possible configuration of the past.

Following Maleczech's death, Fogarty restaged the touring version of *Lucia's Chapters* with Maria Tucci as Lucia. Thus Maleczech's project to reformulate our reception of the past continues. She is now cast among the ghosts of the women she once represented onstage.

3

Family Drama

Love is money, Alex

Hajj

Twenty years before Maleczech was cast in the Joyce family drama, Mabou Mines produced *Hajj* (1983), which features (among other stories) Maleczech's relationship with her father at the time of his death. As with *Lucia's Chapters of Coming Forth by Day* (2007), *Hajj* is a solo piece for Maleczech. Here, however, she plays a version of herself as well as a version of her father. In Mabou Mines's *Lear* (1990), Maleczech transforms the canonical tragic father figure into a mother, reversing inherited notions of paternalistic universalism. These productions reveal Maleczech's interest in unsettling the traditional notion of the father figure, and, by extension, all family roles and relationships. *Hajj* and *Lear* demonstrate Maleczech's determination to expand the boundaries of what women are allowed to say and do, onstage and in life. These productions also probe the uneasy relationship among women, art, power, and money.

Alisa Solomon, who served as dramaturg for *Lear*, questions Richard Schechner's claim that we have arrived at the end of humanism. Instead, she suggests that perhaps we have arrived at "the end of the patriarchy."[1] Maleczech as Lear, Solomon argues, removes universalism from its presumed association with the male perspective and forces audiences to consider the constructed nature of gendered behavior.

If *Lear* disentangles universalism from patriarchy, then *Hajj* unravels the tie that binds paternity to power. *Hajj* began as a poem rather than a performance piece. Breuer wrote it about a friend who committed suicide before Maleczech had the chance to repay a loan of $40. Later, when Maleczech's father took his life before she could repay her debt to him, Breuer adapted the poem into a performance piece for her. The title refers to the annual pilgrimage to Mecca undertaken by devout Muslims. In this work, Maleczech dresses up as her father by placing a latex mask of his face over her own; we recognize him from a projected photograph we have previously seen. Shortly thereafter, she rips off half of the mask to reveal herself. Maleczech colonizes her father's words as she simultaneously resurrects him and takes possession of him. Such permutations chart a troubling course over the rocky terrain of a father/daughter relationship, ultimately unmooring it from traditional power dynamics.

First produced in 1983 at the Public Theater, the project epitomizes Mabou Mines's collective structure and its effort to foster independent thinking among collaborators. According to Maleczech, the members of the creative team worked with an unusual degree of autonomy on their various contributions—she on her performance, Breuer on his text, Julie Archer on her installation, and Craig Jones on video. The mask was created by Linda Hartinian, who also worked with Maleczech the same year to create a hologram for her staging of Samuel Beckett's short story, *Imagination Dead Imagine*. Although Breuer maintains that he was the director for the project, according to Maleczech the original credits for the production did not list a director (a claim supported by archival publicity records). "There couldn't be a singular decider of things" in *Hajj*, said Maleczech, "because it was so complex." The piece came together because "eventually we all bent our efforts to realize the writing."[2] Archer confirms Maleczech's contention that the collaborators worked without a director. "We all worked on it," she says, "and, with the exception of the writing, we all weighed in on all aspects of it. We moved forward collaboratively. We worked by sort of piling on and pulling off and piling on and pulling off."[3] Karen Kandel, whose first project with the company was *Lear*, suggests that the conflicting opinions about Breuer's role may be a question of semantics. The question, she said, is "what does a director mean to Ruth?" The process Maleczech and Archer describe indicates that each of the creators, Breuer, Archer, Jones, and Maleczech, worked on separate tracks, placing their contributions in conversation with each other in the rehearsal room.

In another production characteristic of Mabou Mines's collective process, Maleczech adapted Shakespeare's *King Lear*, transforming familiar perspectives related to patriarchal authority. The company's 1990 production was set in a fictionalized, matriarchal American South when it opened in New York at the Triplex Theater. The production had a single director in Breuer, but it was Maleczech who initiated the process that brought it into being. She wanted the right to speak Lear's words herself, having thought about them for years after sitting backstage as wardrobe mistress for each of Michael O'Sullivan's performances at the San Francisco Actor's Workshop in 1961. Once again, Maleczech took possession of a man's words and performance, not only by playing Lear but also by basing her approach to the role on O'Sullivan's. This time, the father figure was a fictional one.

Hajj and *Lear* are perhaps the two projects that epitomize Mabou Mines's signature artistic approach: *Hajj* began without a director and *Lear* was initiated by a performer. *Hajj*, moreover, in referencing *Vanishing Pictures* (Maleczech's first directing project) and in its use of a collective process, tells a metahistory of the company. "People were quite independent in the pursuit of what they were doing" on *Hajj*, Maleczech said. "I felt quite independent as a performer." Her comments underline the company's commitment to artistic autonomy and flexibility. Mabou Mines "didn't want people to feel that they were stuck in whatever their initial artistic role was," Maleczech explained, "whether it was as a director or as a performer." The company wanted "to formalize the fact" that actors could initiate projects, as David Warrilow did with *The Lost Ones* (1974) and Maleczech did with *Lear*. *Hajj* similarly displays an autonomous and collective process, even if in this case Breuer fulfilled certain directorial obligations. Such autonomy within the collective allowed Maleczech to explore what had become, by the time *Lear* was produced, volatile artistic concerns about money, power, family, and gender. The very nature of the collaborative—and in some instances collective—processes that led to *Hajj* and *Lear* demonstrates structural as well as aesthetic challenges to patriarchal conventions.

This chapter examines the questions these two productions pose about the relationship between patriarchy and power by analyzing the way each engages with money, imitation, appropriation, and cross-gender casting. Although *Lear* comes later in Mabou Mines's production chronology, the discussion begins with this adaptation of Shakespeare's text before moving to the far more enigmatic *Hajj*.

Mabou Mines's *Lear*

Nothing will come of nothing

If *Hajj* and *Lear* are about fathers, they are also about money. In *Hajj* Maleczech is a female performer whose "name is debtor." In *Lear*, she begins as a rich matriarch with the luxury of playing favorites in the division of her earthly possessions and ends in penniless misery. Such financial trouble is part of the family biography of Mabou Mines, not to mention part of the autobiography of almost every artist, including those in the American avant-garde. The Living Theatre, for example, was evicted from its space on 14th Street in Manhattan by the Internal Revenue Service in 1963, and in 2010 left their theater on Clinton Street in the Lower East Side, also for financial reasons. "My life is about money," said Breuer, when asked whether it was significant that both *Hajj* and *Lear* center on financial concerns.[4] In these productions, money troubles are also gendered.

Maleczech and Breuer are no strangers to the drama of financial strain. The focus on this theme in *Hajj* and *Lear* echoes their constant concern throughout the company's history. Iris Smith Fischer's article, "Mabou Mines' *Lear*: A Narrative of Collective Authorship," analyzes the financial complexities the company faced during its development process for this production. She argues that collective authorship extends beyond the company's structure to all of the collaborators in the piece, in which she includes financial considerations. The artistic process for *Lear*, Smith Fischer suggests, took on characteristics of the financial development process itself. Work on *Lear*, she notes, was slow and disjointed because Mabou Mines lacked the funds to keep such a large company together. Smith Fischer also points out that although Mabou Mines was criticized during *Lear* for embracing corporate sponsorship by companies such as AT&T, they, and other downtowners such as La MaMa, had, in fact, received corporate and government funding for some time.[5] Mabou Mines also received sponsorship from the Sony Corporation for *Hajj*, which allowed the company to take advantage of the expensive technical equipment needed for rehearsals.

The staged anxiety over family finances in *Hajj* and *Lear* finds a real-life parallel in Maleczech and Breuer's longtime frustration over Mabou Mines's finances. Maleczech reported that the year after their residency at the Public Theater ended in the 1980s, the company lost $70,000. "We've sometimes had big, big deficits," she said, and those concerns have only grown with time. Only occasionally has Mabou Mines succeeded in covering costs with box office income, as it was able to do by touring *DollHouse*. "We really like earned income," Maleczech explained,

> but you can't always manage it when you are wrestling with these works that are so hard to make and that take so long to develop. And now there's no institutional support for anyone, unless there are subscribers or unless you are really a big multimillion dollar company. We used to get significant support from the NEA and New York State Council for the Arts, neither of which you can get now at a level that would be commensurate with artistic excellence over such a long period of time. I mean, we've had some duds, but for the most part this company is very well respected worldwide. Now you can only really get funding for a specific project from the NEA and NYSCA. This makes it really difficult to continue the operations that make those projects possible—we sometimes don't have the money to employ the right number of staff, for example, or at the right level, so that's become really, really difficult.[6]

For his part, Breuer argues that downtown theater plays a vital role in New York's economy, one for which Mabou Mines and its downtown peers have never been financially compensated. "The city lives on tourism," he says, and

> theater is a gate to tourism and downtown is the key. It's kind of like the laboratory for uptown. Whenever they can come down and steal anything that was invented downtown, they'll take it uptown. So the point is, we should be paid a research and development fee by Broadway. But we're not and that's the whole point. If we were in the car industry and we were inventing a bumper, we'd be paid a research and development fee. But we're not. So that's a little bit of the problem.

The basis of Breuer's complaints has rankled artists since the establishment of off-off Broadway.[7] The evocation of financial strain in *Hajj* and *Lear*, taken together with Maleczech and Breuer's very real concern about keeping the company solvent, reflect an ongoing concern for the company.

Breuer contends that power "is perceived in economic terms" in *Lear*. His view, however, is that the power dynamic in the play is not tied to gender: "the idea and the fundamental question in *Lear* is whether power has its own behavior or whether it is tied to sex or race. My position is that power has its own behavior." [8] I argue that the economics in *Lear* are, in fact, gendered. As the male Regan and Goneril begin to chip away at their mother's remaining assets—her retinue, for example—they are steadfast in perceiving their actions as setting the universe right. In Shakespeare's text, Regan and Goneril use Lear's age as an excuse to undermine their father. The reverse-gender casting tells a second story. It isn't just Lear's age but her gender that makes her unfit to reign. Even in the matriarchal world of this staged society, Regan and Goneril continue to see their mother's economic power as unnatural.

Imitation and appropriation

Breuer was not the only one whose artistic maturity was advanced by the time he and Maleczech spent at the San Francisco Actor's Workshop in the early 1960s. Maleczech, too, was profoundly influenced by what she experienced there. Breuer was given leadership roles (he was Blau's assistant director and directed a few small-scale productions himself), while Maleczech served as a production coordinator and wardrobe mistress. In the 1960s, the San Francisco theater scene was thriving, said Maleczech, and the Actor's Workshop "was serious—very serious," citing their pioneering work on bringing European avant-garde plays to North America. The distinctive approach to theater cultivated by Blau and Jules Irving prompted Maleczech to undertake technical roles she had never considered before. Performing traditional roles in the Bay area—she played Emily in *Our Town* with the Interplayers, for example—was quite different from the post-World War II avant-garde plays Blau promoted. They were different from anything Maleczech had previously encountered. "Those plays," she said,

> don't fit American realism in the way *Our Town* does, even though *Our Town* is a very great play. It is a different requirement from the performer. So I got very steeped in trying to understand what Herb was trying to do. He has a very intellectual and a very brilliant mind, and it was very difficult to get how to apply what it was that he was interested in making these pieces talk about as an actor and a performer.[9]

Her role as a dresser provided her with particularly potent material for later use. Maleczech sat backstage and watched Michael O'Sullivan play King Lear under Blau's direction each night in a production she described as "wonderful." It was so wonderful, in fact, that she memorized it. Breuer, Blau's assistant director on *King Lear*, describes a concept inspired by Celtic Ireland and set in a tribal world of 600 C.E. Echoing Maleczech's praise of O'Sullivan, Breuer calls the performance "genius." O'Sullivan's approach, he said, was "a very large classical interpretation that moved toward Expressionist. He used a lot of Michael Chekhov-ish styles—symbolic gesturing and things like that. He was like a great big spider throughout the stage—a senile spider— and he was quite brilliant."[10]

There were of course barriers to "the dresser Maleczech" striving to achieve prominence in such a performance. One was that, as Maleczech explained, she "wasn't considered good enough to be an actor" at the Actor's Workshop or even to be a paid professional of any kind. "I didn't ask for money to buy soap," she said, acknowledging that her unconditional participation gave her access to work she regarded so highly. Although she performed in several small roles there, one in Alan Schneider's production of *Twinkling of an Eye* featuring O'Sullivan, Maleczech was never one of the company members who received a living wage. She was committed to being part of the Workshop nonetheless. But the lack of financial compensation surely contributed to her feeling that she was a second-class citizen. The other, more obvious reason was that she was a woman.

Inspired by O'Sullivan's performance, "I just wanted to say the words and of course I realized very quickly that there wasn't a way for me to say those words—there wasn't a provision for any woman, not only me, but any woman to say those words." The memory of O'Sullivan's performance, which fueled Maleczech's desire to say words with no provision for her to say them, was the driving force behind Mabou Mines's *Lear*. There is, of course, ample precedent for female performers taking on male Shakespearean roles, the most prominent example being Sarah Bernhardt's Hamlet. But Bernhardt's Hamlet was an adaptation by Marcel Schwob rather than the original and Lear has not been a popular choice for female stars interested in expanding their repertory. Conscious of the history of productions such as Bernhardt's, Maleczech and Breuer were anxious to develop a concept that would speak to contemporary artists and audiences. When Maleczech proposed a production of *Lear* in which she would play the title role, Breuer suggested an entirely cross-cast *Lear* in order to move beyond what he worried would otherwise come across as a Bernhardt-like "star turn." The theatrical world they would create was a matriarchal American South. Mabou Mines is not the only avant-garde company inspired to reconstruct Shakespeare through the lens of American culture—twenty-four years after Maleczech and Breuer's *Lear* production, the Wooster Group incorporated Native American traditions in their 2014 *Cry, Trojans!*, a version of *Troilus and Cressida*.[11]

Although the matriarchal world of the play was largely Breuer's vision, the context for Maleczech's initiation of this project makes clear that the resulting gender-reversed production was a communal undertaking; in fact, according to Maleczech, it was Breuer who "asked if he could direct" the production. Maleczech, in her role as co-artistic director, created the opportunity for herself.

But when asked, Breuer initially contradicted Maleczech's assertion that her performance was based on O'Sullivan's. [12] "The interpretation that I was interested in," he said,

> had almost nothing to do with Michael O'Sullivan's interpretation of that part, and though I think Ruth's was very brilliant and Michael's was very brilliant, I think the concepts were so totally different that any real imitation of Michael O'Sullivan would be destructive to Ruth's performance.

Breuer suggested that imitation on Maleczech's part would be awkward both in the way it would destabilize his directorial conception for Mabou Mines's *Lear* and in the context of Maleczech's physical presence as a performer:

> Michael was six-foot-six and Ruth is five-foot-three and that, in a sense, means that because of their movement structure and their character build, one cannot be an imitation of the other. Plus one took place in 1954 in Georgia and the other took place in 600 A.D. in the Celtic world. I think that what I really feel is that both of us were inspired to do *Lear* by Michael, but as far as imitating any of his stuff, as good as it was, it would be wrong for this concept.

Maleczech's description of her own development process, however, tells a different story.

During the rehearsal process for *Lear*, an early stage of which is captured on film in Jill Godmillow's documentary *Lear '87 Archive*, a reporter from the *Atlantic Monthly* asks Maleczech why she wanted to play Lear. "Because I saw a very great performance of the role," she tells him,

> I saw it fifty-three times in 1962, at a time when performances in the theater were as ephemeral as the theater truly is. There were no videotapes and very few pictures, so no one knows about this performance, but I do. And I wanted to repeat it.

When O'Sullivan played the role of the mythical aging patriach, he was a gay, twenty-seven-year-old man who, according to Breuer, completely dwarfed Maleczech physically. He is, perhaps, an improbable inspiration for a female performer in her late forties. How much will she copy, the reporter wonders? "I'm going to steal as much as I can remember," Maleczech tells him, "and I can remember a lot."[13]

Karen Kandel recalls a rehearsal process for Lear that contextualizes Maleczech and Breuer's differing recollections. Speaking of the workshop sessions marking the first phase of the process, she says, "lots of people said things like, I don't think that's right, I disagree." Recorded scenes in Godmillow's documentary support Kandel's memory. Furthermore, Kandel suggests, it was Maleczech and Breuer themselves who set the tone for this open dialogue among collaborators. "It's a very old relationship, so there was an understanding between them that is clear."

> They would have discussions, differences of opinion, disagreements about something, but it was always very smart and respectful. But it could get heated, and sometimes she would take him out of the room to talk about the project. But the reason they work so well together is because Lee trusts her. He would sometimes get her to go further or do something crazy, which sometimes she would try. It was like shorthand.... Sometimes he would try to convince her, he would try to come at it another way, but sometimes she would say no.

As Kandel's comments indicate, Breuer and Maleczech's ability to incorporate (or, at the very least, tolerate) divergent views is characteristic of the Mabou Mines process. In Deborah Saivetz's book on JoAnne Akalaitis, the former Mabou Mines co-artistic director describes a typical process as one in which everyone gives feedback on everything, which, while occasionally frustrating, empowers actors and designers to do more than simply carry out the director's ideas.[14] Maleczech's performance indicates that she shaped her role to exist within the universe Breuer conceived for the production. Yet the degree of control and manipulation she exerted over her source material, as well as her development process, highlights the freedom and independence of the Mabou Mines performer—the same values Maleczech promoted as co-artistic director.

Maleczech's Lear is a homage to an artist from whom she drew inspiration. But at the same time Maleczech seditiously upends O'Sullivan's performance—along with the convention that prevented her from "saying those words." Maleczech honors O'Sullivan, but she also usurps his performance using her interpretation of his work to promote a politicized theatrical agenda. The value Mabou Mines places on empowerment and autonomy for the performer means not only that Maleczech could initiate a project in order to play a particular part but also that she had the freedom to decide how she would approach the role. In this context, the choice to produce a gender-reversed *Lear* is by no means the "arbitrary gender change" Elin Diamond describes in her 1990 review.[15] Smith Fischer points out that Breuer saw "gender [as] one of many possible analogies," but for Maleczech, gender "was the material obstacle between her and the chance to play Lear...."[16] Considering Breuer's view of the production at the expense of Maleczech's undermines the collective process and the autonomy of the performer that is fundamental to the work of Mabou Mines. Reading the production from Maleczech's point of view posits *Lear* as nothing less than her coming of age from that sidelined performer not worth paying. It also means that her initiation of this project establishes a vital context for a production in which many women could say words traditionally reserved for men.[17]

Performing the gender gap: *Lear*

In 1989, Richard Schechner argued for "a dance and theatre where several different kinds of responses are possible: times when perceiving the race, gender, etc., of performers matter; and times when it should not even be perceived ... because spectators have been trained to be race, gender, age, and body-type 'blind.'"[18] Maleczech's performances in *Hajj* and *Lear* fall into Schechner's first category: in each case, the perception of gender matters; in each case, we perceive what Schechner refers to as the "gap" between the performer and the role she plays. Many performances seek to establish a fusion between the actor and the character he or she plays. Maleczech's carefully designed performances in *Hajj* and *Lear* are calculated to make audience members perceive the distance between the actor and their ideas about the roles she plays. This gap also calls attention to differences in the way we perceive men and women as well as masculinity and femininity.

The strategy is employed differently in each production. In *Hajj* a woman enacts her father; we are aware of the gender gap the moment this part of the performance begins. Maleczech's commanding presence as she enacts her father foregrounds the disruption viscerally. In *Lear* the gender gap exists because of conventional assumptions the audience has inherited about the central role. Borrowing a concept from Brecht, Breuer describes himself as a "dialectical director," explaining that "you're supposed to think and feel two different things and then you're supposed to sit back and analyze the difference between your feeling and your thinking and that is the synthesis." The gender gap in these productions functions as one of Breuer's dialectical strategies. And it functions similarly for Maleczech, which is characteristic of her approach.[19] As Breuer said, "Ruth does understand and work with this dialectical method."

In *Lear* the gap exists between the audience's preconceptions, initiated by the Shakespeare text, and the space of Maleczech's female *Lear*. Without our knowledge of this history, the gap between Maleczech and her Lear would be far less potent—although we still might register the staged presentation of a matriarchal society as subversive. Rather than present the gap between her stage presence and the text, Maleczech's approach to the performance is to embrace the adaptation in its entirety. Solomon writes that, while "the play first sets up a back-and-forth between what I see on the stage and what I recall in my mind," what she describes as "the imposing image of the tradition" quickly gives way to "the live stage experience. The comparisons stop. Lear becomes every inch a woman."[20] This attests both to the seamlessness of the adapted text, which replaces pronouns, changes references to royalty, and tailors the Fool's jokes for contemporary humor, and to Maleczech's ability as a performer to "suspend disbelief."

As dramaturg, Solomon participated in adapting the text and sat through rehearsals and performances; her perception of Maleczech's performance was of course influenced by her involvement in the process. Solomon's evaluation, however, expresses what was for many audience members a strong and dynamic performance (Maleczech received an OBIE Award for her work). One of its most striking aspects is the disruption between Maleczech's ability to suspend disbelief and our cultural awareness of Lear's textual and historical context. The rupture occurs the first moment we see her performance advertised, and it returns at several points throughout the totality of the theater-going experience. The gender gap exists for us in all of the moments—before, during, and after the performance—when we simultaneously register Maleczech as performer and confront the role as originally written and traditionally staged.

Maleczech and Breuer's strategy to invite the audience to accept the performance on its own terms is precisely that: a calculated performance tactic. While it might be more obviously political to play a female Lear at arm's length, so to speak, employing alienating strategies that delineate the distance between text/history and performance or utilizing the feminist gestus Diamond advocates, Maleczech's choice to embody herself in the role fully is in fact deeply political.[21] Breuer's point of view about casting, although less polemical than Schechner's, supports Maleczech's method here. "I don't believe in color-blind and gender-blind casting," he has said. "You can't say you don't see what you see. But I do believe in the idea of conceptualizing a particular production to allow for various races, actors, actresses to take part in this representation."[22]

Maleczech's approach to acting, and indeed that of the entire ensemble, casts her (and them) as integral parts of the representation rather than stationing them outside of the representation in order to point to it. Greg Mehrten, a former company member who created the production's drag-queen Fool, recalls a process in which the actors' task was to work with

Shakespeare's text in order to develop emotionally and psychologically driven characters without overemphasizing ideas about power and gender that were the motor behind the production. Mehrten explains that cast members tried to play their parts as written "and let Lee deal with the overall concept."[23] Maleczech's decision to establish heightened emotional reality for the interval of her performance, to "be" Lear, gives her full possession of the role, the play, and its legendary history.

The cross-gendered production is inherently dialectical (in Breuer's sense of the word), because the audience is confronted with a Lear who was written as a man but is played by a woman. Breuer argues that, in this production, Lear's "power moves" have the "aura of male movement, not the aura of female movement" because Lear has obtained "power in a male-oriented world." Mehrten's interpretation of Mabou Mines's approach to performance supports this notion of a dialectical experience for the audience:

> Mabou Mines's style of acting is not the kind where the actor disappears and you believe that this person is really in the 1950s South but somehow speaking Shakespearian English. It's more that the actors try to find something within themselves that they can grasp onto to portray the character.... It's using yourself.

In this way, the audience must process in performance the biologically female Maleczech playing a behaviorally male Lear. The challenge to the audience is couched subtly because the production does not seek to exaggerate Lear's maleness or Maleczech's femaleness. Rather, Breuer and Maleczech invite the two sides of their Lear to coexist onstage.

Decisions about costume and physical choices were based on Maleczech's female physique. Her *Lear* wears a flowing skirt topped by a business-like jacket and a dainty hat; she stomps around the stage with ease in sensible black heels like a female executive in a china shop. "Look at every powerful woman CEO in New York," Breuer says, "because you're looking at Lear." Maleczech's physical presence, which Diamond describes as a "stocky body" bearing "witness to its own maternal history," is everywhere embraced; she looks "every inch" the aging matriarch the production says she is.[24] While her voice lowers to a growl when she tells us of her "darker purpose," or rises to cloying sweetness when she urges Regan to take her side against the ungrateful Goneril, it is never anything less than a finely honed instrument evoking potent character choices. Breuer's decision to employ body mics (though disliked by some critics) further enhances the range of Maleczech's voice, allowing her to make use of nuanced intonations that would be difficult to project without mechanical amplification. Here the body mic serves a distinctly different purpose than the one hand held in *Hajj*.

Maleczech's unusual resurrection of O'Sullivan's performance as Shakespeare's tragic figure honors his performance while at the same time taking possession of it. Putting Lear's words in her mouth is a colonization, personal as well as political.

A mythological ~~father~~ mother and a fool in drag

In *Lear* Maleczech's is a subtly subversive rebellion, devoid of fiery rhetoric or political posturing. Her insurrection lies in doing the thing in the first place, and doing it convincingly. Maleczech's persuasive performance, taking its cue from O'Sullivan's, musters a high tragic approach, capitalizing on emotionally charged gestures and utilizing the extreme ranges of her natural voice to express heightened psychological states. "I remember her roar," says Kandel, "and I remember her vulnerability. Those extremes were exciting and also different. Where she roared, how she roared, and also how Lear was manipulative with her vulnerability—Ruth just worked every angle of her being." Mehrten recalls that some of Maleczech's choices were derived from O'Sullivan's performance:

> I remember Ruth saying that Michael had used a lot of Delsartian stuff, and she just kind of lifted it from his performance and she did them in the show because they were very classic—kind of grand theatrical gestures. I remember asking her once, "Are you doing that on purpose to look like that?" And she said yes; that it was this system of gestures that came from him, from Michael's performance.

Here, Maleczech adapts O'Sullivan's take on Delsarte to create a physical
and vocal landscape capturing the emotional honesty to be found in
Shakespeare's heightened text. Mehrten previously described "using
yourself" as a crucial element of this strategy. [25]

In the spirit of Delsarte's technique, which pairs an actor's emotional
life with a prescribed corporeal landscape drawn from observation and
heightened for theatricality, Maleczech's physical vocabulary as Lear is
sometimes reserved or abandoned but always controlled. We sense a
certain energy and readiness lurking within her. Her entrance displays
confident bearing, regal but a bit stooped by age. She leans on a cane but
moves as if she owns the space, which, until the close of this opening
scene, she does. Maleczech's Lear retains her composure as she metes
out Cordelion's sentence from a lawn chair, looking as entitled as any
business executive firing a longtime employee. She moves happily and
busily as she multitasks feeding her dogs and breezily hiring Kent, played
by Lola Pashalinski. Her physical state changes only as Lear registers the
newly reduced position her sons have designed for her. At the first sign
that Goneril will enforce a drastic limitation on the number of dogs in
Lear's retinue (here dogs replace men), she staggers forward as if the air
has been knocked out of her (she still has the wherewithal to swat him
on the side of the head using a rolled newspaper). Her reaction displays
an economy of movement, but we will see such physical pluckiness
drain out of Maleczech's Lear as the events of the play unfold. By the
time Cordelion returns to her she is nearly catatonic, and we see her
asleep in a rocking chair on the front porch of the home she no longer
recognizes as her own.

Maleczech's vocal landscape parallels her physical vocabulary,
tracing as it does the full range of Lear's emotional trajectory. In a
tone so low and rough that it could be considered a growl, Lear tells
Cordelion that "nothing can come of nothing." Moments earlier, just
after entering, her voice drips with solicitude as she invites her sons to
express their love for her. When she greets her eldest—after he deigns
to appear before her—"How now, Goneril?" rings with the too-bright
cheeriness of a mother so embarrassingly happy to see her child. Later,

when Lear meets the blind Gloucester, her voice is cautious and feeble, almost gentle, drained as it is of the hoarse raging we hear in the storm scene.

Maleczech's vocal and physical choices chart the rise and fall of Lear's temper and fortunes. They convey a complex emotional life and a complicated, increasingly conflicted, and ultimately ravaged consciousness. Breuer describes Lear as a "mythological mother." Maleczech balances the mystery of this mythical figure, one we can never know intimately, with intense flashes of richly expressive behavior.[26] Breuer suggests that the characters in Mabou Mines's *Lear* may blur the lines between cartoon figures and real people—an interest he pursues in his animations like *The Red Horse, Shaggy Dog,* and *Summa Dramatica* (in which Maleczech performed).[27] Yet the concerns Breuer explores in *Lear* are different from those in the fantasized, humanoid animal kingdoms of his texts. *Lear,* by contrast, gives us Maleczech's detailed portrait of a larger-than-life royal figure.

Despite Maleczech's carefully constructed performance, a female Lear in a cross-cast production was not always enough to dispel concerns voiced by some feminist critics about Shakespearean misogyny. While praising the company for elevating maternal misery to high tragedy, Diamond's concern is that the production doesn't sufficiently distinguish the distance between the company's point of view and the textual boundaries embedded in Shakespeare's patriarchal drama. Diamond directs one of her major criticisms at the portrayal of Lear's madness. The queen's breakdown becomes apparent in the storm scene when Maleczech, hair disheveled, the conventional sign of female madness onstage, retraces the grand tradition of male tragedians. Lear hangs from a telephone pole with her long robes flowing around her, the jaunty jacket and formal skirt having been long discarded. Her voice is labored and her movements disjointed as she rolls her head and moves her eyes from side to side. She dismounts the telephone pole only to circle it on her knees as Kent trails after her carrying an umbrella. Her attention is drawn to Karen Kandel's OBIE-Award-winning Mad Marie, a female, Rastafarian version of Poor Tom, to whom she ascribes a similar insanity. "Thou art the thing itself," she tells Mad Marie with wonder in her voice, the "unaccommodated one" (in place of Shakespeare's celebrated "unaccommodated man"). Maleczech's Lear is relieved to find a kindred spirit. Edna (who replaces Edgar) is, of course, only pretending. Lear, we know, is not.

Such ranting and raving come too close, in Diamond's estimation, to hysteria. "[M]adness is tricky," she writes,

> and Breuer and company can be charged with reinforcing rather than debunking some pernicious social stereotypes. When Shakespeare's Lear complains of womanish "hot tears," he invokes the immemorial equation of women and weakness; when he speaks of "the mother, the hysterico passio" that "swells up toward my heart" he fears being overtaken by the female *hysteron*.... [28]

Additional stereotypes can be found in Shakespeare's text. Lear's response to Goneril after she demands that he rid himself of his one hundred knights is steeped in sexism, even misogyny. He is "ashamed/ That thou hast power to shake my manhood thus,/That these hot tears which break from me perforce/Should make thee worth them."[29]

Mehrten suggests that Breuer intentionally employs stereotypes in order to critique them. Regan and Goneril are played by former Mabou Mines company members Bill Raymond and Ron Vawter as "southern, good old boy types," Mehrten notes. "Those are clichés or stereotypes, and Lee is deliberately using them, but I think it's pretty obvious that it's a critique of that through the mask of the stereotype." However, he says, "you can sometimes sympathize" with these distortions; performers must find some connection to such figures in order to bring them to life onstage. "You have to find some way in," Mehrten says. The juxtaposition of empathy with extremity is part of the critique Mehrten describes—a person we first perceive to be a caricature is suddenly revealed to have sympathetic qualities. Breuer's impulse to explore and document stereotypes onstage is a further manifestation of his fascination with the destabilization that can be found in cartoons.

Breuer describes a distinction between motherhood and matriarchy that is crucial to the interpretation of Lear in this production. Describing Lear's position in relation to her children and to society, Breuer understands that "Lear is queen and mother figure of an extended family and she has neglected the nuclear aspects of being a mother tremendously in order to be a powerhouse in the extended family.... This is a person who is more a king than a father. Or more a queen than a mother."[30] In the stage world Breuer imagines, Lear's position as queen makes her the matriarchal figure for the advisors, the servants, and the entire retinue surrounding her—the full extended family he describes. In this context Lear's fear of the sudden maternal instinct that swells up in her heart also causes apprehension about a potential shift in her priorities, her position in society, and perhaps even in her own personality.

Misogynistic as some lines in Shakespeare's text may be, any interpretation linking Maleczech's high tragic approach to hysteria enforces a double standard in the way she is allowed or expected to present Lear and the way a male actor is allowed or expected to do so. While Maleczech's portrayal of madness in *Lear* is unusual by virtue of her being a woman, her acting choices are no different from what might be expected in a contemporary production by a male actor. And, of course, if Maleczech models her portrayal on O'Sullivan, her interpretation clearly reflects the way he played this scene. Keith Fowler describes O'Sullivan's performance as similarly hyperbolic, calling him "preening, deranged, screeching," and "imbued with primordial divinity."[31] Whether or not this heightened approach to Lear is effective remains a question of personal taste. But if O'Sullivan can play it this way, why can't Maleczech?

"Maleczech's Lear," Diamond argues,

> made no attempt to frame or foreground what patriarchal science has made of her woman's body. A male Lear can argue dialectically against invasive female signs but this female Lear could only struggle against her already flawed (read: female) body. [32]

Mabou Mines's *Lear* does not choose to engage with the way in which female biology and psychology has been characterized in the history of science. Maleczech's approach, instead, merges the performer with the character's reality, rather than creating distance between the two. Maleczech and Breuer ask audiences to look at a reversed-gender Lear differently from the way they are expected to respond to a traditionally cast production. But this does not mean that actors are obliged to play the reverse-gender roles differently than do their traditionally cast counterparts. Maleczech and Breuer's approach is, however, both subtle and subversive. They lure the audience into forgetting, as Solomon says she did, that Lear was not a lead role written for a woman. Spectators are now free to "synthesize" (to use Breuer's term) what they may know about Maleczech and the Lear of Shakespeare's text and what they experience when they watch her perform it. This provides Maleczech the opportunity to play an emotionally engaged Lear, by turns simpering and raging—a figure who has haunted her imagination ever since seeing O'Sullivan onstage. Maleczech plays the role, not the gender.

Diamond calls Greg Mehrten's transvestite Fool's "gestic use of the dildo" (which replaces the coxcomb) a "disruptive" act, comparing it favorably with her overall impression of a passive female Lear struggling from within against the biology that binds her. The dissonance Diamond identifies between Mehrten's alienating strategies and Maleczech's high tragic approach inadvertently uncovers one of the ways the gender gap is represented in this stage interpretation.

In an early rehearsal for the production, captured on camera in Godmillow's documentary, Breuer suggests that Mehrten and his Fool adopt a pose of impersonating Maleczech and her Lear. Besides existing in a metarelationship with Maleczech's replication of O'Sullivan's performance, Breuer's direction suggests an early acknowledgment that Maleczech's Lear will be carefully designed to make such an impersonation possible. It suggests that there will be little distance in performance between Maleczech and her Lear. This proximity between performer and character is what makes Mehrten's parody possible—it is difficult, if not downright impossible, to parody a character already foregrounded with the intrusion of distancing techniques.

Mehrten does more than impersonate Maleczech's Lear and Pashalinski's Kent. Godmillow's documentary records him considering drag icons like Judy Garland, Tallulah Bankhead, and Bette Davis as possible modes for his role. Both Breuer and Maleczech suggest that the young Charles Ludlam, a fellow artist supported by Ellen Stewart at La MaMa during the early years of off-off Broadway theater, served as an inspiration for their interpretation of the Fool. Mehrten's work in rehearsal provides Maleczech with a reverse mirror of her own behavior as Lear as it features the stereotypically feminine behavior (preening, vamping, sashaying) that Maleczech's Lear never displays. Maleczech notes the effectiveness of this trope: "You really get the position that the fool is trying to keep Lear in balance by making her laugh," she says, "by making her look at herself, by pushing."[33] The performance captured on video at New York's Triplex Theater offers us a Fool Mehrten has created with a potent mixture of Maleczech impersonations, movie star inspirations, and his own imagination. By presenting the audience with behavior borrowed from Maleczech's Lear as well as actions we identify as stereotypically feminine, Mehrten is able to fulfill the function Maleczech describes as forcing Lear to examine herself. The position of Mehrten's Fool is crucial in positioning the gender gap so vital to this production. This exists both in the distance between Shakespeare's male character and Mabou Mines's female performer and in Mehrten's exaggerated feminine behavior and Maleczech's performance as Lear. Maleczech's Lear is the woman herself, while Mehrten's Fool plays a constructed femininity.

Mehrten's travesti Fool shows us the trappings of femininity nowhere to be found in Maleczech's female Lear. At his/her entrance, Mehrten's Fool wears a sequined gown, elbow-length gloves, a glamorous blond wig, a boa, strings of pearls, and frighteningly high white heels. Emerging from an outhouse, s/he minces and sways, providing a stark contrast to Maleczech, who stumps across the stage in low, practical shoes. While Mehrten mimics Maleczech's mannerisms, such as the stooped stance s/he adopts for his/her tap dance on a suitcase upon discovering Kent in the stocks, what this Fool shows us reveals as much about who Maleczech's Lear is as who she will never be. In Shakespeare's I.iv, which Mabou Mines's script folds into a continuous opening scene, the Fool provocatively swings a dildo at crotch level. Lear, repeating this movement with insouciance, engages in a similar rhythm and movement with a rolled up newspaper. But while the Fool's dildo never sees any action, appearing as an impotent double of what Mehrten actually does have under his dress, Lear's rolled newspaper becomes an instrument of real power when she uses it to beat Goneril on the head when he tries to deprive her of her canine retinue.

Maleczech's Lear is aggressive; she does not need a penis to prove it. Mehrten's Fool presents us with only superficial trappings of femininity; these turn out to have nothing to do with the traits we see in Maleczech's biologically female Lear. But while Lear may never have been the nurturer her sons may have hoped for, she displays a touching tenderness for the Fool. During a table-work session early on in the development process, Maleczech wonders if the fool in drag could be the daughter Lear never had.[34] Even so, the Fool fares no better than Lear's biological children. S/he is caught up in the storm caused by Lear's actions and swept away because of his/her status as one of Lear's hangers-on, killed in what this production stages as a gay lynching. This horrendous killing and Lear's own downfall are the consequences of failure on the part of these figures to adhere to conventionally gendered behavior.

The fate that befalls Lear is a result of the choices she has made and actively pursued. Mehrten's Fool, a biological man whose behavior is supposedly feminine, plays an ultimately passive role in the action, while the dynamic and demanding behavior of Maleczech's Lear would be traditionally marked as masculine. Maleczech's Lear, however, does not look or sound masculine. Her clothing, physicality, and voice make her recognizable as the mature matron Diamond identifies. Maleczech and Mabou Mines expose the gender gap by exploiting stereotypes to reveal their dangerous and faulty foundations.

Hajj

Money problems are family problems

In Mabou Mines's cross-gendered *Lear*, the matriarch suffers for her presumption that she has the power to control and redistribute land and goods. In *Hajj* the patriarch holds the purse strings and all the power until the performer repossesses both. *Hajj* also configures elements of Maleczech's professional career and reflects the uneasy tensions of her personal financial life.

Several years before *Hajj*, Maleczech offered to work with Beverly Brown, who was then developing a new piece that became *Vanishing Pictures* (1980) at ReCherChez. Brown was one of many artists to benefit from the company's Resident Artists Program, now known as Mabou Mines/Suite. According to Maleczech, who founded the program with Breuer and Raymond, ReCherChez was the namesake of Ray Charles, Cher, and "chez moi." But the colorful portmanteau also evokes the notion and act of research.[35] Maleczech suggests that her work with ReCherChez artists taught her how to look at the work of other artists productively. As a mentor, Maleczech explained, "you learn how to encourage and critically respond to work that is not your own. And in fact, to work that you probably wouldn't ever make, maybe even a kind of work that—not that you didn't like, but that wasn't intrinsic to your artistic growth as you saw it."

At ReCherChez Brown was one of the artists Maleczech mentored. Primarily a French art song chanteuse, Brown created a story for the songs she performed based on research about the murder of Mary Rogers, the New York "beautiful cigar girl" whose history forms the basis of Edgar Allan Poe's "The Mystery of Marie Rogêt." As Maleczech described it, Brown's piece, "was good—really good," but it needed work. Maleczech saw a way she could help, and offered to direct the piece. Wary of spending company funds on her first directing project, she borrowed money from her father to produce the show. Despite Maleczech's initial trepidation about the potential for the project's success under her directorial debut, she and Archer shared an OBIE Award for design.[36]

Maleczech's decision to take the role of director in *Vanishing Pictures* can be read as a parental act—she saw potential in one of her pupils and wanted to nurture and support her talents. Her decision to move from observer to participant deepened her relationship to the project. When the family of collaborators on *Vanishing Pictures* needed money to produce the project, Maleczech turned to her biological family. And when Maleczech's father died before she could fully repay her debt for *Vanishing Pictures*, it paved the way for the creation of *Hajj*, which blends Maleczech's artistic family with her biological one. The decision to theatricalize this personal history highlights the profound connection Maleczech makes between her art and her life. For her, the process of making theater is a family drama.

In a 1982 document describing *Hajj*, Breuer writes that the performance poem is "a simultaneous pilgrimage into the future and the past ... concerned with the relationship between emotional and fiscal debt."[37] Maleczech borrowed $3,000 from her father to produce *Vanishing Pictures*. By the time he died, she had paid back ninety percent of what she borrowed—all but $250. Yet her failure to return the entire sum casts the performer in a disgraceful light in the eyes of her father. Maleczech, as the daughter in *Hajj*, is angry that she has dishonored herself by failing to pay the loan. Perhaps she is angry that she has had to borrow the money in the first place. "We usually don't have enough money to do what we want to do," Breuer said of Mabou Mines:

> usually we get a little bit desperate about trying to put our concepts together because of the lack of funds. And everybody has to learn to deal with that—to cut down or to go into debt or whatever—and I'm really bad at that and Ruth's really bad at that. We both want to have everything, you know, our cake and eat it too.

The money Maleczech borrowed from her father was the means to a highly desired end. In *Hajj*, however, it becomes a source of desperation. Once borrowed and now never to be repaid, it occupies a space of longing and regret—a sort of buyer's remorse—through which the performer must navigate.

Rip off

"I rip you off," says Maleczech as she peels the mask of her father off her face in *Hajj*. This line refers to her stage action as well as her failure to pay back in full the money she owes him. The pun also signifies Maleczech's stage enactment of her father. She impersonates him by putting his face over her own, interpreting his feelings about her unpaid debt. And as she does so she puts words into his mouth by speaking in character as him. He is dead, he can't respond for himself; we are left with the version of events she and Breuer present to us. In this story she owns the character she has created for him, and she says so: "here in the dark box of my throat I bring you back to life." She points out that she has always carried him around anyway—she shares his DNA. "You can't leave me; that plan has a flaw/We'll never sort each other's atoms out."[38] The final portion of the performance poem is a eulogy for Maleczech's father, Alexander Reinprecht (called Lujak in the text), who "killed himself with a deer rifle /In the bedroom of his home" when he was seventy-one.[39] Although Maleczech and Breuer did not indicate why they chose to use the name Lujak in place of Reinprecht, the change signals a distinction between the actual figure and staged version of Maleczech's father—the character we meet onstage is a rip off of Maleczech's father, not the real thing. In *Hajj* Maleczech adapted the technique she observed from the actors in the Berliner Ensemble for her own purposes. These performers unmasked themselves and simultaneously presented the characters they played to underline Brecht's social commentary; Maleczech transforms this technique to expose the nature of gender as representation. In *Hajj* she dons a mask, then removes it, but upon the stage the version of herself she offers is a mask too.

The process for creating *Hajj* mirrors the grieving of a family that has lost one of its own. Just as each family member mourns both individually and collectively, each of the *Hajj* collaborators worked autonomously on his or her artistic contribution, conscious all the while that there were others working independently. Throughout the process separate tracks would repeatedly converge, as creative partners met to discuss the project and to run through their work. As a stipulation of a grant from Sony providing the expensive technical equipment the company needed, rehearsals were open to the public. In this way, the coming together of individual artistic tracks in rehearsal became mirrored acts of public grieving.

While Brown developed a storyline for her series of songs, the *Hajj* artists created a series of multimedia scenes, images and sounds that are interspersed with the narrative of Maleczech's own life. Mabou Mines relied on Sony for the video cameras and television sets that broadcast a live feed of Maleczech. Since the 1990s, this kind of equipment has been regularly incorporated into theatrical performances, but Mabou Mines's relationship with Sony provided support for what was at the time a rare and expensive undertaking. The use of technology in *Hajj* was groundbreaking, as was its use by the Wooster Group in the same period. In this process, technology is used for emotional effect, juxtaposing Maleczech's projected image against her live presence, revealing aspects of her history to us and to herself. As the company project description suggests, "through the medium of performance, it is a poem come alive. The story begins simply: an actress sits at a make-up table and discovers clues to the meaning of her life in the implications of her reflection. She finds a metaphor for her art in terms of 'a pilgrimage of the heart (Hajj)' into her memory and her spiritual history."[40]

As *Hajj* refers to the annual pilgrimage to Mecca, it is a trip, as Maleczech said, "to try to repay an unpayable debt." The actual pilgrimage in the Mabou Mines production is based on a journey Maleczech took as an eight-year-old girl. Smith Fischer describes Maleczech's move from Cleveland to Arizona as "a defining moment."[41] Maleczech made the long drive to the Southwest with her father. Reinprecht, concerned that his daughter would be afraid to sleep in the truck at night, arranged the furniture in the back of the vehicle exactly as it had appeared in Maleczech's bedroom in Cleveland. In Jones's video, one of the independent tracks in *Hajj*, this father–daughter road trip is adapted to one featuring Phil Schenk as the father and Lute Ramblin', the son of Maleczech and Breuer, as the child. Breuer explains that the decision to cast their son was based on his physical likeness to Maleczech rather than any attempt to introduce reverse-gender perspectives. Despite Breuer's remark that the choice has nothing to do with gender, in practice it reveals the way in which masculinity and femininity are played against personal history in this production to challenge the identities upon which conventional family structure is itself predicated.

Maleczech eulogizes her father as she wears his mask on her face. She pays homage to Alexander Lujak by delivering his eulogy and simultaneously rebels against him by holding him hostage to her version of his life. In *Lear* Maleczech transforms her fascination with O'Sullivan's performance into a political statement about what words women have access to onstage. In *Hajj*, her muscular appropriation of her father's character and their shared history places her rather than him into the position of power.

Performing the gender gap: *Hajj*

"The kind of performance that Ruth gives in *Hajj* is too complex to say that it is directed toward having a particular effect," Breuer says. He suggests that Maleczech engages the audience by requiring that they do the work of interpreting her representation. This approach is more directly confrontational than the one she uses in *Lear*; her performance in *Hajj* reminds the audience that even though Maleczech is not her father, she cannot get him out of her system. In *Lear*, Maleczech cradles her fictional son Cordelion (played by her biological son, Ramblin') in her lap. She sits in a rocking chair on a porch as she weeps over his unconscious body. In *Hajj* Maleczech associates herself with the child we see in the video, also played by Ramblin', by speaking the text along with him, her voice sometimes replacing his as he appears to mouth her words. On screen, the child in *Hajj* is cradled in his father's arms as he talks in his sleep, but onstage Maleczech is alone. The audience is made painfully aware of her isolation as she sings a solitary lullaby, cradling herself in her own arms. In *Hajj* the flickering of Ramblin's eyelids as he talks makes us aware that he is only pretending to sleep, while in *Lear* the adolescent performer feigns Cordelion as corpse, limp as Lear mourns over him. The distinction allows Maleczech to expose the theatrical devices used to portray emotion in *Hajj* and to deploy similar but invisible devices in *Lear*.

The diverse formal strategies that allow Maleczech to portray a single character in *Lear* and present a range of characters in *Hajj* dictate the way gender plays out in each production. At the end of *Hajj*, when Maleczech simultaneously eulogizes and enacts her father, her voice is electronically lowered, passing from her own vocal range, through the range of a man's voice, and down to a level we can only imagine is the range in which monsters, aliens, or robots might speak. Electronic alteration also increases the pitch, finally returning us to Maleczech's natural voice for the closing lines of the performance. This aural alteration underlines the fact that Maleczech is not her father and is not trying to make us think she is, even as she plays a version of him onstage. It also exposes the superficiality of our associations with gender at the most basic level—men have low voices; women speak in a higher register. Theater can change all of that. Maleczech dances around the stage in a latex mask of a man's face, sporting an oversized man's jacket and speaking in unrealistically low tones.

Although the means to the end differ in *Lear* and *Hajj*, both gendered performances underscore a key aspect of Maleczech's work. Her choices do not erase gender or create gender ambiguity. Rather, the roles she assumes and the way she represents them reveal and challenge power relationships. Pitting constructs of masculinity and femininity against one another uncovers a false binary.

Dressing up as daddy

In his 1983 review of *Hajj* Gerard Rabkin compares it to the Wooster Group's *Rumstick Road* (first produced in 1977) in its autobiographical exploration of family suicide. "But where *Rumstick Road* never relinquishes the documentary spine of Spalding's mother's suicide," he writes, "*Hajj* does not confront the fact of the suicide of Ruth Maleczech's father (except for premonitory outbursts) until the piece is half over."[42] Indeed, the performance poem guides us through pieces of several alternate narratives before the multiple frames freeze and we focus on the central ritual enacted before our eyes: the performer's delivery of the eulogy for Maleczech's father, her donning of the mask of his face, her sudden transformation, and her reemergence. We are immediately involved in the ritualistic nature of the activities we see and hear. The title itself invokes a religious rite, and Rabkin describes the performer's repetitive activities at the dressing table as a "meditative makeup ritual" which "transforms into a solemn, at times frenzied, ceremony for the dead."[43]

It is apparent early on in the performance that the audience bears witness to a rite that is personal in nature though publicly enacted. The purpose and meaning of this ceremony, however, remains a mystery for some time. If Maleczech's first line, "I have /nothing to /hide," is a clue that we are going to be subjected to deception as much as to revelation, we do not necessarily know that yet. This opening statement sets us up for a series of detours that may come our way prior to the eulogy. Although the video documents the trip Maleczech took with her father as a young girl, on screen we see a boy with his father. When Maleczech dons a blond wig and gold teeth, we wonder if this costume is key to unlocking the mystery of what has unfolded thus far, but instead she offers hints about intimate moments to which we are not privy and shines a flashlight on the faces of audience members, deflecting any possibility of self-illumination.

The choice to use a male child in the video alters Maleczech's actual family history. It creates a staged drama; the father–son relationship plays retrospectively against the damaged relationship we will later learn existed between the performer and her creditor/father. The false parallels between life and art are further advanced by the casting of the video, in which Maleczech's son plays the boy while the father is played by Shenck, not a member of the family. The gender-switching sleight of hand foreshadows the culmination of the live performance:

Maleczech dons a latex mask of her father's face and takes possession of his thoughts, feelings, and history as she delivers the eulogy. Maleczech approaches this takeover from two directions: she hijacks her father's presence by enacting him onstage, and she commandeers his memory by delivering his eulogy, ensuring that the audience, who has never met her father, perceives him from her point of view.

The tantalizing flashes of other histories serve to present, among other narratives, possibilities of other, potentially preferable family relationships. What we see in the video, for example, suggests a wistful parallel to Lujak and Maleczech's positioning as father and daughter. Would the bond between Maleczech and her father have been different if she had been a son? The video does not present the father–child relationship in an especially warm light—the scenes between Ramblin' and Schenk have an eerie, distanced quality. But they also show moments of tenderness: two-thirds of the way into the performance, the child is "held in the FATHER'S arms, being rocked to sleep."[44] Despite the alienating effect of the video, both in its essence as a mediated form and in the distant tone created by the cinematography, these moments serve to underscore the absence of any physical interaction in the live performance. Instead, the performer attempts to create tenderness for herself. Just after we see the video of the child being rocked to sleep by his father, the performer, having altered her appearance to look like the child, "appears to hold herself in the same position." We know this is only a poor substitute for the real thing. She speaks in unison with the child in the video in a vain attempt to make contact with another human being. Tender moments in the video and in the live performance are scarce. Rather, it is the interaction with memory that is given full reign here, suggesting that Maleczech must come to terms with family history as it is, not as it might have been. Memory is mutable, however, and Maleczech can stack the deck in her game of solitaire.

According to Breuer, "there's nothing in *Hajj* that's about gender except the father-daughter relationship." Of course, the father–daughter relationship is what is most crucial to the production. Breuer further suggests that without knowing that the child in the video is a boy, one might think it is a girl. With program in hand, however, those familiar with Mabou Mines collaborators and the Breuer/Maleczech offspring would be sure to know that the child we see is a male. And, as Breuer has said himself about audience reception of cross-gender casting, "you can't say you don't see what you see."

Maleczech's performance in *Hajj* presents an explicit gender gap to the audience. Here, in stark contrast to her emotionally engaged approach in *Lear*, Maleczech holds each of the characters she plays at arm's length. The performance begins with an act that is a representation of artifice as she sits before a three-way vanity putting on makeup. She recites numbers in a dry, world-weary tone, using tape to give herself a temporary face-lift, casually singing a verse from a jaded lullaby: "The man that I marry will come cash and carry." Suddenly the ground seems to shift; Maleczech transforms from a confident character into someone nervous and suppliant who tries to negotiate a schedule for paying back monies owed. In a flash Maleczech shifts tone and mood once again; we hear the low, harsh tones of someone giving a deadline for payment. As Maleczech performs alternating aspects of the power relationship between debtor and lender, she continues applying cosmetics. Her agility in shifting roles and her physical act of making up signal a premeditated superficiality in the presentation of these changing power positions.[45] Maleczech's apparent ease as she adopts and discards roles belies the rigor with which they will be deconstructed as the performance progresses.

As the production unfolds, it becomes impossible to separate the representation of gender with representations of power and money. More than halfway through the performance, Maleczech yells her father's name—"Alex!"—during a blackout. When the lights come back up, she is putting on a big, blond wig—similar, in fact, to the bombshell wig Mehrten wears as the Fool. Maleczech's posture is sexy. "I ain't a good guy," she says, in a matter-of-fact tone of voice. She continues making up. "Love is money, Alex," she says next, in a tone both casual and provocative. We would never know that she is, in fact, talking about the fraught financial relationship she had with her father at the time of his death. She puts on lipstick, then gold teeth. "Once you die you live forever," she says. There is an abrupt blackout, and suddenly Maleczech is holding a flashlight, aimed it at the audience, gold teeth glinting. She points it at different men in the audience, "holding and releasing them with the flashlight beam." Maleczech explains that she was looking for the man in the video who took her on a childhood journey. She lists a number of places connected only by the past—Via Fiorello; Champagne, Urbana; Coldwater Canyon, punctuated by the word "fuck." Place names are delivered in a relaxed voice, full of warmth. Some of the memories recall lovemaking—"in the hot tub, under the water, in front of the fan." The word "fuck" interrupts each flashback, as intermittent as a twitch. In the middle of this sequence, Maleczech begins to dance, holding the flashlight between her legs as she "seduces the audience with its beam."[46]

This dance is uncomfortable to watch. Maleczech flaunts excessive female sexuality by moving suggestively and flirting with individual members of the audience when she selects them with the glow of her flashlight. Perhaps the men Maleczech pinpoints feel uncomfortable too, illuminated and exposed as they are in the otherwise darkened theater. If she is looking for her father, this is certainly an unusual way to do so. Maleczech talks about sex. Her movements, set to jingling music, recall those of a belly dancer. But at the same time, by placing the flashlight at her crotch, Maleczech gives herself a phallus. Maleczech asserts her power by employing two conflicting images: she shows us the size of her penis while simultaneously channeling Salome.

Maleczech's flashlight/phallus dance pre-dates Mehrten's scene with the dildo by seven years. The style and effect in each production are different, and yet both scenes scramble the stereotypical signs of male and female sexuality and power. In a clever bait and switch, Mehrten's drag-queen fool presents us with an artificial phallus even though we know he is in possession of the real thing. The Fool is powerless; in the matriarchal world of Mabou Mines's *Lear* it is clear that being in possession of a penis can leave a man, literally, without a pot to piss in. In *Hajj*, however, money and male genitalia are assurances of authority, and ones that Maleczech must possess symbolically in order to transcend the patriarchal power that has subverted her autonomy.

Maleczech plays dress-up several times in *Hajj*. First she gives herself a face-lift with Scotch tape to appear younger—more like the child we see in the video. Later she prepares for her belly dance with the flashlight by putting on a blond wig and bejeweled false teeth. The final transformation we witness makes her over as her father. Each of these permutations reorients Maleczech's position with regard to gender. The first suggests her physical likeness to the boy in the video, whom we know to be her son. In the second, she displays signs of stereotypically feminine sexuality (blond wig, sexy dancing) while flaunting a phallus. Her final play of dress-up gives her ownership of her father's corporeal presence.

The scene leading up to Maleczech's impersonation and eulogizing of her father is designed to startle and intimidate. We see images of the landscape speeding by from inside a truck. Then video screens go blank. The stage directions tell us that the performer makes "a sign of the devil with her fingers," which is "superimposed over the windshield—the image is of the child riding in the truck. She growls in a devil's voice." Her words are threatening: "ready or not, Al, here I come with cash/ My check's no good, dead man/I come to sodomize you with a roll of Jacksons."[47] The performer begins to dance wildly, spinning, as sounds of the truck engine rip through the theater. Maleczech waves a noise stick. Her voice, electronically altered, is frightening. It rises to a scream as the truck veers, swerving, off the road. The screens go black again, an ominous presaging of Maleczech's usurpation.

In enacting her father Maleczech takes possession not only of male sexuality but also of paternity. Her temporary custody of fatherhood plays out much differently in *Hajj* than it does in *Lear*. In the latter, the rules of Mabou Mines's gendered takeover are apparent from the beginning of the performance because Shakespeare's text is already familiar to the audience. In *Hajj* we never know what is coming, and the production is designed to obfuscate the rules of the game. Furthermore, Maleczech's performance style in *Hajj*, which, in contrast to *Lear*, exposes the theatrical apparatus, makes it possible for us to witness a transformation of gender before our eyes. Maleczech's takeover in *Lear* gave her custody of an imagined mythic father; in *Hajj* this preoccupation becomes personal and real.

Such a deliberate strategy upends the parent–child relationship in *Hajj*, allowing Maleczech to untangle herself from the influence her father had on her. The shift is also significant in terms of gender; Maleczech extricates herself from a personal instance of patriarchal authority in which her father held all the financial power. Had she borrowed money from her mother, the resonances would be different in a society that ties masculinity to power and power to finances. As Breuer comments, an uneven power dynamic is

> part of the father/daughter relationship. It's always who controls what power. And it was all on a very primitive level, of course—this was hunter-fisher-gatherer. You know, this is $200—this wasn't two million. And yet it produced the same inner, spiritual conflict that, of course, it was intended to produce.[48]

Maleczech's performance tilts the balance of power in her favor, disrupting what Breuer describes as "the mythical father-daughter relationship."

With such a potent ending in store, why divert us with parts of alternative narratives rather than engage us early and directly with Maleczech's autobiography, as in *Rumstick Road*? Perhaps these hints of other narratives, other stories are wistful fantasies of what personal history might have been—if only. Or do these invitations into other existences subtly suggest that there is more than one way to live your life? As Maleczech takes possession of her deceased father's story, she presents a version of the past that can never be contradicted, suggesting that memory belongs only to survivors. Using makeovers as a metaphor for spiritual and psychological transformation, Maleczech tries on a number of characters, possessing and discarding each one as she journeys through personalities and power relationships to tell a story that leaves her in control of how she understands her own family history. This final revelation is that Maleczech has the authority to shape a new narrative in which she can confront her father. Challenging his version of the past and retrospectively upending the hierarchy of their relationship exposes the fragility of the foundation upon which the power dynamics of traditional family relationships are based.

A new kind of family fable

Fischer Smith, describing the way in which *Hajj* fits into Breuer's artistic trajectory, writes that "*Hajj* intertwines a recurring theme in Breuer's work, indebtedness, with that of a pilgrimage taken into a person's history to discover the source of that life and the difficult debts owed the past."[49] *Hajj* combines the themes Fischer Smith identifies in Breuer's work with two preoccupations of Maleczech's: the development of artistic work as an autonomous process within a collective, collaborative artistic team, and the reappropriation of male stage and societal power. In *Hajj* and *Lear*, Maleczech does the latter by taking men's words and making them her own; by dissecting and reconfiguring the economy of power, gender, art, and money; and by disrupting the representation of traditionally gendered family relationships.

In *Lear*, Maleczech and Breuer ask audiences to synthesize a male character with a female performer. For Maleczech, the challenge is in making the leap from personal identity to canonical character. "We're unlocking what's already *here* [in the room]," said Maleczech, "and we're putting it together with what's already there—that is the play. So we're making a new play. But we're not going to change [Shakespeare's] play...."[50] Maleczech and Breuer reenvision Shakespeare by placing his *King Lear* in the hands of the people they have invited into the room to breathe new life into his text. They reinvent Maleczech's family history by locating her father's life story within Maleczech's memories. Both couplings expose the conventionally structured family as fractured and deeply flawed, perhaps untenably so. When Maleczech takes control of the mythical father in *Lear* and her biological one in *Hajj*, she ruptures the connective tissue that artificially binds paternity to money and power. She shows us ways in which women can maneuver within the realms of male-dominated theater, family, and the financial world itself in order to explode the questionable logic that sustains them. In their wake lies the potential for a new equilibrium, onstage and in life.

4

Mother–Daughter Collaboration

Who's in who's scenario.

The Shaggy Dog Animation

In 1982 Richard Schechner asked, "Where does 'natural' life leave off and 'artificial' life begin, and what's it got to do with theatre?" As part of a wider ranging essay in *The End of Humanism*, "The Natural/Artificial Controversy Renewed," Schechner comments on two productions: Mabou Mines's *The Shaggy Dog Animation* and Squat Theater's *Pig*. Both productions cast children of the creators in crucial roles and Schechner reads the personal relationships of the creative partners as part of the reception process. *Shaggy Dog* (1978), written and directed by Lee Breuer, featured Ruth Maleczech performing with their then six-year-old daughter, Clove Galilee. Schechner writes that "children are to be seen more than ever" in the avant-garde performance of the late 1970s and early 1980s, and "these children are woven into the fabric of their parents' lives."[1] Furthermore, he argues, such productions blur the boundary between life and art, serving as an

> answer theatre colleagues are giving—maybe not consciously, but still strongly—to the ethical question, the one about the hook of this current century (of atrocities): natural and artificial are transformable/interchangeable quantities. Yes, quantities—like quanta in physics: bundles of relations. And it is natural for theatre artists whose work it is to manipulate behavior across (psychological, cultural, architectural) boundaries.... [2]

Over Mabou Mines's history, parents and children have served as creative partners, most frequently Maleczech and Breuer with Galilee.

This chapter focuses on the ways in which Maleczech blurs the line between family and collaborators, primarily in her work with her daughter and with Breuer, the father of her two children. Although the work generated by the Maleczech-Galilee duo and the pair's work with Breuer is not autobiographical, the impact of the audience's knowledge of these personal relationships enhances the significance of what appears onstage.

Mabou Mines's insistence on a philosophy and practice of overlapping life and work relationships, especially in the early days of the company, set the stage for Maleczech and Breuer's collaboration with their daughter. The proximity of Mabou Mines's children to their parents' work has allowed several of them to step into the creative process, bridging the gap between the natural and the artificial. Galilee describes her two first languages as English and experimental theater.[3] In answer to Schechner's question about where natural life ends and the artificial begins, Galilee says:

> There wasn't much separation in my family between art and life.... I joke that I grew up in a fundamentalist religion, and the religion was art. And my parents were priests. I knew how to walk into a theater, and I knew how to be quiet and sit in the back.[4]

Years after Galilee's performance in *Shaggy Dog*, Maleczech cast her in a 1984 production of *Imagination Dead Imagine*. Maleczech's staging of Beckett's short story pairs the adolescent Galilee's body, in the form of a hologram, with the elderly Ruth Nelson's recorded voice. The hologram of Galilee rotates above a bier in which remains of daily objects appear to have atrophied. Nelson's disembodied voice amplifies the disjunction between live presence and performed absence. Maleczech and Galilee's roles as mother and daughter resonate with the juxtaposition between youth and age represented by Galilee's body and Nelson's voice. The real life roles of the creators enhance the story and relationships hinted at in Beckett's words and Maleczech's staging.

Maleczech and Galilee appeared together under Breuer's direction in Mabou Mines's 2005 production of *Red Beads*, which began as a poem

Breuer composed years earlier for Galilee. Based on a story by Polina Klimovitskaya, *Red Beads* traces the tension that arises in many mother–daughter relationships as daughters enter puberty; here what is usually minor friction is inflated to epic proportions with wind puppetry, opera singers, and aerial performance. The audience's knowledge that the performers are mother and daughter, trained for the stage by the experience and example of the mother, establishes another meaningful and, this time, uncomfortable parallel between stage and life.

Another project on which the family trio collaborated was the development of Breuer's *Summa Dramatica: A Pataphysical Acting Lesson* (2009). *Summa Dramatica* and *Shaggy Dog* are now part of *La Divina Caricatura*, a longer work made up of Breuer's "animations," published in 2003 and produced at La MaMa in 2013, just after Maleczech's death. Galilee originally developed choreography for the hind legs of her mother's character in *Summa Dramatica*; she sits underneath her mother, who was perched on a chair. Maleczech played the professorial Holy Cow, a.k.a. Sri Moo Parahamsa, and Galilee remained hidden beneath her mother's academic robes for the duration of the performance. Maleczech and Galilee's physical position is oddly reminiscent of birthing. Though the role of the hind feet was taken over by another performer following Galilee's move from New York to California, the intimate development process remains a crucial aspect of the performance.

These family collaborations trace dynamic developments in the history of the company as well as in the individual careers of the artists involved. *Shaggy Dog, Red Beads, Summa Dramatica*, and *Imagination Dead Imagine* are characterized by the creators' evolving practice of engaging vocally and physically with design elements and technology in performance; these range here from choral performance to caricatured accent, and from Bunraku-style puppetry to holographic choreography. Each adaptation in physical and vocal approach is marked by a shift in influence among the family collaborators Maleczech, Breuer, and Galilee, underscoring the interaction between theater and life that, as Schechner suggests, "manipulates behavior across boundaries" of the natural and the artificial.

Parents, children, child care, and collaboration

Unbeknownst to Jerzy Grotowski, Ruth Maleczech was pregnant with her daughter when she and JoAnne Akalaitis trained with him in the south of France in 1969. The subterfuge was not limited to Maleczech's pregnancy: Akalaitis brought her baby daughter Juliet Glass along and was giving herself unauthorized intermissions to nurse during the two-week workshop. No one was allowed to leave the room once daily training sessions began, Maleczech explained, and no one knew when the sessions would end. "The door was locked with a key and you could only leave to go to the bathroom." Akalaitis and Maleczech devised a scheme: Akalaitis would climb out of the bathroom window to breastfeed, and "I had to guard the door," Maleczech remembered ruefully. After the Mabou Mines's cofounders settled on New York as the location for their company, the Akalaitis/Glass and Maleczech/ Breuer families lived together in their early days on Houston Street in New York, sharing family responsibilities. These are early instances in which the female creative partners teamed up to create an environment where parents could work and children could be cared for—a pattern that would be repeated throughout their continued collaboration.

Maleczech remembered that the cost of child care was "our first sort of confrontation in Mabou Mines. It happened in Nova Scotia when we realized that Ellen Stewart was paying fifty bucks a week each" for their work on *Red Horse Animation* (1970), developed in residency at La MaMa. "And so," Maleczech explained,

> we each got the same amount of money in our hands but JoAnne and I always had to have a babysitter in order to be able to work. So we pooled our babysitting money and she paid half and I paid half and Juliet and Clove (who at that time were the only children) got to spend time together with the babysitter. And then we realized, gee, we were working for half of what the guys were working for and that didn't seem right to us. So we said, "well, we're going to have to pool all the money and pay the babysitter out of all the money that Ellen gives us—fifty bucks each, five people, is $250 a week. We're going to pool all

that money and then we're going to take $50 a week, which is what it was costing to pay the babysitter, and we'll split the $200 that's left five ways so everybody gets forty bucks a week." And there was a big tangle about it. It was really difficult for a little bit but eventually everybody came around.[5]

Glass and Breuer, the fathers of these children, were less resistant to this idea than David Warrilow, who did not have children of his own. During the debate, Maleczech recalled,

David said—and I thought it was a great argument—"Why should I pay for your chosen life style? I don't ask you to pay for mine." And we said, "Well it really comes down to this: if we don't have the children taken of, we can't rehearse and if we can't rehearse we can't do the play. Now, if you want to work with us you're going to have to help us get the children taken care of." And then later on, when we were touring more and David was really important in the mix, it became clear that there might be things that we could do for him that would be sort of the equivalent. Like he could bring a friend on a tour, someone could bring a girlfriend or a boyfriend, there might be a really even-Steven exchange.

In spite of Warrilow's initial objections, the policy was put in place in the company's first year of existence. "And still is that way," said Maleczech, despite occasional financial obstacles. "Sometimes parents haven't taken advantage of it," Maleczech explained, and

usually it's because the parent feels differently than we felt. They feel that they should be individually and personally responsible for the care of their children. Sometimes it's a matter of ethics, sometimes it's a matter of pride, sometimes they take advantage of the support. Sometimes their kid comes along on tour. And if the other parent comes, then that parent is regarded in the same light as the babysitter would be, so we pay for them to come. It's a way for a family to stay together in touring situations. I had a rule at one time that we wouldn't tour for longer than four weeks because we thought that that was as much as the children could stand, whatever the configuration was. And then eventually when the kids got older they preferred not to come along.

Despite Mabou Mines's progressive views about providing child care, Akalaitis is quick to point out that the conditions of touring with children are far from ideal. "I didn't like it," she says, "it isn't some kind of heavenly situation where you have a little child in rehearsal."[6] The production setting could be hard on children even at home; at the March 2014 memorial service for Maleczech, Akalaitis recalled that Galilee and her own daughter, Juliet, used to sit together on the stairs and cry while the women rehearsed.

In *American Women Stage Directors of the Twentieth Century*, Anne Fliotsos and Wendy Vierow propose some causes for the paucity of female directors in professional theater. They cite studies on gender and communication that point to an association between authority and masculinity, the politics of hiring policies, and the difficulty of balancing a career with motherhood—all cross-disciplinary complaints.[7] Akalaitis, however, rejects the idea that parenting adversely affected her career, saying that conflicts with child care did not have a long-term effect on her professional life. "It has not affected my work at all," she argues, "because it was basically a brief situation, and it got resolved." Maleczech pointed out that the relative difficulty of balancing family and career is tied to the relationship between parents and their ability to share the responsibility of childrearing.

Although the philosophy Akalaitis and Maleczech put into practice by supporting child care resolves one of the concerns about women in the workforce identified by feminist scholars, including Fliostos and Vierow, Akalaitis rejects the notion that there is anything feminist about her approach to this issue. "It's simply common sense," she says,

> that a company, any kind of company—academic, artistic—takes care
> of its community, and that includes its children. If you have a child, let
> me know. I'm going to make sure you're taken care of. Man or woman.
> And it's not a feminist issue. I think it's a humanist issue.

The agreement Maleczech and Akalaitis developed on the issue of employer support for child care and their effort to establish a system for keeping families together on tour extends to their work outside of the company. When in 1989 the Guthrie Theater in Minneapolis hired Akalaitis to direct Jean Genet's *The Screens*, she wanted to cast Maleczech as the Mother. A Guthrie representative called to ask her to take the role; Maleczech told him she would only agree if the theater would cover expenses to visit her children during her three months away. "He said no," Maleczech recalled:

> And I said, "okay, well you just tell JoAnne that I very much want to do it. I'm not going to call her and tell her that you won't give me the money I need so I can't do it. You tell her." So we hung up very cordially but, you know, at a deadlock. And maybe a couple of hours later he called back and said, "no, JoAnne wants you, I'll pay it." I gather that JoAnne was the one who got it put through.

So Maleczech went to Minneapolis for several months, leaving her teenage children with a caregiver. She returned to New York once during that time and her children also visited her in Minnesota.

Akalaitis resists the idea that her position on this issue is anything other than a practical one: "I don't think we're doing good," she says, "I just don't put up with that kind of crap." Despite Akalaitis's view, her efforts set an important precedent for improving child care practices because of her prominence in the field. Nonetheless, Maleczech echoed Akalaitis's argument that touring situations are far from ideal from the point of view of both parents and children. "It was tough," she remembered of her stint in Minneapolis,

> It was hard on them. Those things were never entirely successful even though I tried them—we all did—many times. The most successful— for the adults anyway—was when they got to come along. I'm not sure that it was the most successful for them, but it was the most comfortable for us.

Mabou Mines's approach to supporting child care is financially collective, mirroring the company's structure of shared artistic power. This community- and family-oriented philosophy has led children of creative partners to become collaborators themselves.

At the age of three, Galilee first appeared onstage with Mabou Mines in *The Saint and the Football Player* (1973). Lute Ramblin', Maleczech and Breuer's second child, also made his stage debut when he was three years old in Jean-Claude van Italie's *Naropa*, directed by his father at Yale in 1978; also outside of Mabou Mines, he performed in Robert Wilson's *Einstein on the Beach* (1984) when he was nine. With Mabou Mines, he played the Child in the film section of *Hajj* (1983) and later portrayed Cordelion in *Lear* (1990); he has since developed a career as a puppeteer, working in various Mabou Mines productions. The Akalaitis/Glass children, Juliet and Zachary Glass, appeared in the stage version of *Dead End Kids* (1980); Juliet Glass appeared with Galilee in the film version (1986). Galilee and David Neumann, the son of Fred Neumann and Honora Fergusson, are both current associate artists with Mabou Mines (as was Fergusson). Galilee notes, however, that among the Mabou Mines children, it was she and David Neumann who were most enthusiastic about their participation in the company. Significantly, both Galilee and Neumann have founded their own theater companies and both have been at the helm of Mabou Mines productions.[8] That they are doing so makes them part of a theater tradition stretching as far back as Noh and Commedia dell'Arte family troupes. Such an arrangement, moreover, is not unique to Mabou Mines among American avant-garde companies—Garrick Beck, the son of Judith Malina and Julian Beck, worked with his mother at the Living Theatre and following her death in 2015 has continued in a leadership role with the company.

Proud that her children were part of the family business, Maleczech mentioned it in her correspondence with Beckett regarding *Imagination Dead Imagine*: Galilee was "the young woman in the hologram." She also told him that Ramblin' had performed in the American Festival of the Radio Plays of Samuel Beckett production of *All That Fall* with Warrilow and Billie Whitelaw, directed by Robert Frost. Of her collaborations with Galilee, Maleczech said: "It's great. She's a wonderful performer and she's got ten times the equipment I had. She's got a great voice, a great body, and great training specifically in movement."

Galilee's training in dance began when she was a child and includes ballet, the traditional Indian form Kathak, and Japanese Ningyoburi. She is trained in European and Chinese Opera (she studied the latter as a high school student with the internationally renowned Ye Shaolan) and notes that her studies with Kristin Linklater's technique have been helpful in her vocal approach.[9] Although Galilee's background is in the American avant-garde, Breuer and Maleczech mention Galilee's interest in more commercially viable avenues of performance. As Maleczech said about Galilee's desire to work in modes strikingly different than that of Mabou Mines:

> she wants the opportunity to play in classical plays where maybe more attention is paid to the form of the piece in a more predictable way, more attached to the text. I find it difficult to talk about this because Mabou Mines's work is quite formal and very attached to language. But I know what she means—she means these plays where you play a role first of all. Because we don't usually do much of that in our work, where there's a role and maybe eight people have played that role before and that role has a history in the American theater and the British theater, the Irish theater.... The playwright often provides you with a lot of direction, a lot of blocking. There are sets that people know about and lighting designs that people know about and characters that people are familiar with. And it's different—it's just different.

Galilee suggests that working in this way might give her "a feeling of legitimacy," noting that it wasn't until her first year of college that she took an acting class in which she was asked to do scene work. She also recalls that in her first year at Brown University she performed in a main stage production of *Hecuba* as part of the chorus. She was proud of her work and encouraged her parents to attend. Afterwards, she remembers, she was disappointed by their unenthusiastic response. "Ruth and Lee are amazing," she said with a smile, "but they do have their opinions." Although these ruminations reflect a struggle to find her own point of view, "recently," she says, "I've been turning a corner and feeling, well, this is what you're good at." Galilee has produced and created her own experimental work under the auspices of Trick Saddle, the company she cofounded with her wife, the visual artist Jenny Rogers. Maleczech also described Galilee's increased interest in "vocal acrobatics," a priority for both of them. Before she died, Maleczech brought Galilee on board as the choreographer for Mabou Mines's production of *Imagining the Imaginary Invalid*, based on Molière's play, in which Maleczech planned to star. In fact, Maleczech said, she initiated the project at Galilee's suggestion. "I really came into my own with the Molière," Galilee says of her participation on the project, which is slated to premiere at La MaMa as of this writing with Galilee now serving as the lead artist.

A family trio of collaboration

The Shaggy Dog Animation, *Red Beads*, and *Summa Dramatica* catch the collaborators Galilee, Maleczech, and Breuer at different moments in their careers with Mabou Mines, but enduring artistic concerns of the company can be seen in each iteration of the trio's collaboration. Particularly evident are the vocal acrobatics and interaction of the multiple elements of the physical production, both key values for Maleczech. Finally, the three productions utilize what Maleczech described as "gestural extension," a technique the company has explored since its first production.[10]

In her chapter on *Cascando* (1976), *The Saint and the Football Player*, *Shaggy Dog*, and *Dressed Like an Egg* (1977), Iris Smith Fischer criticizes Randy Gener's 2007 cover story in *American Theatre* for its simplistic characterization of Mabou Mines's production history as beholden to the personal and collaborative relationship between Maleczech and Breuer. While Smith Fischer notes the importance of Breuer's assertion in the article of Maleczech's crucial position in his life and work, she also points out that "in treating Mabou Mines as 'the avant-garde of coupledom,' … Gener overlooks other couples that were central to the company's longevity and plays into Breuer's tendency to place himself at the center of company relationships." Smith Fischer argues for a more complex company history, given the "shift in the company's working methods and character" that "began as early as the mid-1970s when Akalaitis, Maleczech, and Neumann developed their own preoccupations and styles."[11] I extend Smith Fischer's argument to suggest that, in addition to the couples and individuals who made up the company, Maleczech, Breuer, and Galilee form an important trio whose collaborations trace crucial developments in the life of the company as well as marking significant moments in the careers of the artists as individuals. Smith Fischer's chapter includes an extensive discussion of *Shaggy Dog*'s process and production, a work that set a significant precedent for subsequent explorations in *Red Beads* and *Summa Dramatica*.

The Shaggy Dog Animation

The Shaggy Dog Animation, Maleczech said, "is about a dog who wishes she was a woman because she's in love with her master, or she's a woman who feels herself to be a dog because she's slavishly in love with her master."[12] The dog/woman is called Rose; she first appeared onstage in the form of a Bunraku-style puppet operated by four performers with a voice generated collectively by the acting company—Maleczech, Akalaitis, Linda Hartinian, Fred Neumann, Terry O'Reilly, and the six-year-old Galilee. In a technique that Breuer and Maleczech would later use in *Hajj*, the performers' voices were distorted by means of an electronic synthesizer. Although several performers played Rose, Galilee notes, Maleczech's version was central. "Ruth was without a doubt the star of the show." *Shaggy Dog* was awarded a 1978 OBIE for Best New Play.

The characters and situations in *Shaggy Dog* resemble people and events in Breuer's life; he suggests that the performance poem is "'a prototypical love affair circa 1957–1977'"—the same years that mark his relationship with Maleczech. Smith Fischer argues, however, that

> it would be a mistake to identify the events of *Shaggy Dog* too closely with the lives of Breuer, Maleczech, or Leslie Mohn, the namesake of Rose's rival, Leslie. Breuer's insistence on peopling *Caricatura* with characters resembling those to whom he is attached, personally and professionally, constitutes "social archetype," not family history.[13]

Bonnie Marranca made a parallel argument in 1977, suggesting that in his animations

> Breuer's use of autobiography ... goes way beyond a purely narcissistic approach; he is self-projected, not self-centered. By that I mean he situates himself in a social context, and what he writes in his plays relates to the world around him. It is the I in "the world," not the "I" in its own world.[14]

Breuer says that many of his romantic partners have been muses to him—as have his creative partners. "Every writer has a base reality to the characters he puts together," he says, "and some characters are built on two or three of these people. Every writer uses his own family. But I think more important is that you don't see these people, you see your fantasy."[15] *Shaggy Dog*, dedicated to Maleczech and Bill Raymond, is an early example of this approach, which Smith Fischer characterizes as "autograph" rather than autobiography.[16] Though she acknowledges that certain elements are drawn almost directly from real life, Galilee agrees with the assessment that Breuer's work is not autobiographical. "Lee is a really easy target," she says,

> because he's so open with his references in his writing. And he uses animals, so people can say, "oh Leslie [Mohn] was a cow in *Epidog* and Ruth plays a rabbit or a dog—his wife is a dog." But I don't think that's really what he's saying (laughs). I think he uses animals because he's looking for a metaphor to speak through.

Although these texts and productions may not be intentionally autobiographical, that they were inspired by family members and developed with them is, as Schechner points out, a significant factor in audience reception.

Breuer notes his awareness that the people around him serve as bases for fictional writing. He further suggests that the "little dog" in *Shaggy Dog*, inspired by his young daughter, was probably a reductive fictionalization. Schechner puts it another way: "Maybe the grown-ups project on the purer screens of their own children—for these kids aren't actors picked from open calls—clouded (sexual) strategies the better to see them (and work them through)." Citing Mel Gussow's skeptical review of Squat Theater's work in *Pig*, which placed children in similarly complex systems of representation, Schechner notes the complicated reception process for audiences who take in performances featuring parent–child relationships. He describes the way he viewed Galilee in *Shaggy Dog* in equally uncomfortable terms:

> dressed as a grown woman, in a shiny gown, parading on high-heels: there's something not the-child-at-play in this scene: after all, Clover [sic] does it as part of a performance, repetitively, for or at least in front of an audience. Sometimes Clover [sic] utters dialogue not made from an eight-year-old head. There's something porny about it … but not in the 42nd Street way. It's this double action–double agent thing artists feel strongly towards kids.

Distressing though this insight may be, Schechner argues that it is effective to elicit unease in the viewer. Although the "grown-ups" may project ideas onto Galilee, he argues, she remains an autonomous entity. "Obviously she is the synthesis—the only possible synthesis—of her parents; and she is herself too."[17]

Galilee's point of view is that her work on *Shaggy Dog* paved the way for her career in the theater. "The experience of being inside the play was the most fun I've ever had,"

> I've never forgotten anything I got to do in that play. I got to learn how to make cream puffs—JoAnne taught me how. Everything worked onstage and everything was my size because it was for the puppets. Everything in the kitchen worked and I could cook.… I loved it. I really felt the Prop Shop was like home. We would go there every day and we would make the play happen. It was a very magical place for me. Everyone worked a lot and worked really hard and I felt like part of that.[18]

Galilee was five when rehearsals began and eight for the show's premiere; she viewed the company members as her extended family. Rather than feeling uncomfortable with her role in the production, she enjoyed her participation, both because of her level of comfort with the company that surrounded her and because of the activities her job required. From a child's point of view, the opportunity to wear the costumes Schechner describes was a dream come true. "I was so excited," Galilee says, "I got to wear this gorgeous sequined dress that was made for me, I got to wear high heels, I got my makeup done and I got to look beautiful and dance."

In addition to the little dog, Galilee played a twenty-seven-year-old version of Rose—hence the heavy makeup, which she remembers took the entire third act to apply. This mature Rose takes a bubble bath onstage and is lifted out of the tub and carried away by Rose's lover/owner John. Although the content is, as Schechner describes, mature, Galilee says she was unaware of any sexual undertones:

> Lee never said "say that with a sexy voice." He would never say, "this is a come on." He would just say, "say it like you're saying goodnight to me." … I don't think I was aware that I was behaving like an adult, but I was taught. Ruth and Lee taught me from a young age that when you first meet someone you ask them about themselves immediately—what were they working on—so people used to say that I asked these very adult questions. And I used to wear these long black dresses and high heels on a regular basis, all the way from the time I was five, and I still dress like that. It might have been me and it might have been my upbringing.

Yet Schechner's perception that there was "something not the child-at-play" in Galilee's performance is not entirely inaccurate from Galilee's point of view either. "I felt very special—I was the only child," she says, "but I also felt a huge responsibility to act like them, to be a real professional person who thinks about the work.… I really felt akin to the people around me who were forty." Galilee enjoyed the responsibility that came with participating in a professional production, even if she may not have been fully equipped to take it on. "I fell asleep onstage a couple of times," Galilee recalls, "and missed my cues, but it wasn't that big of a deal—it wasn't the kind of high pressure situation I see kids go through now. I imagine that if I really hated it and didn't want to do it, they wouldn't have made me do it."

As Schechner points out, Galilee's participation is complex because she is doing something natural and artificial at the same time—she is a little girl being brought up in the theater and taking on the responsibilities of a mature collaborator in the development process. And, perhaps more importantly for audience reception, in performance she is a little girl playing an adult woman.

The paradox of Galilee's performance goes to the heart of *Shaggy Dog*'s entangled representation of femininity and feminism. *Shaggy Dog* and *Dressed Like an Egg* represent the company's first engagement with questions of gender, an issue that would come to dominate Maleczech's explorations onstage. Smith Fischer suggests that "gender issues that were filtering into the company members' lives and work process" had a major impact on Breuer's work on the animation. She points out that *Shaggy Dog*, with its female narrator, is Breuer's "take on a woman artist's perspective" and deals with "the formation of Rose's feminist consciousness and identity." His interest in taking on the issue of gender coincides not only with the social context surrounding the work but also with his first collaboration with his daughter. While the gendered and sexual aspects of *Shaggy Dog* may not be autobiographical, they are nonetheless personal. In a related argument, Smith Fischer proposes that, for all of *Shaggy Dog*'s nascent engagement with feminism, Breuer "may have been less interested in the feminine than in how female characteristics participate in forming masculinity."[19]

By the time Breuer directed the first part of *La Divina Caricatura*, however, his vision of the role had changed; before her death, Maleczech was to perform Sri Moo, the cow, while Breuer cast the singer Bernadine Mitchell as Rose. *Shaggy Dog*'s relationship to masculinity, femininity, and feminism also appears to have shifted from the exploration Smith Fischer describes in the original production. This may be due largely to the casting; while she is persuasive as a singer, Mitchell lacks Maleczech's power and subtlety as an actor. In her most recent incarnation, Rose was missing the complexity Maleczech, Galilee, and Smith Fischer attribute to her role in the original production. The dynamics of gender and power that Smith Fischer describes in this production have deteriorated with time, leaving us to wonder why Rose, whether human or canine, would bother with John in the first place. There is nothing lacking in the complexity in the puppetry that accompanies her physical presence, however, which is breathtaking in its precision and vibrancy.

The attention to puppetry in *La Divina* finds its roots in *Shaggy Dog*, which featured the company's first extensive use of puppetry in performance (Mabou Mines had already used a puppet in the *B. Beaver Animation*, activating the beaver's robe with sticks held aloft by performers on their backs). Development for *Shaggy Dog* began in 1975 at the Old Prop Shop at the Public Theater, where the production premiered in 1978, making the three-and-a-half year project the longest in the company's history (*Lear* had a similarly long gestation but by six months less). For Breuer, the process was characterized by his desire to exert more control as a director than he had done previously in order to retain authorial control over the text. "I felt that this group collaborative thing was fine for me as a director and not so fine for me as a writer, and when it came to *Shaggy Dog*, I really wanted more control over the thing." The text was published in 1979, with *Red Horse* and *B. Beaver*, as *A Trilogy For Mabou Mines*, edited by Marranca and Gautam Dasgupta.

In her introduction Marranca notes Breuer's attraction to choral performance, a point Smith Fischer makes as well. Mabou Mines's early involvement in choral performance extends far beyond Breuer's written text. It can be observed in a number of performances, indicating that it was as much a function of Breuer's priorities as a writer as it was of the composition and approach of the company, which Maleczech describes in its early days as an intensely close-knit "troupe." In *Dressed Like an Egg*, Akalaitis divided lines taken from Colette's writings among the company; according to Maleczech, three female performers represented young (Ellen McElduff), middle-aged (Akalaitis), and older (Maleczech) versions of the writer—a chorus of Colettes.[20] Sharon Fogarty used the strategy in *Cara Lucia* (2003), an early version of *Lucia's Chapters of Coming Forth by Day* (2007), which featured Maleczech and Galilee as two of three versions of Lucia Joyce. In *Dressed Like an Egg*, as with the collective approach to delivering Rose's dialogue in *Shaggy Dog*, the division of Colette's text serves to amplify and animate the language. Maleczech has said that the *Shaggy Dog* production "used the company of actors that was at the time Mabou Mines, and that company of actors had already worked together for several years, so the coded ways of speaking and working on things were … common knowledge."²¹ There was one significant difference in the group of performers from that of previous productions: David Warrilow had recently left the company.

The "group collaborative thing" to which Breuer refers began with the company's inaugural production, *The Red Horse Animation.* Although Breuer wrote and directed *Red Horse*, the production was developed collaboratively with extensive input from the Akalaitis, Maleczech, and Warrilow, setting the stage for Mabou Mines's commitment to inviting—even requiring—performers to bring their intellect and point of view into the room. Breuer notes that although he began to seek more directorial control over the process at this time, he has continued to value the participation of performers in developing ideas about the production:

> Most actors I work with for the first time are shocked by how much input I do want from them. Most directors don't want to hear a thing from them. You've got people with great ideas, how can you possibly not want to hear them? What I want is permission to say, I'd like to do this, but not that. And sometimes in a totally collaborative situation I don't have that permission.

Maleczech herself noted that collectivity and collaboration do not necessarily equal democracy—someone has to make a final decision. This signals an evolution from Mabou Mines's early days, when, as Breuer says, the director could be outvoted by the rest of the company on creative decisions.

Although the company's early roots in collective development were complicated, they resulted in a cohesive company of actors, capable of activating the choral performances Marranca and Smith Fischer describe. Mabou Mines's interest in chorus extends beyond the performers onstage to all elements of the production. Smith Fischer has noted the importance of the company's use of design and media in storytelling. Maleczech herself says that

> there are moments when you would like a light to say something—not an actor, not a line—or you would like a piece of music to take over some moment. It's mysterious how those judgments are made. It's a kind of eclecticism but it's not arbitrary. It's heartfelt and integrated into the conceptual life of the piece—the existence of elements that make up a piece.

This way of working, Maleczech contends, transcends the various styles of writing, performing, and visual approach that characterize many productions in the company's history. "One of the things that marks the company besides its intense devotion to the language," she said, "is this way of looking for how to say a moment, whether it's said through a gesture or a sound or a piece of video. How the telling takes place."[22] For Mabou Mines's performers and directors, collaboration includes their work with design elements—sets, lights, costumes, props, and sound—which are introduced into the rehearsal room early in the process. Considering performance in this way is a rationale for the company's transition into puppetry, since it can be used to extend the physical presence of the actor or to create a different corporeal presence altogether.

Mabou Mines has also made a habit of exploring the ways performers interact with elements of technology and media to influence the style of performance. In *Shaggy Dog* Smith Fischer describes a process by which performers "listened to recordings, taking verbal tonalities or phrasings indicative of certain singers, and then left the recordings behind" after developing a vocal and rhythmic approach to each of the three sections. These were influenced, respectively, by rock, country-western, and jazz.[23] In an unpublished conversation with Maleczech, Smith Fischer finds similarities between Maleczech's approach to her role in *Shaggy Dog* and the one she used in Patricia Spears Jones's *Mother* (1994), in which she played the title role. From a thematic point of view, both women, Maleczech remarked, are "trying to think their way out of the situation they are in." During performances of *Mother*, Maleczech listened to music through headphones at such a high volume that audience members in the environmental theater staging by John McGrath could hear it as she passed by. According to Maleczech, at certain points the music prevented her from hearing her fellow performers; she had to rely on their gestures and facial expressions to know what was happening in a given scene. Maleczech noted an important distinction between aural and performative interaction in *Shaggy Dog* and *Mother*: the performers relied on music to shape their work in advance of performances for *Shaggy Dog*, while Maleczech continued to listen to music during the actual performance of *Mother*.[24] Both strategies are characteristic of the way Maleczech engages with media, using it to extend her own body and expand her own voice.

As well as relying on musical inspiration for vocal rhythm, tone, and style during the *Shaggy Dog* rehearsal process, Maleczech depended on an additional sonic device during performance. Greg Mehrten, who provided sound effects, fed lines into Maleczech's ear during a particularly dense and lengthy section of text, a technique Maleczech repeated in *Lucia's Chapters of Coming Forth by Day*.[25]

Maleczech had yet to initiate a project with Mabou Mines. The period during which she worked on *Shaggy Dog*, however, is an important prelude to her own full-fledged feminist approach to performing and directing. Galilee, too, was developing her own perspective about the deployment of avant-garde theatrical strategies in staging representations of gender. She would later take on this challenge in her work with her own company, Trick Saddle, and in subsequent Mabou Mines productions.

Red Beads

The arguments Smith Fischer and Marranca make about Breuer's fictionalization of autobiographical source material in *Shaggy Dog* establish a context for considering audience reception of *Red Beads*. While Breuer dedicated *Shaggy Dog* to Maleczech and Raymond, he wrote the poem "Red Beads" for the twelve-year-old Galilee. The piece was based on a short story by Klimovitskaya, one of Breuer's former partners and the mother of one of his sons. It was published with the performance poem version in Breuer's collection *Sister Suzie Cinema* in 1987. The performance poem received its first workshop production in 1982 at Seattle's Empty Space. This was where Kroetz's *Through the Leaves* was to have its English-language premiere; Mabou Mines later staged the play in its own production under Akalaitis's direction featuring Maleczech in 1984 and 1990.[26] The 1982 workshop, directed by Breuer, featured Frank Corrado as the Father, Susan Heldfond as the choreographer and the Mother, Clare Dewey as the Daughter, and Marjorie Nelson as the Narrator. William Spencer composed the music and Thom Cathcart created the design. A photograph of the workshop from Breuer's 1987 anthology shows a spare production, distinct in scale and scope from the 2005 Mabou Mines version performed at New York University's Skirball Center for the Performing Arts, though the text of the performance poem is nearly identical in both. Breuer views the workshop in Seattle as a "preliminary inroad" into the work. "I always do much better when I do something twice," he says, echoing Maleczech's interest in revisiting work. "In fact," he adds, "I don't think I've ever done anything really good the first time."

The Mabou Mines production, also under Breuer's direction, is described on the company's website as

> a gothic, coming-of-age fairy-tale/opera, choreographed aerially. Lee Breuer's performance poem . . . explores the eerie family dynamic of a daughter's transition into womanhood and the gift, from mother to daughter, of the red beads, a metaphor for the passage of power and sexuality. Using only wind, Basil Twist transforms swaths of fabric into luminous, quivering, ephemeral sets and puppets . . . challenging our perception of space and proportion. Ushio Torikai's haunting, dissonant score swells and ebbs, driving the story while evoking the psychological tension one equates with Hitchcock.[27]

Mabou Mines developed *Red Beads* with a 1999 residency in Minneapolis at the Walker Arts Center and Red Eye in association with Three Legged Race. The piece was expanded during two additional residencies at MASS MoCA in 2001 and 2002, with music rehearsals sponsored by a Theatre Communications Group/MetLife Foundation Extended Collaboration Grant. The cast for the full production featured Maleczech as the Mother, Galilee as the Daughter, and Rob Besserer as the Father. Torikai composed and arranged the music, with "animated design and puppetry" by Twist (for which he was selected for the Prague Quadrennial in 2007). Galilee created her own choreography.

During development for the project, Maleczech provided the voice of the Mother but was not physically present onstage. According to Galilee, when the show was scheduled to open at the Skirball Center, Breuer asked Maleczech to perform the Mother's physical presence as well. "It was really difficult for her to do it physically," Galilee says. She remembers that Twist told her mother, "I'm going to make you look incredible." When Maleczech first appears, she dangles from the ceiling of the enormous theater, voluminous silken robes draping to the floor and blowing in the wind. On opening night, this entrance won her an extended standing ovation.

Although it was Galilee who first inspired the poem, Breuer says it was his desire to collaborate with Twist that served as the impetus for this production; Breuer was impressed by Twist's work on *Symphonie Fantastique* (1998). They have since collaborated on several projects, including the 2011 production of *A Streetcar Named Desire* at the Comédie Française. While Breuer's collaborative focus in *Shaggy Dog* was on a group of performers who were responsible for creating the vocal and physical world of the play, in this instance Breuer's major collaborator was Twist:

> The piece was written for Clove. It had been twenty years since I wrote it, and it was good that she still looked young enough to do it. Ruth was a little too old to fly, but she was a great mother. It was fun for her to play the witch. But the real key there was, we wanted to extend puppetry to incorporate decor, and we wanted to use air the way Basil used water in another piece.

Another crucial piece of the puzzle for Breuer was Torikai's music. In keeping with Breuer's aesthetic, the music was, as he describes it, "on the pop edge." The work of the *Red Beads* creative team was favorably viewed by a number of critics. In her review of the production for the *New York Times*, Margo Jefferson lauds it as "theater as sorcery," describing it as "a crossroads where artistic traditions meet to invent a marvelous common language. It is a fairy tale, a puppet play and a chamber opera," noting that the four-performance run was "not nearly enough."[28]

Red Beads tells the story of a girl who, at the approach of her thirteenth birthday, lays claim to what she and her father insist should be rightfully hers: the strand of thirteen red beads her mother wears around her neck. The beads are an obvious metaphor for female sexuality and fertility, and the Mother is loath to give them up. The Daughter experiences a loss of innocence in several stages—her dog dies, then her cat, and she is locked outside of her parents' bedroom door while they have (aerial) sex. Finally her mother tries to strangle her with the beads, but her bird—the proverbial canary in the coal mine—warns her father, who

Photo 4.1 Ruth Maleczech as the Mother and Clove Galilee as the Daughter after an aerial struggle over the contested necklace in *Red Beads* at New York University's Skirball Center, 2005. Photo: Beatriz Schiller.

rescues her, telling her that her mother "was a witch/and I in thrall. Your mother's lost." The Mother's sexuality and primacy in the family are subverted as father and daughter, at the Father's insistence, "vow a vow of fealty/To the rightful lady of the land." This is the Daughter, who is now in possession of the beads. Father and daughter promise to look for the Mother, whom, we are told, they will never find.

Red Beads features vocal as well as aerial acrobatics. In keeping with the conception of production on a vast scale, the three characters have doubles—Chelsea Bacon as the other Mother, Zoe Phillips as the other Daughter, and Terry O'Reilly as the other Father. Not only do the characters have body doubles, their words are doubled aurally. In a variation on the choral dialogue performers used to portray Rose in *Shaggy Dog*, opera singers repeat lines spoken by the Mother, Father, and Daughter in song. Sometimes they do this multiple times, varying the length of words and syllables to musicalize ten short pages of verse into a performance that lasts nearly an hour and a half.

In addition to opera singers, *Red Beads* requires live musicians and teams of puppeteers and aerial operators. When the company assembles onstage for the curtain call, more than seventy people stand before the audience to take a bow. In fact, the company was composed of eighty-five people, twenty-four of them students at New York University. In an interview for an article about the piece that the *New York Times* ran shortly before the show opened, Breuer described his stylistic intentions:

> I wanted to find this meeting ground where the symbolist take of Edgar Allan Poe that goes all the way back to these wonderful high camp ladies on mountains, with ravens on their shoulders and stuff like that. You know, this is Freddy in *Friday the 13th*, when the father comes up with the pick and spade and pulls his daughter down into the grave. So in a way it's a Tim Burton kind of spoof, in a way it's camp, as well as being a very serious operatic statement.[29]

Everything in *Red Beads*—the music, the colors, the huge projected face, the swaths of wind-blown silk that hang to the floor from the limbs of performers dangling from the ceiling of the cavernous Skirball Center—is colossal in scale. Such gigantism supports the style of the poem, which enlarges the tensions between mother and daughter on the eve of the Daughter's ascension to womanhood, making the Daughter's arrival at puberty a battle of epic proportions—for life or death, good or evil.

The atmospheric staging is also, as Breuer indicates, both operatic and threatening. So is the poem. Its gothic quality stems in part from the animation of a deceptively simple story, which allows for the use of elaborate ornamentation to stun the audience and take it by surprise. Because we think we understand where the story is going—a mother's fear of displacement in her husband's affections as her daughter becomes an adult—the impact of the eerie phrases and haunting images catch us off guard. There is also the implication of incest, which further unsettles us. "Incest?" Breuer observed when he spoke to Phoebe Hoban of the *New York Times.* "Of course, it's about a transference of sexuality from the mother to the daughter at puberty."[30] That the family relationships at the heart of the production are familiar further disturbs the nature of the experience, heightening the level of discomfort the production fosters and sustains.

Although a number of Mabou Mines co-artistic directors and creative partners insist that there is no major difference in working with family members than with any other members of their close-knit circle of artists, the observation of family collaborations becomes part of a performance. The reception process now involves reading real-life stories into staged scenes. Hoban begins her *New York Times* article with a discussion of this central set of relationships, which she describes as a "family parable":

> Some families spend Sunday afternoon going to the mall. Not the artistic and biological family at the core of Mabou Mines. Ms. Galilee, a trained dancer who choreographed her own part, is being put through her dangling paces by her father, Lee Breuer.... The performer Ruth Maleczech who ... plays her real-life role as the Mother in the piece, is in the audience, observing the action.... And then there is the

extended family. Polina Klimovitskaya, who wrote the original fairy tale from which Mr. Breuer adapted this "performance poem," is also in the audience. Mr. Breuer first heard the story of "Red Beads" over 20 years ago, when Ms. Klimovitskaya, with whom he lived at the time, told it to their son, Alexander.[31]

Hoban easily elides Maleczech's "real-life role" with the one she plays in *Red Beads*. While the woman and the role she plays are certainly not the same—it is highly doubtful that Maleczech was tempted to strangle Galilee with a necklace when the latter approached puberty—Hoban's identification of such correspondences mirrors the audience's attraction for drawing parallels between theater and life in performance. The title of Margo Jefferson's review for the *New York Times*, "A Girl Caught in an Eternal Family Triangle," also notes the biological family at the core of the production, further blurring the lines separating artifice from reality.

Maleczech, Breuer, and Galilee have at times acknowledged the impact of family ties on their work. Although she reports that she initially had mixed feelings about the poem when it was written, Galilee was nonetheless enthusiastic about the production. She told Hoban: "It's incredible that I have the greatest gift a child can have, which is to grow up and have your parents become your mentors." Breuer concurred: "It's critically important that I worked with the mother of my child and my child. I couldn't have done the piece the same way with other people where I did not have these references." Maleczech elaborated on this point, telling Hoban: "There is a ground base of trust. It's in the air and it's going somewhere and you can trust where it's going." The audience's acknowledgment of these ties enriches the reception process. Galilee has a striking physical resemblance to her mother; it is exciting to see this as the two sit onstage side by side. While the trio's response to predictable questions about family relationships may have been part of a marketing campaign for the piece, their working together was part of the appeal to the press and audiences alike.

Galilee says that collaborating with her mother enhanced her emotional and motivational stage life. "There was no comparison with having my actual mother be the scary mother," she says. Although it might seem that the production's vast scale would render motivational acting choices ineffective (the audience is unable to see the performers' faces closely), "Lee doesn't like you to just dial it in," Galilee says. She recalls that Breuer wanted her actually to weep when the Daughter loses her dog. "It was very hard to do because there's so much technical stuff going on," she explains,

> there's all these people saying, "clip her in!" and I'm saying, "ooooh my dog," and I can't see through the wig.... Lee is really a stickler for combining very real emotions with being surrounded by these hugely extravagant situations. And *Shaggy Dog Animation* was no different.

Maleczech excels at remaining emotionally vulnerable during technically ambitious staging, as she does in *Hajj* and *Lucia's Chapters of Coming Forth by Day*. "Even though her part was small," Galilee says, "she just took over. I learned so much from her."

Not only does *Red Beads* advance the continued collaboration among Maleczech, Galilee, and Breuer, it further engages the company's history with puppetry, which had a profound effect on both daughter and son. Ramblin's worked as a puppeteer with Mabou Mines and also on productions such as *War Horse* when it played at Lincoln Center (2011). Galilee has integrated puppetry into her work with Mabou Mines in a variety of ways since sharing the stage with Rose in 1978. In 2004, she received an Asian Cultural Council grant to study Ningyoburi puppetry in Japan; she brought her expertise to the choreography and performance in *Red Beads*. Ningyoburi has its origins in Bunraku (the style in which the company worked with Rose in *Shaggy Dog*) and is used in Kabuki, especially by Onnagata, the female role played by male actors. In addition to interacting with a puppet dog, cat, and bird in *Red Beads*, Galilee becomes a puppet herself in the tradition of Ningyoburi, performing an intricate dance at the close of Act II, aided by two puppeteers who stand behind her and appear as if they are in control of her movements. The dance underscores the Daughter's distress by linking her to the role of the Onnagata, who typically uses Ningyoburi as a form of expression in moments of emotional turmoil. The Daughter's transitional sexuality—she is caught in her last prepubescent moments—also resonates with the gendered history of the Onnagata. The Daughter must also face sexually charged adversity—albeit of a different nature—as she undergoes the transition from child to woman.

Puppetry, body doubles, aerial performance, and the choral relationship between spoken dialogue and opera in *Red Beads* are techniques that allow the performers, director, and designers to extend and expand expressive gesture and voice. First, there is Maleczech's grand entrance. Later in the performance, the Daughter sails across the stage, strapped into a gigantic, vertical bed, replete with silk bed sheets that spread behind it as it moves forward. Body doubles introduce another way to amplify physical scale through the use of perspective—when we see Galilee glide off stage left and simultaneously see Phillips appear on the same plane stage right, tracing the same path, we have the sense that the Daughter's body is everywhere on the stage, haunting and encircling it. Operatic repetitions of text serve to heighten and underscore certain words and phrases, such as "Save me, Daddy, save me," repeated by both Galilee and the singers as the Daughter hovers before us, waiting for her father to release her from the trap set by her mother.

In *Shaggy Dog*, Breuer and Maleczech naturally wielded greater influence as collaborators than did the young Galilee. In *Red Beads*, however, Breuer and Galilee's contributions are more readily apparent. Though Maleczech's vocal performance—gravelly and electronically amplified—is striking, it is layered within a rich texture of music, voice, wind puppetry, and choreography. In *Summa Dramatica*, the context and composition of collaborative influence among Maleczech, Breuer, and Galilee would shift once again.

Summa Dramatica

La Divina Caricatura, Breuer's epic cycle of animations, includes reworkings of earlier texts, including a musical version of *Shaggy Dog*, as well as new material. *Summa Dramatica*, a more recent addition to the *Caricatura* canon and part of the second half of the epic, takes up self-referential questions about performance and animation. In his review of the published version of *Caricatura*, in which *Summa Dramatica* appears at the tail, Arthur Sabatini writes:

> Far more than a zoo story, Breuer's batty vision is at once biotoonic (biology + cartoons) and mythopreposterous. It is conceived with a concoction that mingles Hinduesque cosmology and snatches of sociobiological hypothesizing with nods to Dante, Disney, and Nietzsche.... He has ... been engendering a substantial mytho-theatrical cycle of plays and a singular approach to acting and performance that brings together world theatre traditions and American pop culture. Moreover, his *comédie animale* descends from a lineup of notable thinkers, most of whom he merrily misreads.[32]

Maleczech played the academic acting guru and cow, Sri Moo Parahamsa, whose lecture, Sabatini notes, "ranges freely into the fields of theory, genetics, spirituality, physics, addiction, and cartoons."[33] *Summa Dramatica* opened in January 2009 on a double bill with *Porco Morto*, performed by Greg Mehrten, as *Pataphysics Pennyeach* at the ToRoNaDa studio in the Public Theater's Under the Radar Festival. *Pataphysics Pennyeach* was also presented the next year at New York Theatre Workshop. Galilee performed in early versions of *Summa Dramatica*, including a 2005 workshop at the Flea Theater; she also provided choreography for the cow, who was subsequently performed by Maleczech with Jessica Weinstein.

This animation, as described by the company,

> features the pontifications of the "eminent acting guru and erstwhile Holy Cow, Sri Moo Parahamsa," on the sorry state of the acting profession. Performance is in crisis due to "the number one health concern of the free world"—animation addiction. What exactly does that mean? It means a four-armed, multi-voiced holy cow, musing on the nature of performance, bovine pearls of wisdom, and a stunning testimonial from recovering animation addict Marge Simpson.[34]

Mohn, who played Sri Moo in *An Epidog* in the 1996 premiere at HERE Arts Center in New York, provided the voice of Marge Simpson.[35] Jay Ansil composed the music and Eamonn Farrell provided the projections, with lighting design by Jason Boyd, sound design by Ken Travis, costumes by Meganne George, and animation by John Infantino. Julie Archer created the mask for Sri Moo—an imposing, bejeweled cow head that obscures most of Maleczech's face.

The use of puppets and masks have an increasingly central place on Breuer's stage in his direction of his own texts, where their presence serves to extend gesture, expand vocal presence, and redirect attention from the performer to the text—all functions of his desire to exert more control over the stage interpretation of his works. In this case, Maleczech's mask deflects attention from her physical presence, although in small theaters with a spartan scenic design, this can be frustrating for the viewer, especially given Maleczech's range of facial expressions designed to create a big impact in an intimate space. For one metatheatrical monologue, however, she does remove the cow's head from her own and talk directly to the audience in a version of herself. Archer relates that the choice was designed "to give Ruth control of when and how much the audience was able to see her face."

Music also plays a crucial role in Breuer's staging of his own texts. This could be observed in the 2013 presentation of the first half of *La Divina Caricatura*, which Breuer reworked for the singer Bernadine Mitchell, as well as in *Red Beads* and in earlier works like *The Gospel at Colonus* (1983). Of the shift from choral performance to pop music, Breuer explains:

> The original Mabou Mines company had no musical ability whatsoever. They couldn't even carry a tune. I remember Philip Glass tearing his hair trying to write a piece of music that Mabou Mines could sing. So if I was going to go into music I was a little limited. But little by little I felt that my writing needed music to be realized. It was more likely that it would work if you sang it than if you said it. So I started getting more and more interested in musical performance.

Breuer comments that in this matter he and Maleczech pursued separate artistic paths. Although he agrees with Maleczech and Akalaitis that Mabou Mines is intensely focused on language, he explains that from his point of view this interest is "pretty literary." Of his move into popular music, he relates that in the 1970s, the company was often introduced to musicians and artists through Philip Glass. "We were kind of moved into the art world and by moving into the art world we were moving into the new dance world and the new music world. And as exciting as all that was, I wasn't really ready to go there." He characterized his post-1970s movement into a variety of musical styles— "anything but avant-garde and classical"—as more evocative of his own aesthetic priorities. In his view, the new, pop music version of *Shaggy Dog* fits more naturally into *La Divina Caricatura*, which also includes *Sister Suzie Cinema*, originally conceived as a "doo-wop opera."

Unlike the *Shaggy Dog* and *Sister Suzie* sections of *Caricatura*, *Summa Dramatica* and *Porco Morto* are spoken, not sung. The pieces were performed by Maleczech and Mehrten, veteran Mabou Mines artists from the company's nonsinging days. *Caricatura* spans Breuer's career as a writer/director both on the page and on the stage. Sri Moo, Sabatini writes,

> applies physics to the soul, eventually concluding that the soul is receptive to light, but behaves like a quanta-particle until it attaches to a role, at which point it becomes animated. Plays, Moo explains, are the cultural entities where roles, in the form of knowable characters (heroes, fools) appear, with historical and social variations. [36]

Sabatini suggests that Breuer links playing a role to having a soul— and who better to play the part of the acting guru who spouts this philosophy than Maleczech, his performance collaborator of more than half a century?

Though Maleczech and Breuer collaborated less frequently in the last years of her career, the performer had a major impact on his plays. Maleczech is "wonderful in terms of her phrasing," Breuer said, explaining that in the earlier years of their collaboration he "was very interested in verbal phrasing. And Ruth's a master of it." Breuer suggests that a divergence in their paths took place when he became more interested in blending his words with music, but at the same time he praises the musicality of her delivery: "as a speaker, she's very musical." This characteristic can be traced all the way back to Maleczech's work at the Tape Music Center in San Francisco, when she worked side by side with musicians who wanted performers "to be a part of their music." Critics have also remarked upon the musicality of Maleczech's stage speech, particularly in her performance of *Happy Days* (1996).[37]

Maleczech's hidden face and stationary position in *Summa Dramatica* direct attention to her vocal work. Breuer's decision to deflect attention from Maleczech's physicality is intentional. He says that Maleczech's limited physical stamina at the end of her life "forced her to become more of a vocal performer." Capitalizing on the musicality of Maleczech's phrasing, Breuer conceptualized the staging of *Summa Dramatica* for the performative qualities he knew were Maleczech's greatest strengths at the time. Aside from her vocal prowess, Breuer emphasizes her affinity for and skill with comedy, underscoring Maleczech's assessment that Mabou Mines has always had a powerful interest in putting humor to work onstage.

Maleczech's facility for vocal acrobatics and comedy are evident in the accent she deploys for Sri Moo, a stereotypical Indian patois that we recognize from television characters like Apu in *The Simpsons*. This brings Sri Moo and the projected figure of Marge Simpson into a shared world of animation. The accent, in Breuer's view, is a "caricature." Though Maleczech used accents in a number of performances including *Through the Leaves, Dead End Kids, Lucia's Chapters of Coming Forth by Day*, this one, Breuer says, is different:

> The Sri Moo accent is a caricature accent. The Polish accent in *Dead End Kids* is not—it's a character accent. The difference is that a caricature accent leads you to a cartoon. The reason for a cartoon is that it is a simplification—it's a parody of that particular life. The other accent is a sociological simplification. In other words, you're classifying yourself with a particular cultural group. Any characterization is an internal,

personalized characterization and a social characterization. You have to bring the two together.

Mehrten suggests that Breuer's use of stereotype is always part of a complex network of social and stylistic signals. In *Lear* the company used southern US accents as part of an overall effort to create fully developed characters. Here, Breuer attempts to move toward the invention of simplified caricature of a being who is not fully human. Sabatini suggests that:

> By inhabiting animals, Breuer's ideas on sex, gender, love, identity, class, family, creativity, and the self-destructive tendencies of human beings are held in arrested development, and comic relief—suspended animation. His animals ... can love, suffer, complain, even die, but the level of self-knowing that they ultimately demonstrate, or the amount of responsibility that they have, is not accountable in fully human terms. After all, what can you expect from a pig?[38]

Or a cow for that matter? Maleczech's use of what Breuer calls a caricature accent allows her Sri Moo to remain in a no-man's-land, somewhere between the human world and the animal kingdom, bringing definition to what Breuer means by "cartoon."

Breuer understands that a performer of Maleczech's caliber uses an accent as only one part of an intricately detailed portrait:

> A good use of an accent is always double. You have to get the social character, and you have to get the personalized character, which is how the social character is different than other members of that social class. The Sri Moo accent is different because it is about being an animated cartoon. Accents are very dangerous because you can stop at having a good accent and you will have a good, generalized theatrical caricature. If you want a real accent, you have to get specific ... the southern accent from upper Mississippi is very different from the southern accent from lower Mississippi, and it usually has to do with social class. An accent is a quick fix on how to direct yourself toward a character. If you stop at an accent, you're dead. It's called caricature. It's a lousy acting choice. Ruth is good enough that she can put a personalized aspect into her accent. But if you don't put a

personalized aspect into it it's a caricature accent. That's why accents work for her and they can kill other actors.

Maleczech's accent for Sri Moo is nothing if not funny. So is the cow's head she wears and the four hooves she and Weinstein control. She uses her voice and her reduced range of movement to maximum effect, creating a cartoon that, by the end of the performance, we know as well as we know the popular character Marge Simpson, a figure who also makes an appearance in this piece.

Galilee moved to California while *Summa Dramatica* was in development. Before her departure, however, she played Sri Moo's bottom half, developing the choreography for the cow's four legs, used as if they are four arms for gestural effect. "That was so easy—easy, easy, easy," says Galilee of the choreographic process: "We just went in and made it." Weinstein took over Galilee's part after her move. Since the performer's face is almost always hidden, however, the choreographic movements designed by Galilee retain the same patterns she established for the role. For Sri Moo's gestures, Galilee drew upon her training in Kathak. "As her daughter, I have a very good feeling for her body," Galilee said, "I would riff on her voice. She had to act above me, so I could do all of the silly illustrative stuff." Acknowledging Maleczech's long history as a skillful performer of movement herself, Breuer noted, nonetheless, that "Clove knows a great deal more about movement than Ruth does, so I think she adds a certain level of sophistication" to the physical landscape. Maleczech, he suggests, knew how to exploit Galilee's choreography in order to create her own major impact, even when the limitations of age and illness threatened to restrict her virtuosity in *Summa Dramatica*.

Shaggy Dog, *Red Beads*, and *Summa Dramatica* offer us distinctive permutations of the Maleczech/Breuer/Galilee creative triangle. These productions, furthermore, chart the evolution of each artist's relationship to movement, voice, and media. Galilee's work under Maleczech's direction and the production that resulted from it, *Imagination Dead Imagine*, is yet another incarnation of the dynamism that can be found in Maleczech's family collaborations.

Photo 4.2 Ruth Maleczech as the "holy cow" Sri Moo Parahamsa and Clove Galilee as her hind legs in a workshop presentation of *Summa Dramatica: A Pataphysical Acting Lesson* at the Flea Theater Downstairs in New York City, 2005. Photo: Julie Archer.

Mother, daughter, and holographic visualization in Beckett's *Imagination Dead Imagine*

While *Shaggy Dog, Red Beads*, and *Summa Dramatica* trace the Maleczech-Breuer-Galilee trio's evolving interaction with puppetry in performance, *Imagination Dead Imagine* shows Maleczech using technology to transform the relationship among performer, audience, and performance. Years after Galilee appeared onstage with her mother in *Shaggy Dog*, and years before they appeared together in *Red Beads*, Maleczech cast her daughter to appear—virtually—in her staging of Beckett's short story *Imagination Dead Imagine*. In a rare case of the writer's willingness to allow artists to repurpose his texts—which he granted on more than one occasion to Mabou Mines—Beckett gave Maleczech permission to stage this prose piece. *Imagination Dead Imagine* was written in French as *Imagination morte imaginez* in the early 1960s and published five years later in 1965 in *Les Lettres nouvelles*. That same year his English translation appeared in the *Sunday Times* in London. J.M. Coetzee writes that Beckett's short stories of this period follow "the narrative premise of *The Unnamable*, and of *How It Is*, in which

> a creature constituted of a voice is attached, for reasons unknown, to some kind of body enclosed in a space more or less reminiscent of Dante's Hell, condemned for a certain length of time to speak, to try to make sense of things. It is a situation well described by Heidegger's term *Geworfenheit*: being thrown without explanation into an existence governed by obscure rules.[39]

Mel Gussow describes the story in his review of Maleczech's production for the *New York Times* as a "futuristic tale of a man and woman confined in a white rotunda."[40]

Mabou Mines had already produced a number of Beckett's works in the early 1970s, including *Come and Go* and *Play* (both 1971), in which Maleczech performed. Fred Neumann's staging of Beckett's novel *Mercier and Camier* was first presented in 1979. Maleczech began working on *Imagination Dead Imagine* in 1981. She asked Beckett for permission to stage his story "as a holographic visualization with the complete text on tape. This would be an installation in a gallery or museum," she explained, "and would not involve any live performer."[41] Maleczech erroneously included a comma in Beckett's title in her letter to him, to which he responded on one of his tiny and immaculate white note cards, pleading that she be mindful of the lack of punctuation but consenting to the staging all the same. He added the caveat, however, that he would like a fuller explanation of what Maleczech meant by "holographic visualization."[42]

Maleczech wrote to Beckett again on March 12, 1984, to describe two possible approaches to the use of holography:

> Process #1—A high contrast black and white film is taken of a figure brightly lit and slowly turning against a black background. The film is developed and projected onto a rear projection screen which then refracts the image through a holographic optical element. As the image passes through this optical element, it takes on the characteristics of a three dimensional body. This three dimensional image appears in mid-air rather than projected onto any surface. The body floats and gently turns above a bier.
>
> Process #2—A film is taken in the same manner as above. The film is then cut and transferred to five 360° celluloid cylinders. These cylinders rest on top of a turning mechanism and are lit by a special high-intensity light. The turning mechanism and the light are both hidden inside the bier. The figure will again appear to be three dimensional and will seem to float in the air, detached from and slightly above the bier.

Anxious to emphasize the artistic concept behind these arrangements, Maleczech added: "If all this sounds very complicated it is, but the goal is a very simple and pure one; to suspend a body made of light above a simple bier, to have it turn gently and seem to emit speech in rays like light is emitted." Beckett responded on March 23 to assure Maleczech of his support, eschewing the possibility of his assistance because of the technical nature of the holographic process and thanking Maleczech for her care in mounting the production.[43]

Although Beckett steers clear of engaging with the technicalities Maleczech describes in their correspondence, his prose piece contains the sort of detailed logistical descriptions that may have attracted the director to the holographic process in the first place. Beckett's rotunda is:

> Diameter three feet, three feet from ground to summit of the vault. Two diameters at right angles AB CD divide the white ground into two semicircles ACB BDA. Lying on the ground two white bodies, each in its semicircle. White too the vault and the round wall eighteen inches high from which it springs.[44]

The density of Beckett's spatial measurements is mirrored by a deceptively simple explanation of the holographic process. According to an exhibit on holography at the Massachusetts Institute of Technology Museum, where Maleczech developed some work for the production,

> holography is a method of recording and reconstructing light waves. When light hits an object, it reflects back in waves that exactly correlate to the object struck, creating a characteristic "wave front" that is recorded on photosensitive film. Projecting light back through the hologram reconstructs the wave front, delivering to the eye the tonal range, color, and 3D form of an object without its material presence.

Further, "holography works by exploiting two light-wave phenomena: interference ... and diffraction."[45] The same could be said of *Imagination Dead Imagine*, which introduces the reader to certain highly descriptive elements while deflecting comprehension by omitting others.

Maleczech's interest in holography also responds to Beckett's use of light as a recurring trope in the piece. Just as Maleczech's holographic image will be, the light in *Imagination Dead Imagine* is active, returning to the space to illuminate the contents and inhabitants in cycles: "wait, more or less long, light and heat come back, all grows white and hot together, ground, wall, vault, bodies, say twenty seconds, all the greys, till the initial level is reached whence the fall began." Taking her cue from Beckett's light, which "makes all so white no visible source," [46] the apparatus that generates Maleczech's holographic image will also be hidden.

In the world of *Imagination Dead Imagine*, all is "white in the whiteness of the rotunda" and there is "no trace anywhere of life," yet Beckett describes figures that are not dead.[47] "Hold a mirror to their lips, it mists," he writes.[48] Holography, which tricks the mind into undergoing the same process it uses to perceive what is actually in front of us, is a sly three-dimensional interpretation of Beckett's figures, who seem to be simultaneously absent and present. As the MIT exhibition notes, "a holographic image engages the eyes and brain in a way that feels like the real world—yet the hologram is simply light; the material is gone."[49]

Maleczech's minimal staging—limited to the interaction among the holographic image, the bier, and the sound recording she describes in her letters—is inspired by Beckett's severe and enigmatic landscape. Linda Hartinian, who collaborated with Mabou Mines on *A Prelude to Death in Venice* and *Wrong Guys* (both 1981), worked with Maleczech to develop the hologram, serving as her major design collaborator. Galilee provided the movement sequence for the hologram. The sound recording, performed by Ruth Nelson, offers us the quiet, strained female voice we hear as the holographic image of a woman's body divided into thirds rotates over a bier, designed by L.B. Dallas. Together, these sights and sounds communicate the eerie and contemplative impression of a space-age reliquary. John Lennon's "Imagine" subtly fades in and out in a sound design by Karen Michel McPhereson, as do the lights, designed by Toby Scott with Anne Millitello and Dallas. The movements of the body in the hologram and the manipulation of sound and light are delicate and highly nuanced, sensitive to Beckett's restrained and minimalist text. In his review for the *New York Times*, Gussow describes some of the visual effects that are lost in the installation's transition to VHS as he reports what the audience of the live performance saw: "a beam of light falls on a catafalque and the intricate design on the exterior changes color and texture as we watch it—from gold to bright white, from sandstone to marble. Faces and objects seem to appear on the surface."[50]

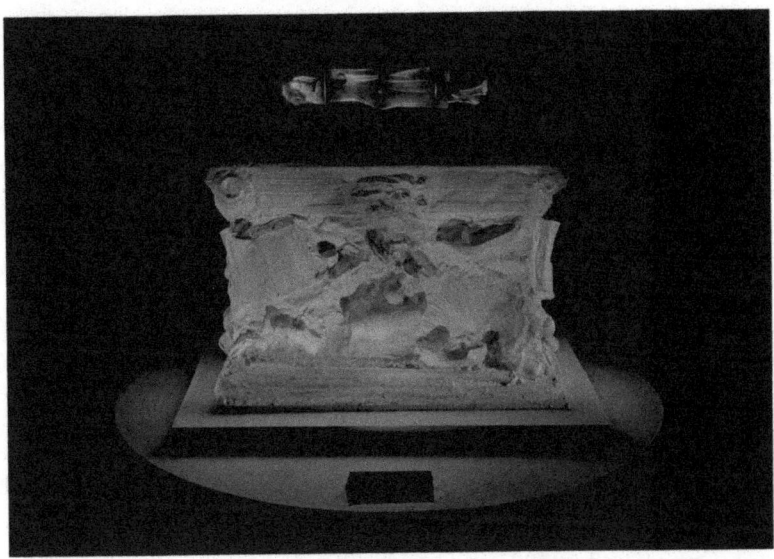

Photo 4.3 Clove Galilee in hologram form levitates above the bier designed by L.B. Dallas in Beckett's *Imagination Dead Imagine* at the Performing Garage in New York City, 1984. Photo: James Hamilton.

Gussow also described the production as something quite different than a traditional theater production, noting that "the starkness and mystery of the vision stimulates visual and aural imagery from Miss Maleczech.... On its most immediate level, the current adaptation is the equivalent of hearing poetry read to sculpture."[51] His impression signals the influence of Maleczech's experience at the San Francisco Tape Music Center in the 1960s, when she and other performers walked around an art gallery to music composed by Pauline Oliveros, among others. Maleczech's idea for holographic visualization also stems from her interest in collaborating with visual artists, as she did with Judy North (then Davis) on *The Black and White Mime Show* and in her early work with Archer, who initially thought of herself as a sculptor. Such nonnarrative pieces, rooted in visual art and music, as well as Maleczech's extensive collaborations with musicians and visual artists, helped to establish the genre in which Maleczech works in *Imagination Dead Imagine*: performance installation. "Because Ruth works so visually," said Galilee, "her work often should be in museums, especially small pieces like *Vanishing Pictures* and *Imagination Dead Imagine*." Considered in this context, *Imagination Dead Imagine* has more in common with work that traverses the line between performance and visual art, such as Carolee Schneemann's or Marina Abramović's, rather than with that of Maleczech's contemporaries in American avant-garde theater. Maleczech's emphasis on technological innovation, however, finds a clear parallel in Elizabeth LeCompte's ambitious mediatized work with the Wooster Group.

Imagination Dead Imagine was Maleczech's third directing project. *Vanishing Pictures* (1980) was her first. As with her staging of Beckett's prose piece, Maleczech worked closely on the design for that piece, for which she and Archer won an OBIE Award. Maleczech's second directing project, a stage adaptation of Jim Strah's detective novel *Wrong Guys*, premiered in 1981 and secured her place as an adept translator of prose for the theater—one that prepared her for the challenge posed by *Imagination Dead Imagine*. The Strah project also foreshadows the incorporation of multimedia Maleczech would exploit in *Imagination Dead Imagine*. Strah himself was familiar with the performance milieu: he worked with the Wooster Group as a writer and performer on LeCompte and Spalding Gray's *Three Places in Long Island* (1975–1979).

Wrong Guys was produced at the Public Theater the same year as *Dead End Kids*, during Mabou Mines's extended residency there. Maleczech's adaptation featured an all-male cast that included Breuer, O'Reilly, and Raymond, full frontal male nudity, and an all-female crew of technicians. Maleczech's adaptation of Strah's book tells the story of two tough guys, Jack (Raymond) and Johnny (Breuer), who are separated in a car crash, and Jack's quest to find Johnny. He eventually finds Johnny in a bathtub, but Johnny has now become a cold-blooded killer. An original pornographic film is interspersed with the live action. In the Wooster Group's *Route 1 & 9*, which premiered the same year, LeCompte similarly makes use of pornographic intervention, which she introduces in sequences drawn from *Our Town*. LeCompte later inserts a pornographic film into the fabric *House/Lights* (1998).

Though *Wrong Guys* was not recorded on video, photographs show a highly visual interpretation experimenting with Archer's designs of light and shadow (a technique Maleczech built into *Imagination Dead Imagine*), projected text, and the judicious use of props such as naked light bulbs, beer cans, a bathtub, and a typewriter in a set design by Michael Kuhling. Photographs reveal nearly nude men in sinewy poses; these sharply contrast with the tough, gangster language in the script. One picture captures all of the gangsters wearing suits in a bathtub; a projection on the wall of words mixed with scribbles gives the impression of a hole made by a gunshot. Another vivid photo depicts the line-up of the all-male cast wearing costumes designed by Mehrten. They are dressed as gangsters with stockings over their heads, holding typewriters instead of guns, part Andy Warhol, part Cindy Sherman.

Wrong Guys received less attention and critical acclaim than *Dead End Kids*. The reviews are mixed. David Sterritt of the *Christian Science Monitor* praised the production for its attempt to recreate film techniques for the stage, "fading and dissolving and jump-cutting from one episode to another. The stagecraft is magical, and its complete visibility—every trick is pulled right before our eyes—makes it all the more ingenious." His review, however, takes *Wrong Guys* to task for its equally "visible problems": overly "sleazy" characters, nudity, and a convoluted plot.[52] A review written by Frank Rich for the *New York Times* has a better sense of Maleczech's intentions, though it, too, is far from encouraging. Rich appreciated the dazzling visual techniques in the piece, describing it as

> a precisely designed mixed media circus in which black-and-white movies combine with live actors, flying lights and a complex network of rope and wire pulleys to take us on a manic descent into a volatile, imaginary criminal underworld.... When we're told of a malevolent black limousine streaking up Eighth Avenue, the cinematic image whips across the wide stage space like a rocket. Rolls of white paper— either dropping from above or ascending from the floor—materialize and disappear in an instant to pick up projected images of the view from a car windshield....

He also praises the feminist message communicated through the juxtaposition between male performers and female technicians who serve them (though one wonders if the message might be just the opposite—that women technicians also have the power to pull the strings) and in the representation of women serving men in the film clips. Rich criticizes the production, however, for resorting to what he describes as overly obvious techniques and dull text, and for failing to present anything "terribly new," ultimately comparing *Wrong Guys* unfavorably with *Dead End Kids*. Some of Rich's uneasiness has to do with Maleczech's choice of material in the first place; he goes so far as to call the language of Strah's novel as "sophomoric."[53]

Despite the project's mixed reception, the Mabou Mines collaborators remember *Wrong Guys* as one of the strongest pieces in Maleczech's repertoire. "*Wrong Guys* was a huge turning point in her work artistically," says Galilee. "She really knew what it was she was making, and she was surrounded by a bunch of really, really talented people who helped her make it."

Eager to stretch herself as a director in a mode and atmosphere different from Strah's wise-guy milieu but also to find a way to energize her emerging feminist perspective and interest in mixed-media performance, Maleczech next turned to Beckett. In doing so she used a similar directorial approach but one which had pointedly different effects. As she did in juxtaposing fully clad female technicians with nude male performers, in *Imagination Dead Imagine* Maleczech is once again playing with binaries. Gussow identifies a sensory binary in his review, writing that "Beckett himself could have been describing the eerie effect of Miss Maleczech's stage piece when he wrote in his text about the striking contrast between the 'absolute stillness and the light.'"[54]

Although it is difficult, in the archival video recording (1984), to take one's eyes off the hologram, Maleczech explained that she conceptualized the "body" of the piece in two parts: the hologram and the bier. The voice would emanate from speakers hidden inside the bier, made from a poured plexiglass mold. When Dallas asked Maleczech what should be in the mold, she told him that she wanted "things from the life of the voice: a clock, a glass, a shoe." Some of these items were, in a metatheatrical turn, from Galilee's own life: "L.B. Dallas put in a high-heeled shoe and a princess telephone," Galilee remembers, "and I had a red princess phone, and I was attached to this phone, I used it all day long, so it was very special to me that there was this phone cord and telephone—that the things in her life were the things in my life."

The other part of the body—the hologram—was four feet, three inches long and at the time it was created the largest of its kind for the theater. Maleczech and Hartinian worked with Hart Perry, "who had something called the Holographic Museum and was the only person working in holography that any of us knew," Maleczech said. His museum was in Soho and, Galilee remembers, "It was a pretty funky little scene up there." Maleczech initially wanted Galilee nude for the recording of the hologram, but, says the latter, "when we met these people, it was me, Ruth, and Linda Hartinian and these two men from the museum in this little room with books everywhere and holograms— it was intense. And Ruth said, 'absolutely not you're not going to do this naked.'" Instead, Galilee was costumed in a vintage Victorian slip and wore her hair in the style of Marie Curie, a habit she and her mother took up after Maleczech portrayed the character in *Dead End Kids*.

"One of the reasons Ruth originally wanted me naked," Galilee explains, "was a practical issue, because they had to connect my body in three sections for the holographic image. They had never made one image that big—that wasn't possible, and just connecting it in three was going to be difficult." Beckett's "bodies" are "neither fat nor thin, big nor small" and "seem whole and in fairly good condition, to judge by the surfaces exposed to view."[55] Maleczech's intention to feature a nude figure in the holographic image was designed to emphasize this corporeal presence. Although that objective was unrealized, the fact that Galilee's figure is presented in three parts fosters an uncanny correspondence to Beckett's female figure, who is "bent in three."[56] Evoking the precision and detail of Beckett's spatial descriptions, Galilee remembers the experience as "incredibly technical. I had to hit the same marks every time." In order to do so, she stood on a stack of books as she rotated herself in a circle and the technicians filmed a third of her body at a time.

Maleczech knew from the beginning of the project that she wanted to pair a recorded voice with the hologram she planned to make with Hartinian. She was careful about clearing her choice to use a recorded voice with Beckett. In the same letter in which she described the approaches to making a hologram, she writes:

> The text of *Imagination Dead Imagine* will be put onto a digital tape system, with the machine and speakers concealed in the bier. This sound system has an extremely expanded range and very low inherent noise, so the voice will sound as close to live speech as is now possible, rather than the quality normally associated with taped speech. [57]

Her plan has its origins in the Mabou Mines tradition of sonic and vocal experimentation, first established in the company's inaugural production: Philip Glass designed the flooring used in *Red Horse Animation* so that it would amplify the sounds of performers' bodies as they made contact with it. Maleczech's interest in recorded voice also has roots in her experience as a voice-over artist for film dubbing in Paris in the 1960s, when, as stated earlier, she often provided the English voice for Catherine Deneuve.

Narrators in Beckett's prose can be ambiguous in gender. Maleczech's female one coincides with Billie Whitelaw's performance of the prose piece *Enough*, directed in 1981 by Alan Schneider (Maleczech worked with him at the San Francisco Actor's Workshop in 1961).[58] Her commitment to putting strong female voices onstage, evident from her earliest directing work, is reflected in her decision to use a female voice in the recording. Maleczech's choice to use a woman's voice follows logically from her perception that Beckett makes more of the female figure in *Imagination Dead Imagine* than he does of her male counterpart. He is described in the text merely as "the partner," reflecting the unenviable role of Willie in *Happy Days*.[59]

Deriving further inspiration from the text, Maleczech sought to achieve a sense of alienation in her vocal work with Nelson. Her voice was more cultured than the one Maleczech envisioned for the recording. She describes Nelson as having been "a starlet in the Group Theatre." The actress was eighty-two when she recorded the voice for *Imagination Dead Imagine*. Her experience in the theater had been rather different from that of the usual Mabou Mines collaborators:

> This very cultured, very talented, uptown sort of person came here and I don't know how she managed to feel okay about being in this studio, such as it is. But somehow she did. She was very honored and thrilled to be saying Beckett's words. And she said them in a very cultured way, much too cultured for me. When you see yourself as a performer in a certain way over many, many years, it's very difficult to change that. And she was really so lovely and her diction was so precise and her voice was so modulated and liquid and it was great. But it wasn't what I wanted.

Maleczech was after a voice that would evoke a more ordinary woman—the kind of woman she herself played in her performance of Winnie in *Happy Days*.[60] In this piece Maleczech displays her sense of the plebian when she uses Lennon's popular ballad, a choice that is further emphasized by the outlines of everyday objects contained in the bier. Maleczech ultimately attempted to unmoor Nelson from her high-class intonations by asking the performer to lean backwards over the back of a chair as she delivered the lines "so she was always under strain.... It's all under a lot of strain. It's still a beautiful, beautiful voice, but under a lot of pressure, a lot of strain, because it's a difficult position to maintain if you're forty, and if you're eighty-two, it's really hard," Maleczech said. In the recording Nelson's voice retains vestiges of its cultivated quality, but it also sounds fractured and overwrought, as if it does not quite belong to the speaker. As such, Nelson's strained voice conveys a subtle aural correspondence to the "agitated light" of Beckett's narrative.[61]

Just as Maleczech establishes a distancing quality in Nelson's voice for the recording, the division of Galilee's body into sections in the hologram sustains a feeling of profound alienation. These sections rotate independently of each other, sometimes turning in contrasting directions and occasionally rotating the segments one at a time. As a result, the body in the hologram is distanced from itself, just as the recorded voice appears to be. It is not until fourteen minutes into the twenty-minute piece that Galilee's body, suspended in beams of light, makes a significant movement on its own. When it does, the choreography we see finds its roots in Beckett's firm description: "with their left hands they hold their left legs a little below the knee, with their right hands their left arms a little above the elbow."[62] Onstage, as "Imagine" begins to play again, we see Galilee in hologram, rotating all the while; she picks up her leg and puts it back down in an understated balletic move. This time the entire track of Lennon's song plays itself out. Galilee's hand, which is cupped in front of her face, begins to move slowly around her face. The hologram is the last thing to fade out onstage.

As Breuer's does in *Red Beads*, Maleczech's staging of Beckett features contrasts in age, juxtaposing the recorded voice of the elderly Ruth Nelson with the body of the fourteen-year-old Galilee in the hologram. By pitting youth against age, Maleczech heightens the sense of distance already established by separating body from voice. She invents the outlines of a visual and aural narrative as counterpart to Beckett's story without overpowering or distorting it. Maleczech, said Galilee, "loves to work with poetry, with language, and her work is very subtle, and that's a perfect example of an incredibly subtle idea taken from an incredibly complicated piece of writing." The bier's detritus of daily life implies that this undead creature of Beckett's was once truly alive. Maleczech's union of youth and age suggests that the enigmatic figure now exists in a purgatorial space. The cyclical nature of Maleczech and Galilee's mother–daughter relationship further enriches this aspect of the staging.

Where Breuer uses puppets to redirect attention from the performer to the text, here Maleczech uses the hologram to the same effect, enhancing our awareness of the figure's presence in a liminal space between life and death. In *Shaggy Dog*, *Red Beads*, and *Summa Dramatica*, however, the introduction of puppets and puppetlike elements establishes a triad of interaction among puppet, performer, and audience. In *Imagination Dead Imagine* Maleczech removes the live performer from the equation, forcing the audience to confront design elements and text without intrusive mediation. This makes *Imagination Dead Imagine* into a landscape play, where, as Gertrude Stein suggests, "the landscape does not have to make acquaintance. You may have to make acquaintance with it, but it does not with you, it is there...."[63] Just as, according to Sabatini, in *La Divina Caricatura* Breuer holds human impulses in "suspended animation," Maleczech stages Beckett's purgatorial world by *virtually* capturing Galilee's body, consigning it to rotate for the duration of the performance.

Maleczech's work on *Imagination Dead Imagine* places her among Mabou Mines's leaders in experimenting with Beckett's work for the stage and makes clear that the writer's influence on the company extends beyond the founding artistic directors' experiments with his texts in the late 1960s and early 1970s. Invested in the possibilities of theater, Maleczech continued to work on *Imagination Dead Imagine* after its New York premiere. The production toured to Florida State University in 1987 and to Radford University in 1988. Maleczech and Hartinian received a grant to work with scientists in an MIT laboratory (the production also played at MIT in 1986) to try to alter the hologram from rainbow color to black and white. "But we never could," Maleczech said. "But they got to blue," says Galilee, "which was pretty beautiful."

Presence, absence, and innovation

Maleczech's use of a large-scale hologram onstage in *Imagination Dead Imagine* was at the very forefront of technological experimentation in the theater, anticipating by nearly two decades the techniques of cyborg performance currently being explored by groups such as the Builders Association. What she was doing, in fact, was so innovative that when Ellen Burstyn visited the Performing Garage during the run of the show as a representative of Actors' Equity, she was flummoxed to discover that there were no live actors present for the performance. "She came," said Maleczech,

> and afterwards she looked in the hallway where these plexiglass drums are that sit on top of the mirror for the hologram and she said, "There is no actor there." I said "no, it's a hologram. It's a hologram in parts. There was an actor, a dancer." "Did she get paid?" Ellen wanted to know. "Oh yes." "And there is a voice?" "Yes, there is." "Did she get paid?" I said, "Oh yes, of course."

Maleczech's investment in technological innovation and in her daughter as a theater artist stem from the same impulse—the one that makes her, as she liked to say, cannon fodder—a figure forging ahead in the avant-garde. Maleczech was a pioneer, forward in her thinking and dedicated to leading the way into uncharted theatrical territory. Her commitment to fostering a new generation of theater makers is evident in her work with Mabou Mines's mentorship programs, begun with her cofounding of ReCherChez in 1979; this continues today with the company's resident artists program, Mabou Mines/Suite. She also demonstrated this commitment in her willingness to consider her daughter as a full partner in the production process, welcoming her into the world of theatrical creation.

Although there are personal disagreements about the success of these collaborations, some of Maleczech's most adventurous work has been created in the company of her daughter and the father of her children. Galilee continues in the family tradition by making her own work with her wife and by collaborating with her Mabou Mines family, where, starting with *The Shaggy Dog Animation*, the trio of Maleczech, Breuer, and Galilee blurred the borders between natural and artificial, working, as Schechner says, to "threaten the peace of mind of those of us who would like to think."[64] Maleczech and Breuer taught Maleczech's performance of *Hajj* to Galilee in 2012, ensuring that the trio's engagement with their nontraditional, metatheatrical family history will continue even in the absence of the mother.

Conclusion: Cannon/Canon Fodder

Prenez bien garde, vous, à vous déhancher comme il faut, et à faire
bien des façons. Cela vous contraindra un peu; mais qu'y faire? Il faut
parfois se faire violence.

Take care, you, that you perform properly, and pay attention to
formalities. That will constrain you a little; but what can you do?
One must sometimes do violence to oneself.

L'Impromptu de Versailles[1]

Ben Brantley's obituary of Maleczech in the *New York Times* underscores
the very issue that prompted Akalaitis to place a call to the newspaper
in the first place: "She occupied the outer margins of established theater
and wore that status as a badge of honor, refusing to join Actors' Equity
until the late 1980s and often seeming to revel in the contumely of the
mainstream press."[2] Don Shewey, a frequent and intelligent reviewer of
Maleczech's work, opened his obituary in *American Theatre* magazine
on a similar note. "Most people don't know that Ruth Maleszech [*sic*] ...
was one of the greatest actors of our time."[3] Only a handful of formal
obituaries materialized, but word spread widely of Maleczech's death on
social media platforms. Among those who contributed informal tributes
on Facebook and via Twitter were notable directors Robert Woodruff,
Joanna Settle, and Rachel Dickstein and critic Alisa Solomon. Director
and Mabou Mines collaborator John McGrath wrote an obituary on the
National Theatre of Wales's blog. La MaMa hosted a standing-room-
only memorial service in the Ellen Stewart Theatre where Maleczech
was eulogized by family and fellow artists.

Of the obituaries in traditional press outlets, Shewey's is most
searching in its attempt to characterize the inimitability of Maleczech's
contribution. He links her to film luminaries Anna Magnani, Jeanne

Moreau, and Judi Dench, all of whom he describes as "consummately skilled actors whose earthiness, authority, intelligence, feminine strength and, at times, scary darkness carved new depths for the portrayal of human experience." Though Shewey describes Maleczech admiringly, he nonetheless falls into the trap of "unhumanizing" her by describing her as the Other: "onstage she was almost frightening in her power, like a witch. Her face was an oriental mask, and her wonderful rich voice came from somewhere far within." Such objectification is later tempered by observing that she was "kind, loving, and extremely honest."[4] Both Shewey and Brantley emphasize Maleczech's physical appearance. "While she cut a striking figure," Brantley says, "with her red hair and sensuous frame and features (critics described her onstage as looking like 'a Technicolor Lucy on a binge' and 'Anita Ekberg on a diet'), Ms. Maleczech never presented herself as an exotic diva."[5] While revealing their discomfort with Maleczech's bodily figure, their commentary inadvertently pays tribute to her lifelong project to provoke the audience to think in new ways about issues of representation. Indeed, Maleczech manipulated her stage appearance as one instrument among many in her theatrical apparatus in order to dramatize issues of masculinity and femininity.

Shewey lauds Maleczech as "extraordinary" and "phenomenally talented," yet he relies on the familiar trope of positioning her importance primarily in relation to Lee Breuer's oeuvre:

> Breuer counted on Maleczech's fathomless resources for the work he created for her to perform. The two of them were like John Cassevetes and Gena Rowlands, or Fellini and Giulietta Masina, or Ingmar Bergman and Liv Ullmann—writer-directors who created impossibly subtle, demanding roles for partners they knew could nail it.[6]

Even as Maleczech was posthumously acknowledged in the press, she remained, in James Harding's terms, "disenfranchised." That is, she was "denied a forum, a venue, or a voice within the dominant structures of social and cultural authority," in this case because, like Lucia Joyce, she is relegated to the role of muse.[7] Maleczech, however, was adept at exploiting what Harding calls the "site that always vacillates between liberty and containment." She was a towering figure who defied inherited patriarchal categorization in the theater. Brantley indicates as much in his obituary. The "proposition" (to use Grotowksi's word) that Maleczech offers us demands nothing short of the "radical shift in focus from a male-dominated canon to the experimental work of women artists ... to excavate a set of norms and values that does not serve patriarchal interests." Harding argues that this is what is required to reenvision American avant-garde historiography.[8]

Maleczech's aesthetic and political priorities converge in her final theatrical endeavor. At the time of her death, she was in the midst of developing *Imagining the Imaginary Invalid*. She conceived the project and was its featured performer, supported by a team of dancers and actors. The piece intercolates Molière's *The Imaginary Invalid* with *Union of Hypocrites*, Mikhail Bulgakov's book about Molière's life, and incorporates texts from the history of medicine as well as original writing on that topic.[9] Although Molière completed his final performance of *The Imaginary Invalid* before succumbing to tuberculosis, Maleczech died before completing her encounter with his play.

As with *Hajj* (1983), Maleczech was attracted to her subject on *Imagining the Imaginary Invalid* for personal—and in this case, medical—reasons. She explained:

> Since I spent six weeks in the hospital having a titanium rod put inside the femur of my leg and dealt a lot with doctors and nurses, I want to make the *Imaginary Invalid*. Molière did it on the commode because he couldn't walk. I can walk, thank God. I know it's everybody's college play, but I still want to do it. And I've never done Molière, so that's a great adventure for me to think about. And I want to do all seven ballets.[10]

Mabou Mines presented workshop performances of the production in July 2012 at the ToRoNaDa studio and a year later at La MaMa Studio. As usual, Maleczech formed a team that includes longtime collaborators and newcomers. Clove Galilee provided choreography and also performed, and Julie Archer designed the sets. Valeria Vasilevski, with whom Maleczech codirected *Fire Works* in 1987—one of her collaborations away from Mabou Mines—worked on dramaturgy and original text. Maleczech had planned to collaborate for the first time with composer Belinda Reynolds, who was slated to create new Baroque-style music. She also consulted with Elaine Elliot as an advisor on classic texts. The supporting cast, at Galilee's urging, was made up entirely of young performers working with Mabou Mines for the first time. At the July 2013 workshop, the cast included Maleczech's granddaughter (Galilee's niece). In a testament to the vitality of Maleczech's vision, the life of the production continues in her absence; Galilee directs a full production slated to open at La MaMa.

Imagining the Imaginary Invalid brings together a number of Maleczech's signature concerns. One of the few actor-managers of her time, Maleczech finally embraced the staging of Molière, one of the most famous actor-managers in theater history. And not only did she perform portions of Molière's play, Maleczech was also doing what Breuer says she did best: crafting her own performance. "When Ruth has the range to come up with a lot of ideas, she comes closer to brilliance," he said.[11] For Sharon Fogarty, *Imagining the Imaginary Invalid* demonstrates Maleczech's investment in considering both history and contemporary politics from a female perspective. Maleczech is "taking this classic play," Fogarty said, "and making a commentary on current medical practices and the history of the medicine."[12] As in *Belén* (1996) and *Dead End Kids* (1980), Maleczech addresses an issue of pressing contemporary concern by offering an original and challenging historiographic point of view. In addition to examining historical material from her feminist perspective, Maleczech takes possession of a canonical text by speaking words written for a man, as she did previously in *Lear* (1990). And as in *The Shaggy Dog Animation* (1978), *Imagination Dead Imagine* (1984), and *Red Beads* (2005), Maleczech collaborated with her daughter. Taking a cue from Molière, who created roles for his wife and sister-in-law, Maleczech elaborated on her family project by including her granddaughter in this work as well. Once again, she transformed an ordinary woman's concerns—this time medical treatment—into an extraordinary theatrical experience, just as she took on everyday preoccupations in *Happy Days* (1996) and *Through the Leaves* (1984).

Maleczech's perspective on hypochondria and medicine is inspired by another of Molière works: *The Versailles Impromptu*, a scripted improvisation in which Molière and Illustre Théâtre company members appear as themselves during rehearsals for a new play. Preparations for a production of the *Imaginary Invalid* provide Maleczech with a frame for her own imprint. Each performer has a dual role: as himself or herself and as the character he or she plays in Molière's text; they are by no means characters in search of an author. Maleczech and Galilee have three roles: Maleczech appears as herself, as Molière's character Argan, and as the actor-manger himself. Galilee, meanwhile, appears as herself, as Argan's maid Toinette, and as Mademoiselle Molière (Molière's wife and a lead actress in their troupe, Armande Béjart). We see actors rehearse scenes and double as technicians, making costumes and building sets. Dancers in baroque-inspired costumes flit across the stage. On one afternoon before the 2012 workshop presentation, the ToRoNaDa studio reverberated with the whir of a sewing machine, the thud of electrical cords dropping from a lofted storage space, and the hammer of nails being driven into wood. This carefully orchestrated soundscape competes with Maleczech's delivery of Argan's opening monologue. The company intersperses scenes from the *Imaginary Invalid* with interludes in an improvisational style that reflects the realities of developing a production. Such practical theater matters are punctuated by the concerns of everyday life—lovers' quarrels, unrequited passions, and access to medical care. In the rehearsal room it became so difficult to distinguish staged rehearsal scenes from the rehearsal itself that the company instituted the use of what Galilee jokingly describes as a safe word, "Oklahoma," so that they could keep the two dimensions clear in their own minds. The atmosphere was chaotic and at the same time focused.

The Versailles Impromptu is an appealing structure for Maleczech to adopt; she spent a career blending stage life and personal reality. Such interlocking worlds deconstructed traditional hierarchies of family and theater. "She's very brave," said Archer,

> she loves to say that she likes things messy and she's really not kidding. I don't think she is interested in following a straight line. I think she's interested in surprises and in uncovering something unexpected. It's incredibly courageous of her. She really puts herself out there.[13]

Galilee says the disordered intersection of life and work that Molière captures in *The Versailles Impromptu* is an apt metaphor for Mabou Mines:

> what this company has been through, and what this company faces, and how this company used to make work. It used to be just like that—no director—and they were very insistent upon that. Five artistic directors, and how the press and grant givers tried to pinhole everybody and put them in categories because it's easier for them. So it's a way to talk about all of these issues and in a very funny way and a scatological way.

Imagining the Imaginary Invalid returns Mabou Mines to its early collective methodology. During a rehearsal-notes discussion session, several performers made suggestions that were incorporated into the structure of the piece. Archer and the stage manager proposed blocking and ground plans that were implemented. Other proposals from performers, Galilee, and Maleczech herself were considered but subsequently rejected.

Maleczech's intuitive process for choosing collaborators—evident in the way she drew Archer and Catherine Sasanov into work with Mabou Mines—allowed her to identify creative partners who can bring unexpected points of view to the process. In turn, artists with strong artistic perspectives have gravitated to her. Archer said of her work with Maleczech that

> there is never any resistance to any idea.... Any idea is worth trying.... She's not intimidated by something that she didn't think of. In fact, she's courageous enough to welcome it into the mix. It's sort of, "Bring it on." She's a dream to work with in that light.

Maleczech especially valued ideas that challenged her own. Although they had known each other for nearly twenty years, Paul Kandel's first collaboration with Maleczech occurred when she invited him to serve as the chorus leader in *Song for New York: What Women Do While Men Sit at Home Knitting* (2007). Though he was happy to defer to Maleczech's wishes as director, the two frequently disagreed about how to proceed aesthetically. "She wanted an aggressive, alternative point of view that she respected," he said, describing their interaction during a residency at the Ucross Foundation in Wyoming to develop the project:

> Ruth is, in fifty different ways, a singular human being. She's at the same time very specific, demanding, and insistent, and within that same person exists the capacity to leave enormous room for other people to do their work in the way they need to do it. She has a huge respect for other artists' process even if it's different from hers. You have this incredibly bright person who brings an enormous spontaneity and passion to her work who has strong opinions and who at the same time can leave room for people who don't agree with her. She'll say, "well, you're wrong," and then she'll leave them room to do the thing she's just told them is wrong. It takes an extraordinary person to coast through life in that way, and happily. So she looks like a one off, she is a one off. There's only one Ruth. There's not another one. [14]

Maleczech's enthusiasm for robust discussion, even disagreement, in the rehearsal room stems from Mabou Mines's early days, when the entire company participated collectively in sculpting the direction of a work (even when a director was in place). She returned to this process in *Imagining the Imaginary Invalid*.

Karen Kandel identifies Maleczech's courage and generosity as crucial to her collaborations. Shortly before the first workshop of *Imagining the Imaginary Invalid*, the pair participated in another Mabou Mines workshop performance: *we would find landscapes*, conceived by Archer and Liza Lorwin. In a structure inspired by Mabou Mines's early collaborations, *we would find landscapes* had no formal director. Instead, Karen Kandel says, she and Maleczech were responsible for developing their own performances within a collective framework for the June 2012 showing at the ToRoNaDa. According to Karen Kandel, the work was characterized by "large fluctuations within a structure and a willingness to play. Ruth said in rehearsal, 'the choices are crazy, but I'm not afraid—I'll do it.' And I think that's how she goes about working, and there are not a lot of people who do that." For Karen Kandel, Maleczech's bravery is inspiring and infectious. In *Lear*, she says:

> I was young and intimidated by Ruth's amazing lack of fear—just going ahead and trying something even if it was completely crazy. Just not saying no to something that seemed outrageous. I had so much respect for Ruth as an artist. I was a little shy, but absolutely amazed by this extraordinary woman with a lot of power, a lot of life force, and she easily shared that with me even in my incredibly shy state. I learned how to grow bolder from my scenes with Ruth and the whole process. [15]

Kandel describes the energy Maleczech offered to her fellow performers. She further identifies Maleczech's inclination to extend trust even when working with an artist for the first time, a quality Archer has noted as well. Maleczech was always confident that her creative partners would rise to the challenge she presented.

Maleczech extends her "proposition" to audiences as well. Because Maleczech's range of sources included her own life, the performances she shared are characterized by a combination of emotional availability and intellectual awareness. Breuer compared her "vulnerability and transparency" to Laurette Taylor's, who, he suggests, was the greatest actress of her own generation.[16] Breuer argues that it was Maleczech's ability to pair transparency with intellectual astuteness that enabled her to create landmark performances. "The real outstanding thing about Ruth's performing," he said,

> is her intelligence. She's really bright, she's really observant, and it makes a special performance. Great performances mean great choices, and if you don't have the chops to make great choices, you can have all the intensity in the world and you're not going to be able to make choices

that astonish people. Really great performers make great choices. This is her number one attribute.... It's ultimately because of these qualities of honesty and smarts that she has this coterie of admirers.

JoAnne Akalaitis has also observed Maleczech's ability to theatricalize intellectual and emotional complexity: "Ruth has a tremendous gift for articulating moments, those crucial moments when everything is crystallized."[17]

Maleczech's liberty in crafting performances that reflect her own point of view on the material—to make great choices for herself, in Breuer's terms—is facilitated by the framework that she developed with other Mabou Mines co-artistic directors. Their mission has been to share, promote, and extend this framework to the many performers who have worked with the company since 1970. This approach, Greg Mehrten says,

demands that the actor take charge of his or her performance.... They try to have you, the actor, connect so deeply to something—you don't even have to tell them what it is, but there's something in the role, in the performance—that you are confident. And you know what you're doing and they just help you get there, and help you be able to get there over and over again, which is not always easy.[18]

Maleczech's decision to refer to herself as a performer rather than as an actor dignifies her power to shape the work she presents to audiences; such terminology underscores her position as an autonomous collaborator of creative significance. It calls attention to her presence as an active mediator for the audience during performance and her insistence that she does not merely play roles. Maleczech chooses not to retreat from confrontation with the audience by disappearing into the roles she plays—her inheritance from Brecht. Although she presents characters to us, she has pursued diverse means to communicate that she—Maleczech—is always there as well.

Maleczech amplified her presence onstage by using the rehearsal process to ground herself physically and vocally as well as intellectually and emotionally in the world of the production. Her concept of the 360-degree awareness that performance requires led Maleczech to remain physically expressive even in the most recent of her last productions, during which she mostly maintained seated positions. She used this strategy in *Imagining the Imaginary Invalid* as well. Maleczech, said Akalaitis, "is very much in her body and needs to know exactly how her body is in the space. I never have to talk to her about that and I never will.... She is ferociously dangerous—she's willing to do all kinds of physical feats without question."[19] Maleczech derived this aspect of her approach from her early training in American mime and her work with Grotowski. She took a similarly multidimensional approach to speech. Karen Kandel, another vocally dexterous performer, comments on the nature of a varied vocal approach: "We both love playing with voices—dancing in our voices." Maleczech's musical approach to text, vocal flexibility, and affinity for accents and highly stylized ways of speaking draw equally upon her voice study with Grotowski, her career dubbing French movies in Paris, and early efforts by the Mabou Mines cofounders to animate Beckett's words onstage. Her nimble approach to movement and voice contributed to the dynamism of her stage presence, helping to distinguish the multiple characters she portrayed in *Imagining the Imaginary Invalid*.

The Molière piece is socially engaged rather than overtly political; this distinguishes Maleczech's work from both Judith Malina's radical activism and Elizabeth LeCompte's assertion of apoliticism. Amid a staged lunch break, the actors sip from water bottles and share stories of childhood medical conditions and difficulties with insurance coverage. Someone passes around a carton of red and yellow cherry tomatoes. One performer tells another that her divorced parents decided to remarry so that her father could receive coverage for the new set of teeth his dentist told him he needed. Maleczech, said Fogarty,

> keeps a pretty close watch on what's going on in the world. She's a voracious reader. She always knows what's going on in the news. She's not in her art world ignoring the outside world. But she's not necessarily directly political. She's not saying, "Oh, this is going on politically in the

world, so let's make this piece." The politics are there and they filter through but she's still operating more on a humanist level.

Maleczech admired the same humanism in Herbert Blau's work in San Francisco, but she likened her emphasis on research to Brecht's insistence that his actors educate themselves about the politics central to his plays. With notable exceptions such as *Dead End Kids*, however, Maleczech's work never employs the stage primarily as an ideological platform. Rather, her multidisciplinary curiosity has led to a nuanced body of projects and performances that are similarly sophisticated in their complexity.

Paul Kandel echoes Fogarty's description of Maleczech as an insatiable learner. "She's a polymath," he said, "I mean, you pick a topic and she'll be able to talk about it in depth. I have never hit on a topic that she doesn't know something about." Maleczech's commitment to research is, in addition to a method for uncovering source material providing inspiration for new work, the key to her preparation for intellectually engaging performances. "I work pretty well dramaturgically," Breuer said, "but Ruth goes through these incredible studies. She does an incredible amount of background reading." Research informs the subjects she stages with a richness of detail, enhancing their valence in performance. Academic studies are a match for her intuitive pursuits. "It seems deceptively like things just come out of Ruth," Galilee remembered,

> but there's a lot of practice that goes on. When she first did the first monologue for Argan, we all thought, "Where did that come from," and I thought back over the week and remembered her sitting up at night with the towel Argan wears on her head and thinking, "Okay, she's been working her ass off to find that voice, to figure him out." She works very methodically through the language. Elaine Elliott tells her the Latin meanings of all the terms. She really wants to understand it. And because of that, the depth of her performances is astronomical. And they're always different because she knows all the different ways that she can work with words. You don't expect it because she's very elegant about how that stuff comes out of her.

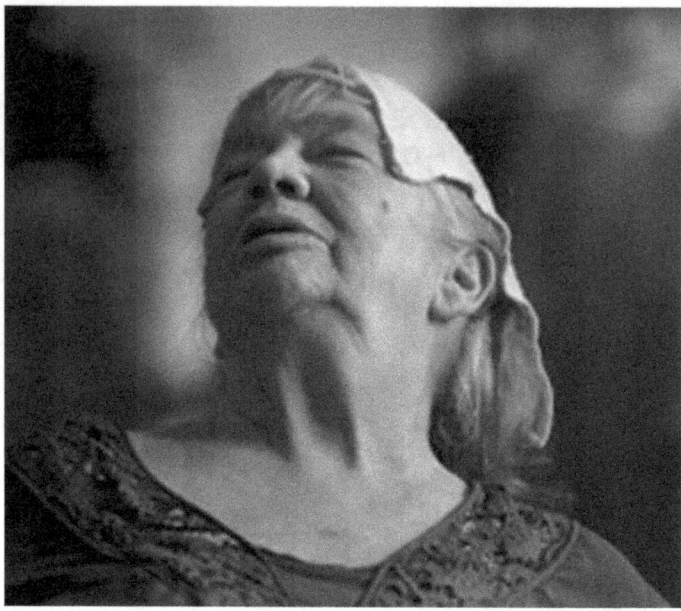

Photo C1 Ruth Maleczech as Molière's Argan in the first rehearsal for a workshop presentation of *Imagining the Imaginary Invalid* at the ToRoNaDa studio, 2012. Photo: Jan Meissner.

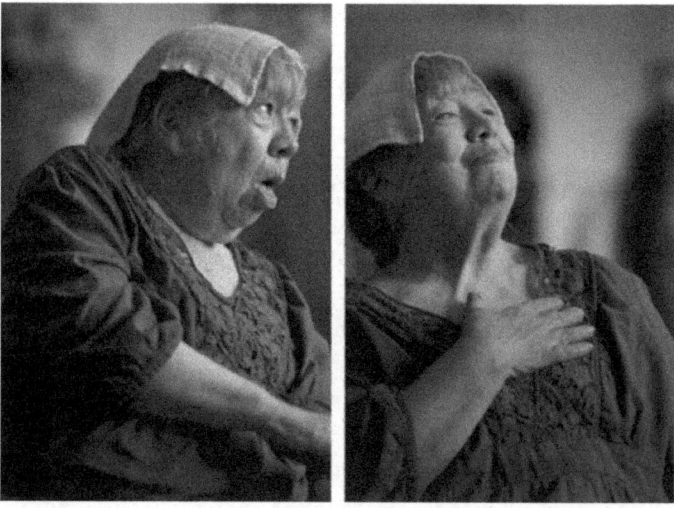

Photo C2 Maleczech used a towel on her head to distinguish Argan from the other characters she played. Photo: Jan Meissner.

While Maleczech's work can be characterized by the refinement Galilee describes, her performances and productions are at the same time unquantifiable. Maleczech's work resists tidy interpretation—the one-to-one correspondence Maleczech said she disliked. Such disjunction is designed to invite the audience to join her in unraveling the elaborate knots her work presents.

Key to this invitation is the relationship between Maleczech's armature of analysis and a determination to greet each performance without preconceptions about what will take place. "When Ruth is in the middle of a script," Akalaitis says, "she's very critical of it—critical of the writing. And then that goes away." Maleczech's ability to appear onstage each night as if for the first time allows her to take risks in performance, even in the context of a theatrical milieu defined by innovation. Her preparation for each production, her facility for collaboration, and her insistence upon remaining physically and emotionally present in each moment onstage enable her to unearth new possibilities in performance—and to share such revelations with fellow performers and audiences. During *Lucia's Chapters*, Paul Kandel recalled,

> Sharon would watch the show and she would give notes, some bold changes, and the next night we would just put them in. Sometimes they were a right turn, and if I turned right, Ruth went right to the right. It was never a question.... You take that little trip and you don't know where it's going to go.... That is essential to her. It's an extraordinary part of what makes her such a dynamic performer.

As well as uncovering unexpected moments in performance, such an inclination for uncertainty can create unanticipated wrinkles. "It also leaves you the possibility that you're going to have a night that's funky," Paul Kandel suggests: "It can happen. You go left, and you hit a wall, and then you get a little bruised and you've got to find your way out. That happens." Maleczech's theater always happens in the present tense and is informed by it. She challenges audiences to confront the terms of this engagement, daring us to risk each instance of live performance along with her.

Maleczech also dared to be funny. Her manipulation of emotional exposure and temporal precision made her adept at comedy as well as pathos. Maleczech deployed humor in service of social commentary, throwing audiences off balance. Surprising them with laughter, she avoided the polemical. Comedy deliberately disturbs the intrigue of Maleczech's emotional vulnerability, preventing sentimentality and self-indulgence from overwhelming both performer and audience. All of Maleczech's performances incorporate humor and, with the exception of *Imagination Dead Imagine*, all of the works she has directed do so as well. Her aptitude for comedy links her firmly to Molière. As the young performers around her sharpened their choreography and the score of background noise in rehearsal for *Imagining the Imaginary Invalid*, Maleczech sat in a chair center stage trying to decide which iteration of "ding-a-ling-a-fucking-ding," "bring-a-bring," or string of "dings," "lings," and obscenities was funniest for summoning Toinette's presence. Maleczech's emphasis on texture and tone in performance is apparent in her dedication to the basic mechanics of comic timing.

Diligence of this kind can also be observed in her work as a manager of the company. For Maleczech the dual facets of producing and artistic work are two sides of the same coin. "I'm sure there's a great deal of overlapping," says Breuer. Karen Kandel agrees that Maleczech's performance and producing work intersect. "I don't think they're different. I think all of those things are happening all the time. She's wearing all those hats, and it's there all the time when she's working." Mehrten, who worked with Maleczech in the Mabou Mines offices in the mid-1980s and 1990s, recalled that

> she was so devoted, and I'm sure she still is, to the idea of Mabou Mines. She had been a legal secretary so she knew how to work in the office, and I did too, and some of the other people didn't. And so it just evolved that we would work in the office. It's like the Soviet system, each according to his needs and to each to his abilities. Wherever your strengths were they tried to utilize those and so Ruth's ability to go to a million readings and really talk about the plumbing or getting the loan or whatever, kind of mundane things, she would do it. Even I would say, "Oh, can we go home now?" I got to really hate meetings

and we had so many. But I never heard her say, "I'm bored, I want to go home." Never. She wanted to fix the problem—she wanted to work. And that's how she approached her theatrical work too. There were these problems that you were trying to solve in the production, and that's what she would work on.

In Breuer's view, however, Maleczech's tenacity in the simultaneity of artistic and producing work was not always an ideal combination. He recalls that rehearsals for *Hajj* were repeatedly interrupted as Maleczech broke to field calls regarding funding for the project. Yet he also notes that Maleczech earned her role as the "elder statesman" of the company as a result of her dedication to managerial concerns. "I don't put in the hours Ruth does just sitting in the office," he said. Where LeCompte and Malina as directors and Stewart as producer were in conventional positions of power in the theater, Maleczech's central role in the organizational structure of Mabou Mines provided her with the license to take an unusual degree of control over her performances. She was a true actor-manager of her own making.

Maleczech's concern for the organizational health of the company is part of her vision of Mabou Mines as an artistic family. She leveraged her prominence in the company to promote equality in the work place, supporting the work of both male and female collaborators and helping to institute and maintain a progressive and enlightened policy on child care. Fogarty recalled a conversation she had with Maleczech about companies and families on the eve of Mabou Mines's fortieth anniversary:

> Ruth said, "How do companies sustain, how do they survive?" And she was talking about the Comédie Française and this other company in Japan that had started out as families, whether they were literally or whether they end up becoming family—how these families operate over time and how that tends to be a recipe for longevity. And they're usually being sidelined. But usually the ones that have considered themselves family or actually have some family involved, they end up surviving. Family is really important to her, whether it's artistic family or personal family. That's key.

Maleczech's dedication to long-term creative partnerships matched her commitment to working with her daughter, her son, and most recently with her granddaughter. Her support for progressive parental polices demonstrated an investment beyond the creative to the family life of her collaborators. For all of these reasons, Maleczech's Mabou Mines is the artistic family Fogarty describes. This obligation prompted Maleczech to put her money, colloquially speaking, where her mouth was. "She saved my butt with a personal loan on *DollHouse*," said Breuer: "We wouldn't have gotten it off the ground without that." Karen Kandel also noted Maleczech's emotional and financial support of fellow artists. "She has been an incredible supporter of whatever I want to do," she said. "I love how she gets excited about young people who are trying to make work. She's generous, offering support. Encouraging. I'll never forget that. She changed my life." Maleczech continued to nurture fellow artists and bring new members into her artistic family through her work with Mabou Mines/Suite. The arrangement for resident artists is unusual among residency programs in New York in providing rehearsal space and financial support as well as mentorship.

Without the funding Maleczech worked to secure, there would be no Mabou Mines, no productions in which to perform, or to direct, especially in a political context that has grown increasingly hostile to arts funding in the United States. Consequently, one of the enduring tropes that emerges in Maleczech's artistic work is a preoccupation with dollars and cents. *Imagining the Imaginary Invalid* is no exception. Molière's play opens with a scene in which Argan itemizes his medical bills and ends by exposing the avarice of Argan's wife. In Maleczech's production, the intercolated material uncovers further links between money and medicine. A performer relates the anecdote about her parents' decision to remarry in order to provide insurance for her father's new set of teeth, explaining that after a dentist removed the crowns from her father's old teeth, her father gave them to her brother. "Gold's worth a lot right now," Galilee says knowingly in response, wondering why her companion does not want to share in this bounty. "He's the eldest," the young woman says of her brother, by way of explanation.

This deceptively casual conversation reveals Maleczech's long attention span for what she sees as an unhealthy association between financial power and masculinity, especially as it relates to family dynamics. Even among the group of women who can be counted among her colleagues in the American avant-garde, Maleczech's point of view in *Hajj, Lear, Through the Leaves,* and finally in *Imagining the Imaginary Invalid* exposes the traditional correlation between patriarchal and financial structures and proposes alternatives with a more balanced distribution of power. Her project to reconfigure the relationship between power and gender extends beyond economics to labor; Maleczech's portrayal of Winnie and Annette and her concern for daily lives in *Belén* champion the significance of quotidian acts that are often women's work. She also suggests that if we are to alter the future, we must first reconsider our interpretation of the past. In *Dead End Kids, Belén,* and *Lucia's Chapters,* her theatricalized historiography disrupts inherited patrilineal narratives. Had she lived to complete her work, *Imagining the Imaginary Invalid* would have been a site of theatrical intersection for Maleczech's many commitments. Such enduring preoccupations both distinguish her work from that of her peers and place her feminist aesthetic innovations within the new paradigm Harding outlines for a fuller understanding of what we mean by American avant-garde performance.

The present study does not aim to undermine contributions of patriarchal figures in the avant-garde but focuses instead on repositioning our understanding to include a much wider field of accomplishments by adding other voices. Such an approach enriches our sense of what happened in the past and how a new avant-garde historiography can sharpen contemporary considerations. Maleczech's work offers us a richer, more expansive, and more encompassing definition of our inherited view of the American avant-garde.

Maleczech liked to remind people that "avant-garde" is a military term for cannon fodder—the soldiers who were first to be shot and killed in battle. "I think that she's a pioneer," says Fogarty, "she embraces the pioneer spirit. She doesn't mind trying new things, whether it means that you'll never work again or never be funded again, it doesn't matter to her. She will follow her artistic and intellectual instincts wherever they lead."

Maleczech presented women onstage who are as unusual and original as she was in life. Maleczech's women are surprising in their behavior, in the way they speak and move, in what they reveal to the audience and what they keep to themselves, in the questions they raise, and in their dislocations of traditionally represented gender and authority. In her work, identity, like power, can be fluid, malleable, changeable, even interchangeable. Her theater shows us what happens onstage when power relations are in flux and challenges audiences to consider what would happen under similar circumstances in daily life. Maleczech wants her audiences and collaborators to meet the women she presents to us halfway; she is above all audacious, daring to sometimes disagree with what anyone else thinks about them in the rehearsal room or on the stage. Maleczech's greatest innovation, finally, is her manipulation of avant-garde theatrical strategies to animate queer and feminist theoretical ideas, to bring them to life on the stage. Bravely, she placed trust for the future of her project in transitory moments of our collective existence:

> Just to think that a kid from the desert in Arizona could be part of this explosion of American art, could be the beneficiary of the generosity of other artists, could continue to pursue the elusive, ephemeral art of live performance—is a miracle of sorts. This work provides no product. There is nothing to sell or own. It is the most transient fleeting experience, and its marks are left only on the grooves of the mind. That is the legacy.[20]

Appendix: The Co-Artistic Directors

JoAnne Akalaitis

A founder of Mabou Mines, JoAnne Akalaitis was the first co-artistic director to shift from performing to directing. After performing in productions including Lee Breuer's *The Red Horse Animation* (1970), Samuel Beckett's *Play* and *Come and Go* (1971), and Breuer's *B. Beaver Animation* (1972), Akalaitis made her directing debut with Beckett's *Cascando* in 1976, which she followed up with *Dressed Like an Egg* (1977), based on the writings of Colette, which received an OBIE Award for Distinguished Production. She continued to perform with Mabou Mines in productions such as Breuer's *The Shaggy Dog Animation* (1978), but had made a permanent move to directing by the 1980s, when she directed *Dead End Kids* (1980) and *Through the Leaves* (1984) for the company. In the early 1990s, Akalaitis resigned from Mabou Mines and spent a brief and tumultuous tenure as Artistic Director of the Public Theater after being named by Joseph Papp as his successor. Maleczech and Akalaitis continued to collaborate following the latter's departure from the company on productions including Jean Genet's *The Screens* at the Guthrie Theater (1989) and his *Prisoner of Love* at New York Theatre Workshop (1995). Akalaitis has had a sustained career as an independent director working at such high profile theaters as the American Repertory Theater (ART), Lincoln Center, the New York City Opera, the Goodman Theatre, the Mark Taper Forum, the Court Theatre, and the Guthrie Theater. In addition to teaching at Juilliard, Akalaitis was a Professor of Theater at Bard College from 1998 to 2012, where she holds the Wallace Benjamin Flint and L. May Hawver Flint Professor Emerita of Drama. Among other prestigious awards, Akalaitis has received an OBIE for Outstanding Achievement and a Guggenheim Fellowship. Akalaitis's work has a reputation for controversy, although little in recent years has generated the storm of her 1984 production of *Endgame* set in a subway car, to which Beckett objected (via a surrogate) because he felt it circumvented his stage directions. The ART production was eventually allowed to go forward, with the caveat that the program must contain a copy of the first page of the play where Beckett's stage directions appear, along with statements by the playwright, Robert Brustein (the ART artistic director at the time), and Barney Rosset (president of Grove Press at the time). Critics have characterized Akalaitis's work as feminist, a label the director eschews. Akalaitis acknowledges the influence of Mabou Mines on her work with actors, in which she asks for the sort of full participation that she herself helped to establish in her early work with the company. Following Maleczech's death, Akalaitis agreed to assist the company by serving as a mentor in the resident artist program, Mabou Mines/Suite.

Julie Archer

Archer served as a co-artistic director of Mabou Mines from 2005 to 2013, although she began working with the company in the late 1970s. Archer has designed a vast number of productions with the company, starting with the OBIE-Award-winning *Vanishing Pictures* in 1980, which she codesigned with Maleczech (also the director). Following this, Archer designed a combination of sets, lights, puppets, and projections for productions including *Wrong Guys* (1981), *Sister Suzie Cinema* (1980), *Hajj* (1983), *Peter and Wendy* (1996), *Belén* (1999), *Ecco Porco* (2002), *Red Beads* (2005), *Lucia's Chapters of Coming Forth by Day* (2007), *Song for New York* (2007), and *Summa Dramatica* (2009). She also presented a 2012 work-in-progress, *we would find landscapes*, based on the landscapes of cornfields surrounding Minneapolis that she remembers from her childhood and conceived in collaboration with longtime Mabou Mines collaborator Liza Lorwin. Archer has received numerous grants and awards for her designs, such as OBIEs for *Peter and Wendy* and *An Epidog*, an American Theatre Wing

Award for her puppets in *An Epidog* (1996) and *Summa Dramatica*, and Best Design in the 1st Irish Festival for *Lucia's Chapters*. Away from Mabou Mines, she collaborated with Breuer on *The Gospel at Colonus* (1985) and on *the CIVIL warS* with Robert Wilson (1984), among other works.

Lee Breuer

Breuer is the only co-artistic director aside from Maleczech who has remained with the company since its founding, and his work has garnered the most critical attention. This is likely due to the visibility, quantity, and quality of his contributions—his work as a writer and director is prominently featured, especially in a theatrical context where substantial contributions of the kind Mabou Mines expects from performers is anomalous. Since 1970, Breuer has written nearly fifteen plays for the company and directed more than twenty productions, not including extensive revivals and tours. His most well-known works as a writer are his animations, the first of which, *The Red Horse Animation* (1970), was followed by many others including *B. Beaver* (1972), *Shaggy Dog* (1978), *Sister Suzie Cinema* (1980), *An Epidog* (1996), *Ecco Porco* (2002), *Summa Dramatica* (2009), and *Porco Morto* (2009). The animations have now been collected into the epic *La Divina Caricatura*, part of which was produced in 2013 at La MaMa; performances were dedicated to Maleczech, who had been slated to appear. Widely known directing works for the company include Samuel Beckett's *Play* (1971), *Come and Go* (1971), and *The Lost Ones* featuring David Warrilow (1975); Mabou Mines's *Lear* (1990); *Peter and Wendy* (1996); and *DollHouse*, an adaptation of Henrik Ibsen's play (2003). High profile directing projects outside of Mabou Mines include *The Gospel at Colonus* (an adaptation of Sophocles, 1985), and a production of Tennessee Williams's *A Streetcar Named Desire* at the Comédie Française (2011). Breuer's work is characterized by his interest in popular culture and interculturalism, his incorporation of live music in production, and his surprising inversions of classic texts.

Sharon Fogarty

Sharon Fogarty became a co-artistic director of Mabou Mines in 1999 after working with the company for more than ten years on projects such as *Cold Harbor* (1983) and *Lear* (1990), in which she performed such odd jobs as holding down Gloucester as her eyes were gouged out and picking up the dogs for each performance. Upon returning to New York from Ireland, where she pursued graduate work, Fogarty took a job managing the Mabou Mines office. In 1996, she became a producer for the company, taking on projects such as *Belén: A Book of Hours* (1999) and *Song For New York* (2007), directed by Maleczech, and Mabou Mines's *DollHouse* (2003) and *Red Beads* (2005), directed by Breuer. Meanwhile, she spent several years as the artistic director of Daedelus Theatre Company, specializing in Irish plays. Fogarty's first project as a Mabou Mines co-artistic director was to write and direct *Cara Lucia*, later reimagined as *Lucia's Chapters of Coming Forth by Day*, featuring Maleczech and based on the life of Lucia Joyce. *Cara Lucia* premiered at HERE Arts Center in New York in 2003, and the revised version, *Lucia's Chapters*, has been produced a number of times since, including as part of New York's 1st Irish Festival at PS 122 in 2011 and on tour in Finland in 2013. As of this writing, it is slated to be presented at the Brighton Festival in the UK in 2015 with Maria Tucci as a replacement for Maleczech. In 2010, Fogarty directed *FINN*, also rooted in Irish culture and based on the stories of the Irish folk hero Finn McCool. *FINN* premiered at New York University's Skirball Center, where the company had produced *Red Beads*. As of this writing, Fogarty is developing Goethe's *Faust 2.0*, slated to premiere in Mabou Mines's newly renovated theater in 2016. Fogarty is on the faculty at Barnard College and has also taught at New York University and elsewhere in the US and abroad.

Philip Glass

Glass, who was married to Akalaitis from 1965 to 1980, was a cofounder of the company and composed and sometimes performed music for Mabou Mines in the 1970s and into the 1980s, mainly on projects directed by Breuer and Akalaitis, such as *Red Horse* (1970), *Music for Voices* (1972), *The Saint and the Football Player* (1973), *The Lost Ones* (1975), *Cascando* (1976), *Dressed Like an Egg* (1977), *8Dog* (1979), *Mercier and Camier* (1979), and *Dead End Kids* (1980). Before cofounding Mabou Mines, he founded the Philip Glass Ensemble. Per Maleczech's request before her death, the group performed Part 10 of *Music in Twelve Parts* at her memorial. Glass has composed a number of important works for theater and opera outside of Mabou Mines, including *Einstein on the Beach* (1976), directed by Robert Wilson, and *Satyagraha*, which premiered at New York's Metropolitan Opera in 1980 and was remounted there in 2007–2008, and he has collaborated with choreographers such as Twyla Tharp, filmmakers such as Woody Allen, and musicians as diverse as Yo-Yo Ma and Paul Simon. He composed *Overture for 2012*, which was part of a commemoration of the War of 1812 and premiered simultaneously in his hometown of Baltimore and in Toronto. His music has been profoundly influential across the fields of art and academia. Although critics have referred to his work as minimalist, he has regularly described it as "music with repetitive structures."

Karen Kandel

Karen Kandel first collaborated with Mabou Mines on *Lear* (1990). She played Edna (a female version of Shakespeare's Edmund) in the cross-gender production and won an OBIE for her role. Kandel played the lead in the company's celebrated and often-revived *Peter and Wendy* (1997), for which she garnered an OBIE, an Edinburgh Fringe Festival Golden Herald Angel Award, a Helen Hayes Nomination, a Drama League Citation, a San Diego Craig Noel Award, a Dramalogue, and a Connecticut Critics Circle award. Other Mabou Mines performances include roles in Brecht's *In the Jungle of Cities* (1991) and Breuer's *Ecco Porco* (2001) and *La Divina Caricatura* (2013). Maleczech commissioned Kandel to write the "Queens Song" for *Song For New York* (2007). She became a co-artistic director in 2015. Outside of Mabou Mines, Kandel has worked with Akalaitis in productions including Racine's *Phèdre* at Bard Summerscape (2003); *Eh Joe/Beckett Shorts* at New York Theatre Workshop, a production that also featured Mikhail Baryshnikov, Bill Camp, and Mabou Mines Associate Artist David Neumann (2007); and Euripides's *The Bacchae* at Shakespeare in the Park, which featured music by Philip Glass (2009). She collaborated with Anne Bogart on productions including a staged version of Gertrude Stein's *The Making of Americans* at Lenox Arts Center (1985) and Lillian Hellman's *The Women* at Hartford Stage (1994). Other notable productions include Julia Cho's *BFE*, directed by Gordon Edelstein at Playwrights Horizons (2005). Kandel has also worked with Elizabeth Swados, Tina Landau, Anna Deavere Smith, Ong Keng Sen, and Peter Sellars. She is most widely known for her virtuostic vocal performance, but she is also a visual artist and writer. She created an original work with miniature puppets, *A Woman of a Certain Age*, for the Toy Theater Festival at HERE Arts Center (2000) and the installation/performance piece *Portraits: Night and Day* for Theater for the New City (2005).

Terry O'Reilly

After seeing Mabou Mines perform in Memphis in 1971, Terry O'Reilly became fascinated with the company. He joined them in New York in 1973, becoming a co-artistic director in 1974. O'Reilly has been a performer and puppeteer on projects including *Shaggy Dog* (1978), *Dead End Kids* (1980), *Wrong Guys* (1981), *Pretty Boy* (1984), *In the Jungle of Cities* (1991), and *Red Beads* (2005). He is also a writer and a director; his plays include *The Bribe*, an adaptation of several radio plays directed by Maleczech in 1990, and *Animal Magnetism (A Live Cartoon in Animal Drag)*, which Breuer directed at St. Ann's Warehouse in 2000. O'Reilly also worked with the Ming Ri Institute for Arts Education and the Guangxi Puppet Art Troupe of China to develop a new puppet play for Mabou Mines entitled *Brer' Rabbit in the Land of the Monkey King* (2010), which draws on folklore from Asia, Africa, and the American South. O'Reilly's training is in dance and his work is particularly engaged with internationalism, a strain of interest he shares with Breuer and, to some extent, Maleczech. Away from Mabou Mines, he has collaborated regularly with the Creation Company and on plays by Jim Neu, and he has taught extensively at colleges across the country.

Fred Neumann

Fred Neumann began working with Breuer and Maleczech in the 1960s in Paris, including a staging of Bertolt Brecht's *Mother Courage* in which Maleczech played Kattrin. He began his formal relationship with Mabou Mines in 1971, becoming a noted interpreter of Beckett's texts. Neumann met Beckett in 1976 and the two remained in communication about Neumann's staging of the writer's works for the remainder of Beckett's lifetime. These stagings included *Mercier and Camier* (1979), which Neumann performed in and also directed; *Company* (1983), which Neumann codirected with his late wife and Mabou Mines associate artist Honora Fergusson; and *Worstward Ho* (1986), which was given to Neumann by the noted Beckett scholar Ruby Cohn with Beckett's approval. Neumann also performed in an extensive number of Breuer's animations, most famously in *B. Beaver* (1972), but also in *Shaggy Dog* (1978), *The Warrior Ant* (1988), and *Ecco Porco* (2002). In 1984, he and Maleczech were awarded OBIEs for their performances in Franz Xaver Kroetz's *Through the Leaves*, which played at the Public under Akalaitis's direction. Neumann has also performed widely outside of Mabou Mines; those projects include Robert Wilson's *the CIVIL warS* (1984) and José Quintero's 1985 Tony-award-winning production of *The Ice Man Cometh*. Neumann remained an artistic director of the company until his death in 2012.

Bill Raymond

Bill Raymond joined Mabou Mines in 1971, though he had met the cofounders in California in the 1960s. He performed in productions including *Dressed Like an Egg* (1977), *Shaggy Dog* (1978), *Wrong Guys* (1981), *Cold Harbor* (1983), *The Lost Ones* (1975), *Cascando* (1976), and *Mercier and Camier* (1979). At Mabou Mines Raymond also collaborated with his wife, the writer and visual artist Linda Hartinian, who worked closely with Maleczech on *Imagination Dead Imagine*, for which she helped create the hologram, and *Hajj*, for which she created the mask of Maleczech's father's face. Raymond played Goneril in Mabou Mines's *Lear* and left the company in 1990 following that production, subsequently developing an extensive resume in theater, film, and television on projects ranging from the popular HBO series *The Wire* to a 2008 Broadway revival of *Gypsy*. He remained close with Maleczech, however, and spoke about their friendship and collaboration at the memorial service organized by her family.

David Warrilow

Cofounder David Warrilow, the only non-American artistic director of Mabou Mines, was born in Staffordshire and began working with his cofounders in Paris, where they first tried their hand at Beckett. He performed in a number of early productions including *Red Horse* (1970), *Play* (1971), and *B. Beaver* (1972). Warrilow was widely acclaimed for his performances of Beckett's texts in both English and French, including his one-man staging of *The Lost Ones* (1975), on which he collaborated with Breuer, and *Mercier and Camier* (1979), on which he collaborated with Neumann. Warrilow won rare approval from Beckett for his performances of the writer's work, and Beckett wrote *Piece of Monologue* for him, which the actor premiered in New York in 1979. Warrilow left Mabou Mines in the late 1970s and worked regularly with the well-known American director of Beckett, Alan Schneider, on productions including *Ohio Impromptu* (1979), *Catastrophe* (1983), and *Born in What Where* (1983). He also collaborated with Maleczech on a 1987 production of Khlebnikov's *Zangezi*, directed by Peter Sellars, in one of the few projects outside of Mabou Mines that Maleczech elected to take on. Warrilow performed with Billie Whitelaw in *All That Fall* in 1989 and was awarded OBIEs for his Mabou Mines work in *Dressed Like an Egg* (1977), *Southern Exposure* (1979), and his revival of *The Lost Ones*. He died of AIDS in 1995 at the age of sixty, performing regularly even during illness in the last year of his life.

Additional co-artistic directors and artistic associates

The other former, nonfounding co-artistic directors of the company are Ellen McElduff, L.B. Dallas, B-St. John Schofield, and Dawn Gray. As of this writing, associate artists are Clove Galilee (daughter of Breuer and Maleczech and founder of her own company, Trick Saddle), Maude Mitchell (Breuer's partner), and David Neumann (son of Fred Neumann and Fergusson and founder of his own company, advanced beginner group).

Notes

Introduction

1   James Harding, *Cutting Performances: Collage Events, Feminist Artists, and the American Avant-Garde* (Ann Arbor: University of Michigan Press, 2012), 16.

2   "Mission + History," La MaMa website, accessed June 2, 2015, http://lamama.org/about/mission-history/.

3   "Poor Theater," The Wooster Group company website, accessed June 5, 2015, http://thewoostergroup.org/twg/twg.php?poor-theater.

4   For more on Bogart's work, see Scott T. Cummings, *Remaking American Theater: Charles Mee, Anne Bogart and the SITI* (New York: Cambridge University Press, 2006).

5   Unless otherwise noted, all quotations of Maleczech in this chapter are taken from interviews conducted by the author between March 2009 and March 2012.

6   Iris Smith Fischer, *Mabou Mines: Making Avant-Garde Theater in the 1970s* (Ann Arbor: The University of Michigan Press, 2011).

7   Mel Gussow, "Mabou Mines Inhabits Beckett Landscapes on Jane St.," *New York Times*, Thursday, October 23, 1975, Family/Style section, 46.

8   Theodore Shank, *Beyond the Boundaries* (Ann Arbor: University of Michigan Press, 2002), 297.

9   All quotations of Sharon Fogarty in this chapter are taken from interviews conducted by the author, October 2011.

10 All quotations of Breuer in this chapter are taken from interviews conducted by the author in July 2011 and May 2012.

11 Maleczech in conversation with Nick Westrate, "Process and Performance," New York Theatre Workshop, April 23, 2012.

12 Smith Fischer, *Mabou Mines*, 33. For a thorough discussion of the prehistory of Mabou Mines, see Iris Smith Fischer's chapters "Coming Together: San Francisco, Paris, New York" and "Play, Come and Go, The Lost Ones: Staging Beckett, 1965–1975," 28–59.

13 As described on the Mabou Mines website, *The Red Horse Animation* company "is about the process of performing—the building and sustaining of an image. The medium is theater and so the image is one that materializes only in performance. Three performers play parts. These parts combine to form and animate the red horse. The red horse, once animated, attempts to create itself. The piece is composed of these processes moving along simultaneously," "The Red Horse Animation," Mabou Mines company website, accessed June 8, 2015, http://maboumines.org/productions/red-horse-animation.

14 Quotation taken from a recording of an unpublished interview with Maleczech by Iris Smith Fischer, October 2001.

15 Ibid.

16 Smith Fischer makes this suggestion to Maleczech in the October 2001 unpublished interview.

17 Ruby Cohn, "The Becketts of Mabou Mines," in *Samuel Beckett and the Arts*, ed. Lois Oppenheim (New York: Garland Publishing, Inc., 1999), 219.

18 Ibid., 220.

19 For a thorough account of Mabou Mines's early experiments with Beckett, see Smith Fischer's chapters "Coming Together," in *Mabou Mines*, 28–59 and 99–119.

20 Liza Lorwin was the producer for *Peter and Wendy* (1996), *Song for New York* (2007), and the workshop production *we would find landscapes* (2012).

21 Harding, *Cutting Performances*, 19.

Chapter 1

1 All quotations of Douglas Stein in this chapter are taken from email correspondence with the author March–May 2012.

2 Maddy Rooney in *All That Fall* marks an earlier expansive female role for radio. Beckett would pursue such roles for women in his late plays for the stage. See Linda Ben Zvi, ed., *Women in Beckett* (Urbana: University of Illinois Press, 1990).

3 All quotations of JoAnne Akalaitis in this chapter are taken from an interview conducted by the author in December 2011.

4 Enoch Brater, *Why Beckett* (London: Thames and Hudson, 1989), 102.

5 Ben Zvi, *Women in Beckett*, xiii.

6   Downey writes that the "postwar German theatre had been explicitly
    designed as a sanctuary, a place devoted to the classics, to Goethe and
    Schiller, to Shakespeare, Shaw and Sophocles, to the 'poetic realism'
    of Williams and Miller, the enameled fancies of Giradoux and Fry.
    If critical attitudes to contemporary society were expressed at all, it
    was allegorically, through the neo-Expressionism of writers like the
    Swiss authors Frisch and Dürrenmatt. But by the mid-Sixties, a post-
    war generation full of nothing but contempt for *Kultur* and its smug
    consumers was ready to take on contemporary reality again. In Franz
    Xaver Kroetz they found a dramatist eager not only to portray reality,
    but rub his audience's nose in it." "Introduction," in Franz Xaver Kroetz,
    Through the Leaves and Other Plays, trans. RogerDowney (New York:
    Theatre Communications Group, Inc., 1983), ix.

7   Iris Smith Fischer, "Happy Days," review of Beckett's *Happy Days* by
    Mabou Mines, ToRoNaDa Studio, New York, 1999, in "Women, Nations,
    Households, and History" special issue, *Theatre Journal* 51, no. 1 (March
    1999): 97.

8   Both Maleczech and Breuer acknowledge that many of the ideas they
    took from Brecht find their origin in one of Brecht's influences, Erwin
    Piscator. For more on Malina's training with Piscator, see Judith Malina,
    The Piscator Notebook (New York: Routledge, 2012).

9   As quoted in "Ruth Maleczech," DVD, Mabou Mines Archive, Fales
    Library & Special Collections, New York University, Series IX, Box:
    Media.

10 Ibid.

11 All quotations of Paul Kandel in this chapter are taken from an interview
    conducted by the author in August 2012.

12 Maleczech in conversation with Nick Westrate, "Process and
    Performance," New York Theatre Workshop, April 23, 2012.

13 All quotations of Galilee in this chapter are taken from an interview
    conducted by the author in August 2012.

14 Maleczech in conversation at "Process and Performance."

15 As quoted in *Ruth Maleczech*, DVD.

16 Michael Greif served as artistic director of La Jolla Playhouse from 1995
    to 1999.

17 Michael Feingold, "Judith Malina and the Award-Season Rush (Part II),"
    Thinking About Theater, TheaterMania (website), accessed June 5, 2015,

http://www.theatermania.com/new-york-city-theater/news/judith-malina-and-the-award-season-rush-part-ii_73099.html.

18 Michael Greif, as quoted in Jan Breslauer, "Beckett's Her Hole Card," *Los Angeles Times*, August 4, 1996.

19 Maleczech's production notebook for *Happy Days* includes dramaturgical research and her notes from Woodruff. It is stored in the Mabou Mines office archive.

20 Beckett's production notebook from *Happy Days* is available in an edition edited by James Knowlson: Samuel Beckett, *Happy Days: Production Notebook*, ed. James Knowlson (London: Faber and Faber, 1985).

21 S.E. Gontarski, *Beckett's Happy Days: A Manuscript Study* (Columbus: Publications Committee, Ohio State University Libraries, 1977), 43.

22 Billie Whitelaw, as quoted in Linda Ben Zvi, "Interviews: Billie Whitelaw," in *Women in Beckett*, 6.

23 As quoted in Breslauer, "Beckett's Her Hole Card."

24 Julio Martinez, "Happy Days," *Daily Variety*, August 13, 1996.

25 Laurie Winer, "Love and Marriage, According to Beckett," *Los Angeles Times*, August 13, 1996.

26 Wilborn Hampton, "When Everything's Normal, and All of It Is Absurd," *New York Times*, March 24, 1998, 13.

27 Smith, "*Happy Days*," 86.

28 As quoted in Brater, *Why Beckett*, 102.

29 Smith, "*Happy Days*," 87.

30 Billie Whitelaw as quoted in Ben Zvi, "Interviews: Billie Whitelaw," in *Women in Beckett*, 7–8.

31 This and subsequent notes from Woodruff are from Maleczech's production binder.

32 JoAnne Akalaitis to Margot Lewitin, March 6, 1985, Mabou Mines Archive, Fales Library and Special Collections, New York University, Series IIIA, Box 10, Folder 424.

33 Spence Halperin to Margot Lewitin, December 19, 1984, Mabou Mines Archives, Fales Library and Special Collections, New York University, Series IIIA, Box 10, Folder 424.

34 Undated correspondence, Franz Xaver Kroetz to JoAnne Akalaitis, Mabou Mines Archive, Fales Library and Special Collections, Series IIIA, Box 10, Folder 424.

35   Robert McNamara, "Franz Xaver Kroetz: A New Voice from Europe," *Washington Review*, August/September 1985, Mabou Mines Archive, Fales Library and Special Collections, New York University, Series IIIA, Box 10, Folder 453.

36   I refer to the characters Maleczech and Neumann played as "Annette" and "Victor" in this chapter.

37   Franz Xaver Kroetz, *Through the Leaves* in *Through the Leaves and Other Plays*, trans. Roger Downey (New York: Theatre Communications Group, Inc., 1983), 4.

38   Ibid.

39   Michael Feingold, "Lover's Meatings," *Village Voice*, April 3, 1984.

40   *Through the Leaves* is the fourth and final treatment of the same material by Kroetz. The first version, *Man's Work*, "ends with an almost expressionistically extreme scene of double murder/suicide." Kroetz, *Through the Leaves*, 3.

41   Alisa Solomon, "Parallel Fantasies," *Village Voice*, October 2, 1984.

42   Feingold, "Lover's Meatings."

43   Frank Rich, "Through the Leaves," *New York Times*, April 6, 1984.

44   D.J.R. Bruckner, "A Revival of 'Leaves,' Grimmer Than Ever," *New York Times*, September 18, 1990.

45   Kroetz, *Through the Leaves*, 12–13.

46   Interview conducted by the author in July 2011.

47   Feingold, "Lover's Meatings."

48   Kroetz, *Through the Leaves*, 14–15.

49   McNamara, "Franz Xaver Kroetz: A New Voice from Europe."

50   Kroetz, *Through the Leaves*, 17–18 and 29–30.

51   Deborah Saivetz, *An Event in Space* (Hanover: Smith and Krauss, 2000), 36.

52   Solomon, "Parallel Fantasies."

53   Maleczech appeared in small roles in a limited number of commercial films such as *The Crucible*, directed by Rebecca Miller (1996), and *Sleepers* (2008) as well as television shows including *Law & Order* and *ER*, but never in high-profile roles such as Malina's in *The Adams Family* film (1991) or *The Sopranos* television series.

54   As quoted in Saivetz, *An Event in Space.*

55   Maleczech in conversation at "Process and Performance."

Chapter 2

1   Peter Weiss, "Notes on the Contemporary Theater," in *Essays on German Theater*, trans. Joel Agee (New York: Continuum, 1985), 294.

2   Roger Bechtel, *Past Performance: American Theatre and the Historical Imagination* (Lewisberg: Bucknell University Press, 2007), 16.

3   Freddie Rokem, *Performing History: Theatrical Representations of the Past in Contemporary Theatre* (Iowa City: University of Iowa Press, 2000), xi.

4   Felipe was born in Argentina, though she lives and works primarily in Mexico.

5   All quotations of Sharon Fogarty in this chapter are taken from interviews conducted by the author in October and November 2011.

6   All quotations of JoAnne Akalaitis in this chapter are from an interview conducted by the author on December 18, 2011.

7   All quotations of Ruth Maleczech in this chapter are from interviews conducted by the author between July and September 2011.

8   The Renaissance physician Paracelsus is credited with founding toxicology and studied alchemy and the occult, among other fields. General Leslie Richard Groves oversaw the secretive American government initiative to develop atomic weapons during the Second World War, known as the Manhattan Project.

9   All quotations of Greg Mehrten in this chapter are from an interview conducted by the author in July 2011.

10 Elinor Fuchs, "Staging the Obscene Body," *TDR* 33, no. 1 (1989): 36.

11 This is discussed in more detail in Chapter 1.

12 Fuchs, "Staging the Obscene Body," 36.

13 *Dead End Kids*, directed by JoAnne Akalaitis (New York: Cinema Guild, 1986), VHS.

14 Ibid.

15 Ibid.

16 Ibid.

17 *Belén: A Book of Hours* (Mabou Mines, 1999), DVD. Copy provided to the author by Mabou Mines.

18 All quotations of Julie Archer in this chapter are from an interview conducted by the author in November 2011.

19 This is discussed in more detail in the Introduction.

20 Archer remembers that work on *Wrong Guys* began before work on *Vanishing Pictures*, though the former opened in 1981 and the latter in 1980.

21 All quotations of Catherine Sasanov in this chapter are from email correspondence between Sasanov and the author, November and December 2011.

22 *Song For New York* featured poems by Migdalia Cruz, Maggie Dubris, Patricia Spears Jones, Karen Kandel, and Imelda O'Reilly.

23 Program, *Belén: A Book of Hours*, presented at Teatro de La Capilla in Mexico City in 2000, Mabou Mines office archives.

24 *Belén: A Book of Hours*, DVD.

25 Alisa Solomon, "Prison Prayers," *Village Voice*, May 25, 1999.

26 Ibid.

27 *Belén: A Book of Hours*, DVD.

28 Roslyn Costantino, "Embodied Memory in *Las Horas de Belén: A Book of Hours*," *Theatre Journal* 53, 4 (December 2001): 608.

29 *Cold Harbor* premiered in 1983 at the Public Theater in New York.

30 All quotations of Paul Kandel in this chapter are from an interview conducted by the author in August 2012.

31 For differing accounts of Lucia Joyce's relationship with Beckett, see James Knowlson, *Damned to Fame: The Life of Samuel Beckett* (New York: Grove Press, 1996), 106, 109–11, 120, 134, 544; and Carol Loeb Shloss, *Lucia Joyce: To Dance in the Wake* (New York: Farrar, Strauss and Giroux, 2003), 6, 16, 176, 187–96, 204, 205, 215–16, 220, 225, 308, 335, 342, 345, 380.

32 Shloss, a Stanford University scholar, was embroiled in litigation with the Joyce Estate, which sought to prevent online publication of *To Dance in the Wake*. The suit was settled in Shloss's favor, as was a subsequent suit in which she sought restitution from the Estate for $240,000 in attorney's fees.

33 Sharon Fogarty, *Lucia's Chapters of Coming Forth by Day*, 2. Mabou Mines office archives.

34 Ibid.

35 Costantino, "Embodied Memory in *Las Horas de Belén: A Book of Hours*," 608.

36 *Belén: A Book of Hours*, DVD.

37 Catherine Sasanov, *Belén: A Book of Hours*, production program supplement by Mabou Mines, Mabou Mines office archives.

Chapter 3

1 Alisa Solomon, *Re-dressing the Canon: Essays on Theatre and Gender*
   (Ann Arbor: University of Michigan Press, 2002), 137. Solomon also
   argues that, likewise, the choice to cast black actors in the roles of
   Gloucester and Edna/Edgar challenges *Lear*'s link to whiteness.

2 Unless otherwise noted, all quotations of Ruth Maleczech in this chapter
   are taken from interviews conducted by the author between July and
   September 2011.

3 All quotations of Julie Archer in this chapter are taken from an interview
   conducted by the author in November 2011.

4 Unless otherwise noted, all quotations of Lee Breuer in this chapter are
   taken from an interview by the author conducted in July 2011.

5 Iris Smith Fischer, "Mabou Mines's 'Lear': A Narrative of Collective
   Authorship," *Theatre Journal* 45, no. 3 (1993): 279–302.

6 The NEA is the National Endowment for the Arts. NYSCA is an
   abbreviation for the New York State Council for the Arts.

7 See Stephen Bottoms's extensive discussion of this subject in his book
   Playing Underground (Ann Arbor: University of Michigan Press,
   2004).

8 Lee Breuer as quoted in Gabrielle Cody and Lee Breuer, "Lee Breuer
   on Interculturalism," special issue, *Performing Arts Journal: The
   Interculturalism Issue* 11/12, no. 3/1 (1989): 62–63.

9 Although elements such as Thornton Wilder's use of the stage manager
   distinguish *Our Town* stylistically from realism, Maleczech suggests that
   the acting approach of the performer in *Our Town* has more in common
   with what is required for realism than with what is asked of the Beckett
   performer, for example.

10 Konstantin Stanislavski described Chekhov (1891–1955), the nephew of
   Anton Chekhov, as his most outstanding student. Chekhov worked with
   Stanislavski at the Moscow Art Theatre and subsequently developed his
   own psychophysical acting method.

11 *Cry, Trojans!* was originally part of a coproduction with the Royal
   Shakespeare Company and codirected by Mark Ravenhill. The RSC
   commissioned the production for the World Shakespeare Festival held in
   conjunction with the 2012 Olympic games.

12 Although in interviews Breuer dismissed the notion that Maleczech had imitated O'Sullivan's performance, at a 2014 event honoring Maleczech's contribution to the theater he suggested that, to the detriment of the production, she did indeed base her approach on O'Sullivan's. "Ruth Maleczech: Art & Impact," presented at the Martin E. Segal Theatre Center, CUNY, New York, NY, April 7, 2014.

13 Ruth Maleczech in *Lear '87 Archive*, disk 1, hour 2, directed by Jill Godmillow (Laboratory for Icon & Idiom, Inc., 2001), DVD.

14 Deborah Saivetz, *An Event in Space: JoAnne Akalaitis in Rehearsal* (Hanover: Smith and Kraus, 2000), 63.

15 Elin Diamond, "Review," *Theatre Journal* 42, no. 4 (December 1990): 484.

16 Smith Fischer, "Mabou Mines's 'Lear': A Narrative of Collective Authorship," 285. The only other analogy Smith Fischer cites for Breuer's interest in telling a story about a struggle for power is that of dogs, because, according to Breuer, "'in a sense it's a play about the dog-eat-dog of it all.'" However, at a 2014 event honoring Maleczech's contribution to the theater, he suggested another possible obstacle between the performer and her role: age. Breuer noted that, in retrospect, the middle-aged Maleczech may have been too young to play the part effectively. Maleczech herself suggested in conversation with the author that she would welcome the opportunity to revisit the role as an older performer, suggesting a retrospective reconsideration on her part as well. "Ruth Maleczech: Art & Impact."

17 The opportunities Maleczech's production created for female performers garnered an OBIE Award for Karen Kandel's performance of Edna, who is the Mabou Mines's *Lear* version of Edgar.

18 Richard Schechner, "Race Free, Gender Free, Body-Type Free, Age Free Casting," *TDR* 33, no. 1 (Spring 1989): 9.

19 See Chapter 1 for an account of her strategies for engaging the audience.

20 Solomon, *Re-dressing the Canon: Essays on Theatre and Gender*, 139.

21 In *Unmaking Mimesis*, Diamond suggests that Brecht's concept of gestus—an action on the part of the character that reveals a crucial aspect about social and political context—could be adapted as a valuable technique for feminist performance. Elin Diamond, *Unmaking Mimesis: Essays on Feminism and Theater* (New York: Routledge, 1997).

22 Breuer, "Lee Breuer on Interculturalism," 62.

23 All quotations of Greg Mehrten in this chapter are taken from an interview conducted by the author in July 2011.

24 Diamond, "Review," 483.

25 François Delsarte (1811–1871) suggests physical poses designed to stimulate emotion in the performer in his "System of Expression."

26 Lee Breuer in *Lear Archive '87*, disk 3, hour 5.

27 For further discussion of Breuer's animations see Chapter 4.

28 Diamond, "Review," 483.

29 William Shakespeare, *King Lear*, ed. R.A. Foakes (London: Arden Shakespeare, 2001), 1.4.288-91.

30 Lee Breuer in *Lear Archive '87*, disk 2, hour 3.

31 Keith Franklin Fowler, *A History of the San Francisco Actor's Workshop* (DFA diss., Yale University, 1969), 512.

32 Diamond, "Review," 483.

33 Ruth Maleczech in *Lear '87 Archive*, disk 1, hour 1.

34 Ibid.

35 In Iris Smith Fischer's thorough account of ReCherChez, she quotes Maleczech as tracing the name of the program to the "'colloquial French,'" meaning "'a bit old-fashioned.'" The two descriptions by Maleczech are not, of course, mutually exclusive. For Smith Fischer's discussion of ReCherChez and *Vanishing Pictures*, see *Mabou Mines: Making Avant-Garde Theater in the 1970s* (Ann Arbor: The University of Michigan Press, 2011), 163–99.

36 Archer recalls that discussions about *Wrong Guys* (1981), which Maleczech also directed, were also underway when Maleczech approached her about designing *Vanishing Pictures*. About the pair's shared OBIE award, she suggests that the "committee wanted to acknowledge the obvious close collaborative nature of the process, but in doing so unfortunately excluded the third, equally essential collaborator, Stephanie Rudolph, who designed the photographic images."

37 Production Files, Mabou Mines Archive, Fales Library and Special Collections, New York University, Series IIIA, Box 9, Folder 368.

38 Lee Breuer, "Performances: *Hajj*," in *Sister Suzie Cinema: The Collected Poems and Performances, 1976–1986* (New York: Theatre Communications Group, 1987), 122.

39 Ibid., 119. Hereafter cited as *Hajj*.

40 "*Hajj* Project Description," Production Files, Mabou Mines Archives, Fales Library and Special Collections, New York University, Series IIIA, Box 9, Folder 367.

41 Smith Fischer, *Mabou Mines: Making Avant-Garde Theater in the 1970s*, 37.

42 Gerard Rabkin, "Review," *Performing Arts Journal* 7, no. 2 (1983): 57.

43 Ibid., 58.

44 Breuer, *Hajj*, 115.

45 The immediacy with which Maleczech shifts roles in *Hajj* is an early example of what she will later do in *Lucia's Chapters of Coming Forth by Day*, discussed in Chapter 2.

46 Ibid., 116–17.

47 Ibid., 114.

48 The $200 Breuer refers to is the balance of the loan Maleczech had yet to pay off at the time of her father's death. In an interview with the author, Maleczech remembered the amount as $250.

49 Smith Fischer, *Mabou Mines: Making Avant-Garde Theater in the 1970s*, 37.

50 Ruth Maleczech in *Lear '87 Archive*, disk 1, hour 2.

Chapter 4

1   Richard Schechner, *The End of Humanism* (New York: Performing Arts Journal, 1982), 79 and 91–92.

2   Ibid., 91–92.

3   Paraphrase of Galilee taken from my notes on the panel "Staying Power: Mabou Mines after Forty Years" on November 21, 2010, at the 2010 ASTR/CORD conference "Embodying Power: Work Over Time" in Seattle, WA.

4   Unless otherwise noted, all quotations of Galilee in this chapter are taken from an interview conducted by the author in August 2012.

5   Unless otherwise noted, all quotations of Maleczech in this chapter are taken from interviews conducted by the author between July 2011 and March 2012.

6   All quotations of JoAnne Akalaitis in this chapter are taken from an interview conducted by the author in December 2011.

7   Anne L. Fliotsos and Wendy Vierow, introduction to *American Women Stage Directors of the Twentieth Century*, ed. Anne L. Fliotsos and Wendy Vierow (Urbana: University of Illinois Press, 2008), 13–27.

8   Mabou Mines coproduced David Neumann's *I Understand Everything Better* (2015). Following Maleczech's death, Clove Galilee took artistic leadership on *Imagining the Imaginary Invalid*, slated to perform at La MaMa. Galilee's work with Mabou Mines is the most extensive among the group of offspring. Aside from projects such as *The Saint and the Football Player* (1973), *Shaggy Dog*, and *Dead End Kids*, she appeared in versions of *The B. Beaver Animation* (1990), *An Epidog* (1996), *Animal Magnetism* (2000), and *Ecco Porco* (2002). Galilee performed with her mother in *Cara Lucia* (2003), an earlier incarnation of *Lucia's Chapters of Coming Forth by Day*, and played France in Lear (1990).

9   See Kristin Linklater, *Freeing the Natural Voice: Imagery and Art in the Practice of Voice and Language* (1976; reprint, London: Drama Publishers, 2006) and *Freeing Shakespeare's Voice: The Actor's Guide to Talking the Text* (New York: Theatre Communications Group, 1992) for information on her technique.

10 Quotation taken from a recording of an unpublished interview by Iris Smith Fischer, October 28, 1994, side 1.

11 Iris Smith Fischer, *Mabou Mines: Making Avant-Garde Theater in the 1970s* (Ann Arbor: University of Michigan Press, 2011), 120.

12 Interview by Smith Fischer, October 28, 1994, cassette side 1.

13 Smith Fischer, *Mabou Mines: Making Avant-Garde Theater in the 1970s*, 138.

14 Bonnie Marranca, introduction to *Animations: A Trilogy for Mabou Mines*, Bonnie Marranca and Gautam Dasgupta, ed. (New York: Performing Arts Journal Publications, 1979), 7.

15 Unless otherwise noted, all quotations of Breuer in this chapter are taken from an interview with the author conducted in May 2012.

16 Smith Fischer, *Mabou Mines: Making Avant-Garde Theater in the 1970s*, 137–38.

17 Schechner, *The End of Humanism*, 86–87.

18 Galilee's reference to the "Prop Shop" describes the Public Theater's converted performance space where *The Shaggy Dog Animation* premiered.

19 Smith Fischer, *Mabou Mines: Making Avant-Garde Theater in the 1970s*, 134 and 138. Maleczech suggests to Smith Fischer in the October 28, 1994 interview, side 1, that Breuer continues to examine incarnations of the female perspective through Rose in *The Warrior Ant and An Epidog*, which, along with *Shaggy Dog*, constituted a trilogy. That trilogy is currently incorporated into *La Divina Caricatura*.

20 For more extensive discussion of *The Shaggy Dog Animation* and *Dressed Like an Egg*, see Smith Fischer, *Mabou Mines: Making Avant-Garde Theater in the 1970s*, 120–62.

21 Interview by Smith Fischer, October 28, 1994, cassette side 1.

22 Ibid., cassette side 2.

23 Smith Fischer, *Mabou Mines: Making Avant-Garde Theater in the 1970s*, 135.

24 Interview by Smith Fischer, October 28, 1994, cassette side 1.

25 This strategy is discussed in Chapter 2.

26 Mabou Mines's *Through the Leaves* is discussed in detail in Chapter 1.

27 Webpage, "Red Beads," Mabou Mines digital archive, accessed June 21, 2012, http://www.maboumines.org/productions/red-beads.

28 Margo Jefferson, "A Girl Caught in an Eternal Family Triangle," *New York Times*, September 22, 2005.

29 Phoebe Hoban, "An Allegory Unfolds in the Air," *New York Times*, September 18, 2005.

30 Ibid.

31 Ibid.

32 Arthur Sabatini, "From Dog to Ant: The Evolution of Lee Breuer's Animations," *PAJ: A Journal of Performance and Art* 26, no. 2 (May 2004): 52–53.

33 Ibid., 59.

34 Webpage, "Summa Dramatica," Mabou Mines, accessed June 21, 2012, http://www.maboumines.org/productions/summa-dramatica-pataphysical-acting-lesson. Marge Simpson is a character from the popular American television cartoon series *The Simpsons*.

35 Mohn is another of Breuer's former partners; their son is Wah Mohn.

36 Sabatini, "From Dog to Ant: The Evolution of Lee Breuer's Animations," 59.

37 See Chapter 1 for a discussion of critical reception in Maleczech's *Happy Days*.

38 Ibid., 58.

39 J.M. Coetzee, Introduction to *Samuel Beckett: The Grove Centenary Edition*, vol. 4, Samuel Beckett, ed. Paul Auster (New York: Grove Press, 2006), ix–x.

40 Mel Gussow, "'Pretty Boy' and a Beckett," *New York Times*, June 15, 1984.

41 Samuel Beckett, December 16, 1981, Mabou Mines Correspondence, Mabou Mines Archive, Fales Library and Special Collections, New York University, Series IA, Box 1, Folder 8.

42 Ibid., December 24, 1981.

43 Ibid, March 23, 1984.

44 Beckett 2006, IV, 361.

45 Curatorial statement displayed in *The Jeweled Net: Views of Contemporary Holography* exhibit, MIT Museum, Massachusetts Institute of Technology, Cambridge, MA, opened June 27, 2012, and continuing indefinitely.

46 Beckett 2006, vol. 4, 361.

47 Ibid.

48 Ibid., 363

49 "The Jeweled Net."

50 Gussow, "'Pretty Boy' and a Beckett," 1984.

51 Ibid.

52 David Sterritt, "A Play That Tries to Be a Movie, and Pulls Lots of Stage Tricks to Do So," *Christian Science Monitor*, Boston, May 22, 1981.

53 Frank Rich, "Wrong Guys: A Mixed Media Circus at the Public," *New York Times*, May 15, 1981.

54 Gussow, "'Pretty Boy' and a Beckett," 1984.

55 Beckett 2006, vol. 4, 363.

56 Ibid., 362.

57 Mabou Mines Correspondence, Samuel Beckett, March 12, 1984, Mabou Mines Archive, Fales Library and Special Collections, New York University, Series IA, Box 1, Folder 9.

58 For a further discussion of Beckett's narrators of ambiguous gender, specifically in *Enough*, see Enoch Brater, *The Drama in the Text: Beckett's Late Fiction* (London: Oxford University Press, 1994), 58–61.

59 Beckett 2006, vol. 4, 363.

60 *Happy Days* is discussed in detail in Chapter 1.
61 Ibid.
62 Ibid.
63 Gertrude Stein, "Plays," in *Gertrude Stein: Writings 1932–1946*, ed. Catherine R. Stimpson and Harriet Chessman (New York: Literary Classics of the United States, Inc., 1998), 263.
64 Schechner, *The End of Humanism*, 92.

Conclusion

1 Original translation developed in consultation with Henri Van Laun, *The Dramatic Works of Molière* (Philadelphia: Gebbie and Barrie, 1879), 459.
2 Ben Brantley, "Ruth Maleczech, Beacon of Stage Avant-Garde, Dies at 74," *New York Times*, October 2, 2013, accessed July 1, 2015, http://nyti.ms/18vfQqj.
3 Don Shewey, "In Memoriam: Ruth Maleczech," *American Theatre*, January 2014, accessed July 1, 2015, http://www.americantheatre.org/2014/01/22/in-memorium-ruth-maleczech-1939-2013/.
4 Ibid.
5 Brantley, "Ruth Maleczech, Beacon of Stage Avant-Garde, Dies at 74."
6 Shewey, "In Memoriam: Ruth Maleczech."
7 James Harding, *Cutting Performances: Collage Events, Feminist Artists, and the American Avant-Garde* (Ann Arbor: University of Michigan Press, 2012), 4.
8 Ibid., 4 and 19.
9 Bulgakov also wrote a play with the same title.
10 All quotations of Maleczech in this chapter are taken from interviews conducted by the author between July 2011 and March 2012.
11 All quotations of Lee Breuer in this chapter are taken from an interview conducted by the author in May 2012.
12 All quotations of Sharon Fogarty in this chapter are taken from interviews conducted by the author in October and November 2011.
13 All quotations of Archer in this chapter are taken from an interview conducted by the author on November 11, 2011.

14 All quotations of Paul Kandel in this chapter are taken from an interview conducted by the author in August 2012.

15 All quotations of Karen Kandel in this chapter are taken from an interview conducted by the author in August 2012.

16 Taylor was best known as the original Amanda Wingfield in Tennessee Williams's *The Glass Menagerie* (1944).

17 JoAnne Akalaitis, as quoted by Ross Wetzsteon, "Queen Lear," *Village Voice*, January 30, 1990.

18 All quotations of Greg Mehrten in this chapter are taken from an interview conducted by the author in July 2011.

19 All quotations of JoAnne Akalaitis in this chapter are taken from an interview conducted by the author in December 2011.

20 Ruth Maleczech, "Untitled," *Foundation for Contemporary Arts 2011 Booklet*. Foundation for Contemporary Arts, accessed May 19, 2014, http://www.foundationforcontemporaryarts.org/about/essays/ruth_maleczech.html.

Bibliography

Interviews and Correspondence with the Author

Akalaitis, JoAnne. Interview, December 2011.

Archer, Julie. Interview, November 2011.

Breuer, Lee. Interviews, July 2011–May 2012.

Fogarty, Sharon. Interviews, October–November 2011.

Galilee, Clove. Interview, August 2012.

Kandel, Karen. Interview, August 2012.

Kandel, Paul. Interview, August 2012.

Maleczech, Ruth. Interviews, April 2008–March 2012.

Maleczech, Ruth. Interviews, July–September 2011.

Mehrten, Greg. Interview, July 2011.

Sasanov, Catherine. Email correspondence, November–December 2011.

Stein, Douglas. Email correspondence, March–May 2012.

Other Interviews

Maleczech, Ruth. Unpublished interview by Iris Smith Fischer, October, 1994.

Maleczech, Ruth. Unpublished interview by Iris Smith Fischer, October, 2001.

Maleczech, Ruth. In conversation with Nick Westrate, "Process and Performance." New York Theatre Workshop, April 23, 2012.

DVD/Video

Guthrie Theater. *The Screens*. Directed by JoAnne Akalaitis. Chicago, IL: The Guthrie Theater. Video recording, 1989. New York Library for the Performing Arts, Theater on Film and Tape Archive.

La Jolla Playhouse. *Happy Days*. Directed by Robert Woodruff. San Diego, CA: La Jolla Playhouse. Video recording, 1996. New York Library for the Performing Arts, Theater on Film and Tape Archive.

Mabou Mines. *Belén: A Book of Hours*. Directed by Ruth Maleczech. New York: ToRoNaDa Studio. DVD, 1999. Mabou Mines office archives.

Mabou Mines. *Dead End Kids: A Story of Nuclear Power*. Directed by JoAnne Akalaitis. New York: The Public Theater. Cinema Guild. Video recording, 1986. Mabou Mines Archive, Fales Library and Special Collections, New York University.

Mabou Mines. *Hajj: A Performance Poem*. By Lee Breuer. New York: New York Theatre Workshop. DVD, 1986. New York Library for the Performing Arts, Theater on Film and Tape Archive.

Mabou Mines. *Imagination Dead Imagine*. Directed by Ruth Maleczech. New York: The Performing Garage. Video recording, 1984. Mabou Mines Archive, Fales Library and Special Collections, New York University.

Mabou Mines. *Lear '87 Archive*. Directed by Jill Godmillow. Laboratory for Icon & Idion, Inc., 2001. DVD.

Mabou Mines. *Lucia's Chapters of Coming Forth by Day*. Directed by Sharon Fogarty. New York: HERE Arts Center. DVD, undated. Mabou Mines office archives.

Mabou Mines. *Lucia's Chapters of Coming Forth by Day*. Directed by Sharon Fogarty. New York: PS 122. DVD, 2011. Mabou Mines office archives.

Mabou Mines. *Mabou Mines' Lear*. Directed by Lee Breuer. New York: Triplex Theater. Video recording, 1990. Mabou Mines Archive, Fales Library and Special Collections, New York University.

Mabou Mines. *Red Beads*. Directed by Lee Breuer. New York: Skirball Center for the Performing Arts. DVD, undated. Mabou Mines office archives.

Mabou Mines. *The Red Horse Animation*. Directed by Lee Breuer. New York: The Guggenheim Museum. Video recording, 1970. Mabou Mines Archive, Fales Library and Special Collections, New York University.

Mabou Mines. *Sueños*. Directed by Ruth Maleczech. New York: The Triplex Theater. Video recording, 1989. Mabou Mines Archive, Fales Library and Special Collections, New York University.

Mabou Mines. *Through the Leaves*. Directed by Ruth Maleczech. New York: The Public Theater. Video recording, 1990. Mabou Mines Archive, Fales Library and Special Collections, New York University.

Ruth Maleczech. DVD, undated. Mabou Mines Archive, Fales Library and Special Collections, New York University. Series IX, Box: Media.

Other Sources

Akalaitis, JoAnne. JoAnne Akalaitis to Margot Lewitin, March 6, 1985. Mabou Mines Archive. Series IIIA, Box 10, Folder 424. Fales Library and Special Collections, New York University.

Bechtel, Roger. *Past Performance: American Theatre and the Historical Imagination*. Lewisberg: Bucknell University Press, 2007.

Beckett, Samuel. *Happy Days: Production Notebook*. Edited by James Knowlson. London: Faber and Faber, 1985.

Beckett, Samuel. Mabou Mines Correspondence, Mabou Mines Archive. Series IA, Box 1, Folder 8. Fales Library and Special Collections, New York University.

Ben Zvi, Linda, ed. *Women in Beckett*. Urbana: University of Illinois Press, 1990.

Bottoms, Stephen. *Playing Underground*. Ann Arbor: University of Michigan Press, 2004.

Brantley, Ben. "Ruth Maleczech, Beacon of Stage Avant-Garde, Dies at 74." *New York Times*, October 2, 2013.

Brater, Enoch. *The Drama in the Text: Beckett's Late Fiction*. London: Oxford University Press, 1994.

Brater, Enoch. *Why Beckett*. London: Thames and Hudson, 1989.

Breslauer, Jan. "Beckett's Her Hole Card." *Los Angeles Times*, August 4, 1996.

Breuer, Lee. *Animations: A Trilogy for Mabou Mines*. Edited by Bonnie Marranca and Gautam Dasgupta. New York: Performing Arts Journal Publications, 1979.

Breuer, Lee. *La Divina Caricatura: A Fiction*. Kobenhavn and Los Angeles: Green Integer #43, 2003.

Breuer, Lee. *Sister Suzie Cinema: The Collected Poems and Performances, 1976–1986*. New York: Theatre Communications Group, 1987.

Bruckner, D.J.R. "A Revival of 'Leaves,' Grimmer Than Ever." *New York Times*, September 18, 1990.

Butler, Judith. *Gender Trouble: Feminism and the Subversion of Identity*. New York: Routledge, 1990.

Catlett, Mallory, Martha Elliot, Karen Houppert, Melanie Joseph, Theodora Skipitares, Joe Stackell, and Nick Westrate. "Being the Imaginable Ruth Maleczech: A Tribute." Brooklyn Rail digital archive. November 5, 2013. http://www.brooklynrail.org/2013/11/theater/being-the-imaginablef80ruth-maleczech-a-tribute.

Case, Sue-Ellen. *Feminism and Theatre*. New York: Routledge, 1988.

Cody, Gabrielle and Lee Breuer. "Lee Breuer on Interculturalism." Special Issue, *Performing Arts Journal: The Interculturalism Issue* 11/12, no. 3/1 (1989): 59–66.

Coetzee, J.M. Introduction to *Samuel Beckett: The Grove Centenary Edition*, Volume 4. Edited by Paul Auster. New York: Grove Press, 2006.

Cohn, Ruby. "The Becketts of Mabou Mines." In *Samuel Beckett and the Arts*, edited by Lois Oppenheim. New York: Garland Publishing, Inc., 1999.

Costantino, Roslyn. "Embodied Memory in Las Horas de Belén. A Book of Hours." *Theatre Journal* 53, 4 (December 2001).

Diamond, Elin. "Review." *Theatre Journal* 42, no. 4 (December, 1990).

Diamond, Elin. *Unmaking Mimesis: Essays on Feminism and Theater*. New York: Routledge, 1997.

Dolan, Jill. *The Feminist Spectator as Critic*. Ann Arbor: University of Michigan Press, 1988.

Feingold, Michael. "Judith Malina and the Award-Season Rush (Part II)." Thinking About Theater. June 5, 2015. TheaterMania digital archive. http://www.theatermania.com/new-york-city-theater/news/judith-malina-and-the-award-season-rush-part-ii_73099.html.

Feingold, Michael. "Lover's Meatings." *Village Voice*, April 3, 1984.

Fliotsos, Anne L. and Wendy Vierow, eds. *American Women Stage Directors of the Twentieth Century*. Urbana: University of Illinois Press, 2008.

Fliotsos, Anne L. and Wendy Vierow, eds. *International Women Stage Directors*. Urbana: University of Illinois Press, 2013.

Fogarty, Sharon. *Lucia's Chapters of Coming Forth by Day*. Mabou Mines office archives.

Fowler, Keith Franklin. "A History of the San Francisco Actor's Workshop." DFA diss., Yale University, 1969.

Fuchs, Elinor. "Staging the Obscene Body." *TDR* 33, no. 1 (1989).

Fuss, Diana. *Essentially Speaking: Feminism, Nature, and Difference*. New York: Routledge, 1989.

Gontarski, S.E. *Beckett's Happy Days: A Manuscript Study*. Columbus: Publications Committee, Ohio State University Libraries, 1977.

Gussow, Mel. "'Pretty Boy' and a Beckett." *New York Times*, June 15, 1984.

Halperin, Spence. Spence Halperin to Margot Lewitin, December 19, 1984. Mabou Mines Archives. Series IIIA, Box 10, Folder 424. Fales Library and Special Collections, New York University.

Hampton, Wilborn. "When Everything's Normal, and All of It Is Absurd." *New York Times*, March 24, 1998.

Harding, James. *Cutting Performances: Collage Events, Feminist Artists, and the American Avant-Garde.* Ann Arbor: University of Michigan Press, 2012.

Hart, Lynda, ed. *Making a Spectacle: Feminist Essays on Contemporary Women's Theatre.* Ann Arbor: University of Michigan Press, 1989.

Hart, Lynda and Peggy Phelan, eds. *Acting Out: Feminist Performances.* Ann Arbor: University of Michigan Press, 1993.

Hoban, Phoebe. "An Allegory Unfolds in the Air." *New York Times*, September 18, 2005.

Jefferson, Margo. "A Girl Caught in an Eternal Family Triangle." *New York Times*, September 22, 2005.

The Jeweled Net: Views of Contemporary Holography exhibit, curatorial statement, MIT Museum, Massachusetts Institute of Technology, Cambridge, MA, opened 27 June 2012 and continuing indefinitely.

Knowlson, James. *Damned to Fame: The Life of Samuel Beckett.* New York: Grove Press, 1996.

Kroetz, Franz Xaver. Franz Xaver Kroetz to JoAnne Akalaitis, undated. Mabou Mines Archive. Series IIIA, Box 10, Folder 424. Fales Library and Special Collections.

Kroetz, Franz Xaver. *Through the Leaves and Other Plays.* Translated by Roger Downey. New York: Theatre Communications Group, Inc., 1983.

Linklater, Kristin. *Freeing the Natural Voice: Imagery and Art in the Practice of Voice and Language.* London: Drama Publishers, 2006. First published 1976.

Linklater, Kristin. *Freeing Shakespeare's Voice: The Actor's Guide to Talking the Text.* New York: Theatre Communications Group, 1992.

La MaMa. "Mission + History." La MaMa digital archive. http://lamama.org/about/mission-history/.

Mabou Mines. *Belén: A Book of Hours.* Program. Presented at Teatro de La Capilla in Mexico City in 2000. Mabou Mines office archives.

Mabou Mines. *Hajj.* Production Files. Mabou Mines Archive. Series IIIA, Box 9, Folder 368. Fales Library and Special Collections, New York University.

Mabou Mines. "*Hajj* Project Description." Production Files. Mabou Mines Archives. Series IIIA, Box 9, Folder 367. Fales Library and Special Collections, New York University.

Mabou Mines. Mabou Mines Correspondence, Samuel Beckett, March 12, 1984. Mabou Mines Archive. Series IA, Box 1, Folder 9. Fales Library and Special Collections, New York University.

Mabou Mines. "Red Beads." Mabou Mines digital archive. http://www.maboumines.org/productions/red-beads.

Mabou Mines. "Red Horse Animation." Mabou Mines digital archive. http://www.maboumines.org/productions/red-horse-animation.

Mabou Mines. "Summa Dramatica." Mabou Mines digital archive. http://www.maboumines.org/productions/summa-dramatica-pataphysical-acting-lesson.

Maleczech, Ruth. "Am I Dying While I'm Devouring Life?" *Performing Arts Journal* 6, no. 1 (1981).

Maleczech, Ruth. "Untitled." *Foundation for Contemporary Arts 2011 Booklet.* Foundation for Contemporary Arts. http://www.foundationforcontemporaryarts.org/about/essays/ruth_maleczech.html

Malina, Judith. *The Piscator Notebook.* New York: Routledge, 2012.

Marranca, Bonnie, ed. *The Theatre of Images.* Baltimore: John Hopkins University Press, 1996.

Martin, Carol, ed. *A Sourcebook of Feminist Theater and Performance: On and Beyond the Stage.* New York: Routledge, 1996.

Martinez, Julio. "Happy Days." *Daily Variety*, August 13, 1996.

McGrath, John. "My Friend and Mentor Ruth Maleczech, Rest in Peace." National Theatre Wales digital archive. October 1, 2013. http://community.nationaltheatrewales.org/profiles/blogs/my-friend-and-mentor-ruth-maleczech-rest-in-peace.

McNamara, Robert. "Franz Xaver Kroetz: A New Voice from Europe." *Washington Review*, August/September 1985. Mabou Mines Archive. Series IIIA, Box 10, Folder 453. Fales Library and Special Collections, New York University.

Molière. *The Dramatic Works of Molière.* Translated by Henri Van Laun. Philadelphia: Gebbie and Barrie, 1879.

Murray, Christopher. "Queen Lear: Ruth Maleczech Exits the Stage." *Huffington Post* digital archive. October 1, 2013. http://www.huffingtonpost.com/christopher-murray/queen-lear-ruth-maleczech_b_4020299.html.

O'Sullivan, Sibbie. "Ruth Maleczech: Art & Impact." Presented at the Martin E. Segal Center Theatre Center, CUNY, New York, NY, April 7, 2014.

Rabkin, Gerard. "Review." *Performing Arts Journal* 7, no. 2 (1983).

Rich, Adrienne. *Blood, Bread, and Poetry: Selected Prose, 1979–1985*. New York: W.W. Norton & Company, 1994.

Rich, Frank. "Through the Leaves." *New York Times*, April 6, 1984.

Rich, Frank. "Wrong Guys: A Mixed Media Circus at the Public." *New York Times*, May 15, 1981.

Rokem, Freddie. *Performing History: Theatrical Representations of the Past in Contemporary Theatre*. Iowa City: University of Iowa Press, 2000.

Sabatini, Arthur. "From Dog to Ant: The Evolution of Lee Breuer's Animations." *PAJ: A Journal of Performance and Art* 26, no. 2 (May 2004).

Saivetz, Deborah. *An Event in Space*. Hanover: Smith and Krauss, 2000.

Sasanov, Catherine. *Belén: A Book of Hours*. Production program supplement by Mabou Mines. Mabou Mines office archives.

Savran, David. *Breaking the Rules: The Wooster Group*. New York: Theatre Communications Group, 1988.

Schechner, Richard. *The End of Humanism*. New York: Performing Arts Journal, 1982.

Schechner, Richard. "Race Free, Gender Free, Body-Type Free, Age Free Casting." *TDR* 33, no. 1 (Spring, 1989): 9.

Sedgwick, Eve Kosofsky. *Tendencies*. Durham: Duke University Press, 1993.

Shakespeare, William. *King Lear*. Edited by R.A. Foakes. London: Arden Shakespeare, 2001.

Shewey, Don. "In Memoriam: Ruth Maleczech." *American Theatre* digital archive. January 2014, http://www.americantheatre.org/2014/01/22/in-memorium-ruth-maleczech-1939-2013/.

Shloss, Carol Loeb. *Lucia Joyce: To Dance in the Wake*. New York: Farrar, Strauss and Giroux, 2003.

Simonson, Robert. "Ruth Maleczech, Founder of Mabou Mines, Seminal Downtown Theatre Group, Dies at 74." *Playbill* digital archive. October 1, 2013. http://www.playbill.com/news/article/ruth-maleczech-founder-of-mabou-mines-seminal-downtown-theatre-group-dies-a-210108.

Smith Fischer, Iris. "Happy Days." Review of Beckett's *Happy Days* by Mabou Mines, ToRoNaDa Studio, New York, 1999. In "Women, Nations, Households, and History." Special Issue. *Theatre Journal* 51, no. 1 (March 1999).

Smith Fischer, Iris. "Mabou Mines's 'Lear': A Narrative of Collective Authorship." *Theatre Journal* 45, no. 3 (1993).

Smith Fischer, Iris. *Mabou Mines: Making Avant-Garde Theater in the 1970s.* Ann Arbor: The University of Michigan Press, 2011.

Solomon, Alisa. "Parallel Fantasies." *Village Voice*, October 2, 1984.

Solomon, Alisa. "Prison Prayers." *Village Voice*, May 25, 1999.

Solomon, Alisa. *Re-dressing the Canon: Essays on Theatre and Gender.* New York: University of Michigan Press, 2002.

"Staying Power: Mabou Mines after Forty Years." 2010 ASTR/CORD conference "Embodying Power: Work Over Time." Seattle, WA. November 21, 2010.

Stein, Gertrude. "Plays." In *Gertrude Stein: Writings 1932–1946.* Edited by Catherine R. Stimpson and Harriet Chessman. New York: Literary Classics of the United States, Inc., 1998.

Sterritt, David. "A Play That Tries to Be a Movie, and Pulls Lots of Stage Tricks to Do So." *Christian Science Monitor*, Boston, May 22, 1981.

Weiss, Peter. "Notes on the Contemporary Theater." Translated by Joel Agee. In *Essays on German Theater.* New York: Continuum, 1985.

Wetzsteon, Ross. "Queen Lear." *Village Voice*, January 30, 1990.

Winer, Laurie. "Love and Marriage, According to Beckett." *Los Angeles Times*, August 13, 1996.

The Wooster Group. "Poor Theater." The Wooster Group digital archive. http://thewoostergroup.org/twg/twg.php?poor-theater.

About the Author

Jessica Silsby Brater is a visiting assistant professor and the Theater Program Director at the University of New Haven, where she teaches courses in contemporary performance, theater history, directing, and theater for community impact. She also serves as an Assistant Dean of the UNH College of Arts and Sciences. Her writing has appeared in publications including *Theatre Journal*, *Samuel Beckett Today/ Aujourd'hui*, and the *Journal of Beckett Studies*. Forthcoming publications include a chapter on Mabou Mines in *Women, Collective Creation, and Devising* (Palgrave Macmillan). She is the founding Artistic Director of Polybe + Seats, a Brooklyn-based theater company that often partners with other cultural organizations to produce site-specific work. She holds a BA from Barnard College, Columbia University and a PhD in Theatre Studies from the Graduate Center, City University of New York.

Index

locators followed by n refer notes.